Praise for *Follow You Down*

"If James Crumley got lost and ended up in the ramshackle backwaters of rural Michigan he might have written a book like *Follow You Down*. Deputy Meg Shaw, navigating tattoo parlors, strip bars, and biker clubs in search of a missing teenage girl, is one of the most believable and compelling investigators I've read in contemporary crime fiction. *Follow You Down* is at turns funny and horrifying, and Hyatt's prose is taut as piano wire, run through with an amphetamine hum that refuses to stop, even long after the book is finished."

—Augustus Rose, author of *The Readymade Thief*

"*Follow You Down* is everything a crime novel should be—it's grounded, it's full of well-earned surprises, and it's tough enough that it doesn't need to read like a fantasy. More than that, it's a story of well-drawn, carefully observed human behavior, lending real weight to the idea that average people can end up as participants in horrific crimes. Like the town of Pike Lake in which it's set, *Follow You Down* has an edge that cuts deep. I cannot recommend it highly enough."

—David Peak, author of *Corpsepaint*

FOLLOW YOU DOWN

Also by Geoff Hyatt

Birch Hills at World's End

GEOFF HYATT

FOLLOW YOU DOWN

Down & Out Books
3959 Van Dyke Road, Suite 265
Lutz, FL 33558
DownAndOutBooks.com

Cover design by JT Lindroos

ISBN: 1-64396-084-9
ISBN: 978-1-64396-084-5

For Karen

CHAPTER 1

Where the roads run dark and the stars shine bright, folks don't think much of the law. Despite all that, not a single speeder had crossed Deputy Meghan Shaw's radar in the hour she'd spent gazing through her windshield at the line of oaks and maples beyond the two-lane blacktop. Her radio's squawk broke her vigil: Dispatch needed her out at Julie Wells's place because Julie's daughter, Bree, "might've got herself in a bit of trouble again." Meg scratched those last two words along with the girl's name in her notepad as she called back her ten-four. Then she pulled her cruiser out from behind the auction yard's billboard and onto the county highway. She didn't need to ask for the address.

When Meg arrived, Julie poured two glasses of Diet Cherry 7-Up and carried them to the kitchen table, placing one on the checkered tablecloth in front of the deputy before sitting down with her own. The table was too big for the trailer's kitchen, and the mismatched chair pressed uncomfortably against Meg's gun belt, but it was a pleasant, clean place. Dishes dried in a rack beside the sink, and blue-and-white-checkered hand towels hung from the cabinet knobs.

Meg thanked her before asking, "So, where's Bree

tonight?"

"Wish I knew. She stormed out after a fight we had on Sunday. Haven't seen or heard from her since."

"Five days ago?" Meg kept a neutral tone. "Any reason you waited so long to call us?"

"I figured she'd be staying with a friend, sulking around until she cooled down. It's just—" Julie's mouth pinched. Beyond the window screen over the sink, choruses of tree frogs and crickets chattered in the summer twilight. "She's a wild one. Always has been. I do the best I can."

"I know." Meg gave a sympathetic nod. She glanced around the kitchen. A faded print of Jesus carrying a lamb hung beside the back door. Beneath it was a framed school photo of a striking, green-eyed teen in a high-necked black dress, her sneer painted with blood-red lipstick. A heart-shaped magnet depicting the same girl but younger—gawky and acne spotted, with an uneasy, gap-toothed smile—affixed a photocopied Alcoholics Anonymous serenity prayer to the fridge. "It's a hard age," Meg said. "I remember it well."

After a search of Meg's expression, Julie gave a sullen sigh and took a sip of her pop. "So after three days, I wasn't feeling great about it, but she's done this before. So I waited a couple more days. Didn't want you guys thinking I was overreacting."

"What changed?"

"Her boyfriend came by today asking about her, and I really got worried. He's almost never over here, and when he is, he hardly says a word. Russell McCreech. From her school." She lit a cigarette, then reached over and took an ashtray from the countertop. "Leon McCreech's kid. You know Leon?"

Now in his late forties, he was also known as "Bloody Leon," the president of the Ironwolfs Motorcycle Club. Russell was his youngest son, and though Meg didn't know him well, she knew the family. Leon's oldest son was killed in a motorcycle accident five years ago, shortly before Meg returned to Pike Lake, and the middle son just wrapped up a prison sentence for assault and battery. One of their uncles was still inside. The McCreeches had a long-standing rivalry with the Hornweens, another clan with a criminal reputation going back for generations. Folks said that McCreeches or Hornweens had a hand in every dirty deal or bad scene around Pike Lake. It was hard to tell how much of that was a local legend and how much an ugly truth.

"Oh yeah, I know Leon. Biker. Owns the Hobble Inn, tends bar there sometimes. Don't know much about Russell. Is he like his dad?"

"Doesn't strike me that way. Skinny. Long, reddish hair. Shy. Looks like a heavy metal kid. Didn't know that was still a thing. Of course, I thought that about mohawks until my daughter came home with one." Julie sighed out a plume of smoke. "Russell asked if Bree was home or if she had been sick. He wanted to make plans with her, but he didn't know where she was."

"What did you and Bree fight about the last time you saw her?"

"She wanted to go to some festival or something. In Chicago. For a whole weekend." She rubbed her face. "You know how many people get shot in Chicago every weekend?"

"More than in Pike Lake."

"Right. And Bree, with a bunch of teenagers in a big city none of them know? I'm not crazy. I said no."

"You think she's gone to Chicago? Maybe she went

anyway."

"If she did, she went without any of her friends. She's not the type these days. Does everything with people, especially Sam—Samantha Black. The two of them are like peas in a pod. Russell says Sam hasn't seen or heard from Bree, neither."

"Did she pack any clothes?"

"No. But who knows if she's been in and left again while I was at work." Julie clucked her tongue. "I know it might be nothing, but do you think I should file a missing person report?"

"It can't hurt." Meg sipped her pop to be polite, even though she never drank the stuff. She forced down the aspartame sweetness and fake cherry flavor. "I'll write down as much as I can, and then you come to the office first thing in the morning. I'll be in at the end of my shift at eight a.m. Bring a couple recent photos, or email them to me."

"I remember this," Julie said, "from last time. I'm so sorry."

Meg had worked on that case as well. Two years ago, Bree ran off with a hippie-type from out of state who met her online and picked her up at a field party on the Hornween property. The guy promised to take her all the way to Colorado but instead left the fifteen-year-old with twenty dollars and a prepaid calling card at a Motel 6 outside South Bend. Taking a minor across state lines was a major crime, but once the child was found, Sheriff Cunningham decided it would be best to drop it. To let the girl get on with her life. Besides, he said, pursuing an arrest would have meant the challenges of digital forensics, out-of-state law enforcement, and an uncooperative teenage victim—and who needed that? Meg didn't agree, but it wasn't her call.

"Don't worry, Julie. It's what we're here for. Now, let's get some of this down."

According to Julie, Brianne "Bree" Wells was wearing a green T-shirt with a silver foil skull design on its front, black stretch pants, and combat-style boots. Her hair was auburn, long on top and shaved on the sides, and sometimes she wore it up in a mohawk style. She was about five-foot-six and one-hundred-ten pounds. She had a piercing in her lower lip, tongue, navel, and multiple in her ears. There was a purple birthmark on her left hip about the size of a thumbprint. Her mother didn't think Bree had any tattoos, but it was possible. Kids do dumb things. She wasn't prescribed any medication nor known to be a user of hard drugs, but her mother had concerns.

"Oh," Julie said as Meghan finished writing the last lines in her notepad, "and she wears a pendant with a big, curly silver *B,* like the letter. For 'Brianne.' I got it for her sixteenth birthday. One of the only things I ever gave her that I think she actually liked."

"Thank you, Julie, that's helpful."

The women stood—Meghan in her uniform and boots, towering over Julie who, in her bathrobe, with her sunken eyes and nervous flitting gestures, looked like someone who still fretted when she should be too tired to care. Meghan handed off her card, said her goodbyes, and headed out to her patrol.

It was a pretty slow night. She pulled over a teenage couple driving back from a late show at the multiplex in Birch Hills, a few towns over. They had a taillight out, and she let them off with a warning. After that, she came across a roadkilled deer blocking a lane on the 54, so she got the pleasure of dragging its carcass to the shoulder for animal control to maybe (or maybe not) pick up in the morning. There was a noise complaint at White Brook Apartments; she knocked on the door, and the thumping rap song abruptly ended. The terrified and clearly stoned occupant offered his apologies.

This was the sort of policing she was used to, the kind she expected when she came back stateside to Pike Lake after her second deployment: cooling down domestics now and then, nailing the more egregious DUIs, chasing teens away from the crumbling railroad bridge. But the whole of Stanley County had more grime now than it did when she was a kid. Murder was rare but not unheard of; the last one was two years ago, a road-rage incident that ended in gunfire. Much of Pike Lake's Main Street stood empty, including some of her childhood haunts: the Pike Cinema, Ethel's Ice Cream Parlor—gone, along with the stamping plant and most of the farms. With that decay came methamphetamine and, more recently, heroin—not what the news would call a "scourge," but nothing you would have seen ten years ago. Overdose rates were climbing, even in the nearby bedroom community of Birch Hills. Pike Lake was still a decent place but rougher around the edges. And those edges could cut deep. Especially if you were a kid like Bree Wells.

She drove out to the Hobble Inn, hoping to track down Russell or one of the other McCreeches. Not that any of them ever said much to anyone with a badge. The bar was still a trouble spot these days, its lot packed with gleaming Harleys and mud-caked trucks, but it wasn't quite the legendary hellhole it was before the Ironwolfs opened a separate clubhouse out by the river.

The patrons lowered their voices when she strode in but otherwise ignored her. The jukebox blared an old Motorhead song, the bass like a jackhammer, the vocals like broken glass. Leon McCreech, looking like a red-bearded, weathered berserker, leaned behind the bar. He gave her a barely visible nod.

She walked over to him and said, "Leon."

"Deputy." He dunked a pint glass into a basin of gray water and plopped it onto a rubber mat. "What you need?"

Leon, chatty as ever.

"Hear your youngest is close with Bree Wells. Green eyes, head shaved on the sides. Lip piercing. Seen her around lately?"

"Nope." He leaned over the bar top and rumbled, "Girl like that's gonna wander."

"How's Russ with that?"

"He's got his feelings. Boys, you know?"

"What about them?" She asked.

"Always falling for girls they don't know a damn thing about."

"That is a fact. But I suppose it goes both ways." She hooked her thumbs in her belt. "Where's Russ tonight?"

"No idea. I'm working." He swept his arm around at the bar and said, "And it's busy for a weekday."

"Bree's mom can't find her, and she's making it my problem. If you see her, I'd consider it a favor if you let me know."

"Sure," he grunted.

After she left the Hobble, her hands stayed steady on the wheel as she cruised the back roads, but her mind drifted back to Julie Wells. A single parent, Julie worked two jobs daily—twenty miles apart—just to keep the debt collectors from her door. She left home before dawn and often didn't return until after dark. The county had lots of next-level latchkey kids like her daughter. It wasn't unusual for them to bounce from house to house, staying with a string of boy-friends, girlfriends, and relatives for weeks at a time. Julie Wells hadn't laid eyes on Bree in days, and it wasn't a re-markable situation.

But the fact that it was so commonplace is what made it so dangerous. Meg knew kids like Bree could fall into dark places, and no one would notice until it was much too late. Bree was very young, unconventionally beautiful, and deeply unhappy—all things men notice much too soon. She'd been lured away and taken miles from home once before already. The girl was lucky that when she'd been left behind in that motel room, she was still alive. It could have just as easily gone the other way.

Meg rolled by a couple of the boat launches on the lake, the railroad bridge, the pool hall, the Gas-Go and Dairy Queen parking lots, but there was no sign of Russell or any of his clique. A night of chasing McCreeches around was standard operating procedure for a Stanley County sheriff, and tonight she was one step behind. The night shambled onward toward dawn.

By the time an early-rising farmer out on Windmere Road reported his lawnmower stolen, Meg already had a solid tip that it was probably sitting in Jesse McCreech's driveway. It was just before dawn when the call came in, about three hours after she'd stopped by the Gas-Go to fill her tank. The clerk told her that Jesse McCreech—Leon's nephew and Russell's cousin—had come in with an unsecured mower in his truck bed, swaggering and shirtless as he paid for his gas, talking up his time in county lockup and how many shots he'd done at the Hobble Inn. Jesse's criminality and alcohol abuse would have made absolutely no impression on anyone he'd been drinking with earlier at the Hobble.

The clerk wasn't exactly dazzled, either.

She turned off the 54 onto Gooseberry Road, rolling through the tree-swarmed dark before dawn, to close out the night's last call.

Jesse's place was pretty far out in the country. She strode from her patrol car toward a rusted truck parked half on the driveway's morning-damp gravel, half in the knee-high grass. Condensation lacquered the pickup's windows and the suspicious push mower lurked in its bed. The deputy leaned over the Chevy's tailgate to verify the lawnmower's model. Sure enough, it was a high-end Honda recycler, worth about seven hundred bucks new. Leave it to Jesse McCreech to know when something was worth stealing but not know enough to hide what he stole.

An underfed pit bull at the end of its chain barked across the yard, its doghouse surrounded by dried shit and a worn patch of mud. The grass, shot with thistle and glistening with dew, rippled in the wind. Perhaps Jesse had been inspired to get some yardwork done last night. The place certainly needed it.

The deputy looked to the house, its yellow paint sloughing like dead skin, the porch on the edge of collapse, a television glowing beyond the thin curtains. Both the storm door and the inner one hung partway open. The pit bull grew hoarse as birds chattered in the misty woods surrounding the property. She made a mental note to have animal control come check out the dog after she put Jesse away this time.

Meghan radioed in to let them know she'd be bringing a guest back.

Darla radioed back, "Jesse again? Some people never learn, eh?"

"But we keep teaching them, don't we?"

"You want another car out there?"

"Negative on that. I brought him in last time. He knows the drill."

Darla laughed. "Go get 'em, hon."

When Meg walked up onto the porch, the steps creaked a warning. Dead leaves and broken bottles littered the planks. Corroded wind chimes clanged overhead, and a battered pinwheel struggled to spin. A rocking chair, its wicker back and seat a tattered ruin, teetered with her every step.

A body in the corner of her vision gave her a start, and she spun to face it, setting her hand on her pistol.

A rotting scarecrow, probably kidnapped from some local garden, slumped against the railing. Its stitched smile and single eye greeted her with morbid amusement. A huge corncob phallus protruded from its overalls, both work-gloved hands wrapped around it. The deputy took a breath and tucked her thumbs into her gun belt. As she called out "Sheriff!" to the door, she noticed the frame was splintered where it had been kicked in, and scattered buckshot holes riddled the storm door's Plexiglass. Then she spotted the blood spatter.

The droplets, tinged purple in the morning light, glistened on the porch's planks. Ragged barking echoed across the yard. She called again, and the half-open storm door groaned in the breeze. The wind chimes rattled.

Meg drew her pistol. She took out her flashlight and reached around the storm door, nudging open the inner one with the Maglite's black head. It drifted open onto a vacant hallway cluttered by a listing coat tree and a bike with two flat tires. She stepped around the open storm door and crept down the hallway, squeezing past the crippled bike, her pistol drawn and flashlight spotting. The sour reek of garbage mixed with the gritty tang of cigarette smoke, the air stagnant despite the open front entrance. Wallpaper surrounded her with printed flowers muted by a film of grime.

The television's blank glow did little to illuminate the living room, only deepening the pits of shadow. Pale light pressed against threadbare curtains. An afghan lay heaped on the torn couch. A long glass pipe, clouded with resin, rested beside some wads of foil and an overflowing ashtray on the end table. Jesse McCreech slouched in a recliner, his overalls soaked with blood from chest to knee, his gray-toothed mouth gaping. One tattoo-sleeved arm hung over the side, fingers dangling above a cracked-open double-barrel and some scattered shells on the floor. The other hand was shoved in his pocket. She kept her weapon and light trained on him, yelling for him to raise his hands. He did not respond. Not even a little.

She radioed for an ambulance and backup, edging toward Jesse until she could kick the shotgun away. She set the light down on the table in front of the couch, keeping it on him.

Meg reached over to feel for his pulse. She stepped back when he took a sharp, rasping breath.

Hinges squealed in the dark kitchen beyond the doorway across the room. A boyish voice called out, "Jesse? Hello?"

She aimed her weapon on the kitchen doorway with one hand and reached over to snatch the flashlight with the other. The beam swept up to the shadowy figure creeping toward the room.

"Sheriff! Freeze, hands up!"

The light blazed on a wide-eyed boy in a sleeveless black T-shirt. Shoulder-length bronze hair hung from beneath a backward baseball cap, and loose-fitting blue jeans bunched at his ankles over heavy black work boots. Russell McCreech. He turned his face from the light and saw his bloodied cousin.

"Jesus *Christ*." He raised his thin, sunburned arms to put his hands in the air. "Did you—"

"Found him like this. Keep your hands where I can see them, Russell." Meg glanced to Jesse and back to Russell again, a coil tightening in her chest.

"Don't you point that gun at me! What the hell is going on?"

"I have to get you out of here." She lowered the weapon, slightly. "Whoever did this might still be nearby. Ambulance and backup are on the way."

Jesse gurgled and wheezed as he began working his left hand out from his pocket.

"Don't move, Jesse," she shouted, setting her pistol's sights on him. His hand fell from his pocket and laid open and limp in his lap. Jesse squinted through the glare of the flashlight, and something glinted in his palm.

"Wasn't me," he said, holding it out.

And then, with a spasm, he slumped over. A thread of red spittle dripped from his still lips. She swept the flashlight to his hand. Russell gasped.

There, in the center of the dead man's blood-smeared palm, gleamed a silver pendant in the shape of the letter *B*.

Russell McCreech's ass ached from hours of sitting in a plastic chair at the sheriff's office. After they'd swabbed his hands and fingerprinted him, the lady sheriff, Deputy Shaw—Meg—said she'd be back in a few minutes. He'd sat alone in the windowless room ever since, the air conditioning keeping the place cold as a meat locker. He shivered in his sleeveless shirt, feeling half-dead from his adrenaline crash, tucking his ink-blackened fingertips up under his armpits and leaning his elbows on the table.

He'd watched his cousin Jesse die holding the one thing Bree was never without: that goofy B pendant she got for her sweet sixteen. Russell hadn't seen her for days. They were all supposed to be in Chicago right now—him and Bree, Sam, Alex—driving out there, crammed in a car, and then crashing out in a hotel room after partying their asses off at BlocksFest, rolling, tripping, just friends kicking off the summer with a ton of sick music in a real city.

But no. He was still in Pike Lake, or some weird, nightmare version of it. Maybe he would be shivering in this empty room, isolated and out of his mind, with the ventilation buzzing and the fluorescent lights ringing in his ears, forever. Maybe this was Hell.

Finally, the door swung open. Deputy Meg kind of reminded Russell of a deer or an antelope; she had long legs and arms and a narrow torso, but her shoulders were broad for a lady. She had a boyish round face with big blue eyes, thin lips, and short blonde hair. White, crooked teeth. Some people said Meg Shaw was a dyke, but most didn't give her too hard of a time, her having grown up in Pike Lake and come back after being in the war.

"Are you okay? How are you feeling?" She set an unopened can of Mountain Dew on the table and sat across from him. "I'm so sorry you had to see that this morning, Russell."

You weren't supposed to take anything cops gave you. You weren't even supposed to talk to them. But his cottonmouth was killing him. He cracked the pop and took three long gulps before clanking the can on the table.

"You have to write up a lot of stuff when something like this happens," the deputy said. "Took a while. I need to ask you about some more things."

"You know what I know," Russell said. "I don't got nothing to add to it."

"Okay, sure. But help me out here. Do you know anyone who had a problem with Jesse?"

"A lot of people had a problem with Jesse. My mom don't even let him in the house, and Dad don't blame her. He was even banned from the Hobble for a couple years, and my dad *owns* it."

"Anybody seem like they were out for him lately?"

"No more than usual." Russ took another drink. "I ain't supposed to talk to cops without our lawyer."

"You're not a suspect. We're just talking."

"That why you took my prints and swabbed my hands?"

"It's procedure, Russ. We need to be able to exclude your prints from the actual assailant's and rule you out as the shooter. That means I have to get statements too. For instance, I need to put down the reason you were on your way to your cousin's house before seven in the morning."

He'd fallen asleep last night with his phone turned all the way up and set on the pillow just in case Bree texted or called. The text that came through at 4:35 a.m. still didn't wake him up. The message-waiting chime finally stirred him around six. He snatched the phone and blearily squinted at the screen in the dark. It was from a blocked number:

Russ itz ur cuz Jesse com ovr az s%n az u git DIS
I nEd 2 TLK 2 U v IMPORTANT

His cousin Jesse didn't have a phone, hadn't since he got locked up for a stretch as far as Russell knew. His house was just a short walk away. At six in the morning, Jesse might've still been up from the night before, all spun out, so within minutes of seeing the message, Russ scrambled through the old orchard and crossed the pasture to his cousin's place. He never imagined he'd be greeted by the muzzle of a cop's gun as Jesse died in the living room.

"I told you. Woke up and couldn't get back to sleep. Thought Jesse might be up too. Sometimes we watch movies together." Which was true. They also smoked a ton of weed.

"Have trouble sleeping?"

"Don't everybody?"

"Bree Wells's mom, Julie, just filed a missing person report. Have you heard from Bree lately, Russ?"

He shook his head, looking down at the table. "Nobody has. She ain't been online neither. But that was her necklace in Jesse's hand. I'm sure of that much. That blood—you didn't—" He took a breath and tried again. "Was she there?"

"The necklace is all we have so far." The deputy asked, "Were you and Jesse close?"

"Like I said, I'd drop in and hang out now and then." Russ folded his arms. "I know he had problems, and I get why people didn't like him. But he was okay to me. Never made fun of me for doing my thing. Like, I make masks and stuff, and he always thought it was, I dunno. He was cool about it."

"You make masks?"

"Yeah, you know. Old-school special effects like latex, prosthetics. Aliens. Monsters. I want to work for the movies." He wound a lock of his hair around his finger. "CGI ain't all that. Practical effects are coming back."

The deputy nodded. She probably didn't know what he was talking about. People usually didn't when it came to that.

"What about you and Shane?" she asked. "How's that?"

"Weird having him back after being gone for so long. We get on each other's nerves, but I mean, he's my brother."

She said, "He's a bit of a rough character."

"He did what he did. Was years ago."

"Listen. I know folks have run-ins with the law, time to time, and that can make for some bad feelings. But I hope we can put those aside for a minute. Shane went away because he hurt a couple of people pretty badly."

"Shane didn't do this."

"Well, we'll need to talk to him. Whoever killed your cousin is still out there."

"You think I don't know that?"

They wouldn't get away with it. Dad, Shane, and Uncle Duane would make sure of that. Whoever did it better hope the law caught him first.

"Russ, I need to know something. This is important: Did Brianne Wells ever hang around Jesse?"

"Bree? With Jesse? Hell no. He couldn't hardly get with any of them broke-down bitches from the Hobble. Excuse my language, ma'am. Sorry, but what would a girl like her do with a guy like him?"

"Her mom told me you were looking for her, and now Jesse's dead. That necklace being there is strange, don't you think?"

"I don't know nothing," he said, "other than there ain't no chance in hell Jesse ever spent five minutes with Bree. She thought he was a creeper. So him having that necklace, yeah, that's real *strange,* Deputy." He took a swig of the Mountain Dew, swallowed, tried to relax his shoulders. "Ain't there an actual detective around this place? Somebody whose job ain't writing speeding tickets and hassling skateboarders? 'Cause my cousin is dead and Bree's gone and I really just—"

When he ran out of words, he suddenly felt as if a python was constricting his ribs. Panic crushed the air from his lungs.

"I know you're angry." Her tone was even, calm. "And this is some scary stuff. But I have reason to think that Bree—"

The door squeaked open, and an old, dumpy-looking lummox in a wrinkled blazer stepped in, a manila folder in his hand.

"Detective Stoltz," she said, looking like she was trying to smile while someone stood on her foot. "An interview is in process here—"

"You get a statement?"

"Yessir. I was just about to wrap this up."

The detective grunted. "Yeah, go type up what you have. He can go."

"Sir?"

"The kid's mom is out there to pick him up." He waved the folder at the door. "You can grab him up later if we need to ask anything else. You know where he's at."

"We done?" Russ felt as if he could breathe again. Part of him didn't want it to be done—he hadn't told them about the text message, and maybe he should, or maybe there was something else he hadn't thought of that might help find out who killed Jesse or figure out where Bree was, and people said Deputy Meg was one of the good ones, far as cops went...

"Go on now, head on out," the detective said, hitching

his thumb at the door. "We'll take care of this, son. You can count on that."

Russ looked over his shoulder as he walked out of the room, seeing the deputy shaking her head with her fingers pressed against her temples. The detective caught his gaze a moment before reaching over and pushing the door closed.

"Look, Shaw," Detective Stoltz said with a shrug as she followed him down the hall, "he's had a rough morning as it is. He's printed. We swabbed his hands and took a statement."

Stoltz looked like he'd been up for a week. Over fifty years old and still closing cases, he never seemed rested, not since his wife passed away. His eyes glared, red with bloodshot, from a stubbly face the color of milk.

"Gunshot residue, Detective? Really? All a positive for that will prove is that he fired a gun at some point," Meg said. "Or that he was around someone who did. Which puts him in the same camp as just about anybody around here. Could have been weeks ago. That's something a prosecutor can sell to a jury, but it doesn't tell us jack."

Stoltz turned to her and pressed the heel of his hand against his head. "What are we going to get by holding him longer, other than his family buzzing around like hornets?"

"Let them buzz a bit, then. I just can't believe he's the only one on the scene, and we—"

A loud throat-clearing interrupted them. They looked over to see the sheriff standing in his doorway with his hands on his hips. He jerked his head toward the office and walked back inside. They followed. Sheriff Dale Cunningham gestured at two brown swivel chairs, and the deputy and the detective sat.

"Well." He lumbered behind his desk, an old football player with heavy-lidded eyes and a booming voice. "I got the rundown of the McCreech killing, but it seems you two are still in discussion about it. What's the issue?"

"Sir," Meg said, "are you aware that a pendant belonging to a missing minor was found in the victim's hand?"

"I know he had a necklace or something, yes."

"Sir," Meghan said. "Her mother identified it from a picture I took. Julie Wells filed a missing person report while Russell McCreech—that's her daughter's boyfriend—was held for his statement."

"Are you trying to give the woman a heart attack, Shaw? And you're giving her info from an ongoing investigation?" Detective Stoltz gaped at her. "Jesse McCreech was in shock. Dying. Who knows what he was trying to tell us?"

"I can't believe I'm hearing this." Meg clutched the chair's armrests as she checked her temper. "We have a missing girl. We have a murder. We have a necklace from the missing girl at the scene."

"There's nothing at the scene to suggest someone was held there," Stoltz said.

"I think someone might have kidnapped her, or this was a deal gone bad with her. Maybe we'll be rounding up rednecks for this shooting while the girl is locked up in a basement somewhere."

"You mean like a *Silence of the Lambs* sort of deal?" Stoltz rolled his eyes. "You watch too many movies."

"Things like that happen," Meg said, evenly. "Maybe not in that way, but they do."

"Maybe the girl is the one who shot him. That'd be a good twist, eh?"

"Take it, easy, Ed," the sheriff warned.

"Okay." Stoltz clasped his hands. "Let's say it's a cover-up for some dirty business, or payback for doing it. Let's say this was done as part of a kidnapping. Why does the guy hold on to the necklace?"

"I don't know." Megan scratched behind her ear, thinking. "Maybe he had it as proof of capture. Maybe I interrupted them. Maybe it was planted there."

Stoltz scoffed. "There's no evidence of any of that. And why would you plant evidence for a girl everyone thinks ran away to begin with, and then kill the guy you planted it on? I think we're looking at two or three different things here, and the case isn't going to benefit from us mixing them all up."

"What do you suspect, Detective?" Sheriff Cunningham asked. "I'd like to hear it."

"Somebody had a scrap with Jesse McCreech at his house last night after he came back with the stolen mower. Maybe this person helped him steal the thing, and they argued about how to split it. Maybe he was a dealer Jesse owed who just showed up." Stoltz propped his elbows on his knees. "They have words about something. Could be anything; they're out of their heads by this hour, probably. This is out front. Maybe they trade punches, maybe the other guy pulls a gun. Jesse runs inside. Tries to lock himself in. The guy busts the door open, bam. Jesse has got his shotgun, blasts at him, but the door bounces back from hitting the inside wall. Most of the spread hits it. The guy opens up on Jesse with his pistol, then flees, seeing that this has all gone way south. Something like that."

"There is blood outside, I'll give you that," Meg said. "We don't know whose yet."

"Or maybe the guy was gunning for him and just kicked

the door in." Stoltz mimed a kick and pointed a finger-gun. "People around here—even people like Jesse—don't bolt their doors, not usually. If it wasn't an altercation out front, it seems Jesse might have been expecting it. Point is, it could have happened a lot of ways. Word will get out about what went down, and we'll lean on the right people. It's only been a few hours."

"What about Bree?" Meghan said.

"What about her?" Stoltz replied. "Brianne Wells has run away before. She has MIPs, shoplifting. Fights with other girls. Jesse is a junkie and a thief as a matter of record. Maybe she traded the necklace for drugs or sold some of her stuff to fund a new adventure."

"Any sightings of her since Sunday?" Cunningham asked.

"No," Stoltz said. "But I bet it won't be long till her money runs out, or she gets spooked, and Mommy gets a weepy phone call from some Motel 6 again."

"Teenage girls with smartphones and online profiles don't just vanish. People notice them. They call or text. They Instagram funny signs and take goofy selfies," Meg said. "This girl has gone dark. We had someone at the scene who knew both her and the victim, and you let him walk out of here."

"Dale, what was I supposed to do?" Stoltz looked to the sheriff. "I had Alice McCreech in here like hell-on-jets, cursing a blue streak and demanding her son back. She'd already called that bastard attorney they keep on retainer. The whole family is out for blood, and there's probably a war-party gathering at the Hobble or the Ironwolf clubhouse right now—all looking to hang it on someone, probably one of the Hornween crew—or maybe on the good deputy here. We got a murder that could be on the news tonight and will be in the paper tomorrow. We have a ton of legwork to do, lab work to process, statements, and a ton more."

"And?" Cunningham asked.

"And all I'd be doing by holding that kid is making it worse. It would piss off every McCreech, most of the local bikers, along with every girlfriend, boyfriend, spouse, ex, common law, and everyone else who ever got a free drink from Leon at the bar. I need them to talk, and it's too early to get aggressive. These are people that, as a rule, don't talk to police. And if I make this about Brianne Wells too, the town's going to go loony. We'll be chasing leads in all directions with nothing to show for it. This is a *murder*. That is a true fact. If more shakes out, we'll deal with that when it comes. I can't make investigating a runaway girl who wanted to go to some rock concert a priority right now."

"I don't think she's a runaway," Meg said. "And if she is, it's because she's running from something."

Sheriff Cunningham sucked on his cheeks, mulling it over. "How about this: Detective Stoltz, you work the homicide, fine, that's what you do here. And you, Deputy, you seem pretty worked up about this missing person. It's Julie's girl, right? You helped out last time she up and went?"

"Yessir."

"Sure, sure. How about you look into that. You know the town as well as anybody. Ask around, see what you can find, but keep the details close. Keep it professional. And for God's sake, hold off on stirring up the McCreech folk about it, at least until they get their kin buried. You think you can do that?"

"Yessir, thank you."

"And both of you, help each other out." Cunningham hacked out a cough. "Alright, get to it."

Stoltz gave the deputy a stiff nod before walking out. As Meghan was about to leave, the sheriff called out, "Oh, and Meg, one more thing?"

"Yes, sir?"

"Call Paul Stephens and let him know we got his lawnmower back. He can pick it up at the property garage. I'm not charging a dead man." Sheriff Cunningham rubbed his eyes. "At least we have that part solved."

Russell slouched in the passenger seat as his mother, Alice, shook out a Kool 100, pinched it between her lips to pull it from the pack, and lit it all in a single motion while squealing her red '72 Camaro through an illegal left turn out of the sheriff's office parking lot. The radio was set to a Lansing station, blaring static-punctured Southern rock.

"Glad you called me." She cracked the window. "Who knows how long they would have tried to screw with you if you hadn't."

"Can I have one of those?"

"Since when you smoke menthols?"

"Since now."

Alice held out the pack. "How many times have we told you to stay away from Jesse? What were you doing over there at that hour, boy? Jesus. It could have been you shot full of holes in there. You know how close you came? What is wrong with you?"

Russ cranked his window down. "I dunno." He shrugged and lit up, dragging in the minty smoke's sting.

"You better know. At least one of my kids is gonna finish high school. If I don't see you in a cap and gown next summer, you're not gonna be long for this world, you can bet your skinny ass on that. I will end you. Swear to God."

"Roy was gonna go back for his GED."

"Well," Alice said quietly, "he probably would have. But you can graduate with your class. Don't drop out, and don't make the same mistakes. And you wear a helmet if you start riding again, you hear me?"

"Dad don't."

"He should, but he's set in his ways. You still got time."

Russell grunted. He didn't like motorcycles. He was sick to death of the damn things, and all the Billy Badass bullshit that went along with them, even before his brother Roy died on one.

"But Jesse, what a sad shame." She took a drag. "Never the sharpest knife in the drawer, that boy, but I never thought he'd go out like that. A fool killed by some other fool."

"How then?"

"Figured he'd do it to himself, trying something stupid. Drugs. Or like when he nearly blew his balls off trying to make that flamethrower."

"It worked for a minute," Russell said.

"How it ends is all that matters. That's all you're left with. Don't you ever forget it." Alice glanced into the rearview and scraped away a clot of eyeliner with a curved pink fingernail. "The detective ask you about your missing girlfriend, too?"

"How you hear about that?"

"You and Sam and Julie Wells have been asking all over town, and Pike Lake ain't exactly New York City, hon."

"Detective didn't ask me shit about shit. Just Deputy Meg."

"You have anything to say?"

Alice ran her hand through her bangs, then coasted to a stop at the light by the vacant ice cream parlor downtown. A row of fliers had been stapled onto the plywood over the window, each one with MISSING in bold black across the top and Bree with a gap-toothed smile below. Russ knew that soon he would see them everywhere: taped on the Shell station's glass door, tacked onto the Waffle Palace bulletin board, pasted to lampposts in the park, and taped on the Dairy Queen window. Bree's mom was in full-on freak-out mode.

"I didn't say nothing. Nothing other than I'm looking for her." He pressed his shaking hands flat against the dash, the cigarette jutting from between his knuckles. "Why you asking?"

Alice didn't respond.

"Mom? Why you asking about Bree?"

"Because you need to keep your head on straight, and nothing scrambles a boy's brain like his dick. Listen." She glanced over and wagged her finger, her gold bracelets flashing in the sunlight. "There are two kinds of trouble-people in this world. People looking for trouble, and people that just *are* trouble. And the people looking for trouble are usually the ones that cause problems."

"That don't make sense." He exhaled a stream of smoke.

"Sure does. Look at Jesse. For that boy's whole life, he was always looking for trouble. Doing the dumbest shit just to do it. Always getting himself into something. Sure enough, he found somebody who *was* trouble. And that's the end of that."

"What's that got to do with Bree?"

"Because that little one, she's looking for trouble, too. I know it. That's why she likes you so much."

"I ain't trouble half as much as most."

"Then she was smart to pick you," she said with a smirk. "And I think she was looking for trouble with more than just you. I think, just like Jesse, she might've really found it."

A freight train crossed the road ahead. Red lights flashed beneath the white, X-shaped sign as the bell clanged its alarm. When he lifted his cigarette to take a drag, it had burned out. His hand wavered as he reached to drop it out the window. Alice stopped at the crossing and reached over to squeeze Russell's knee.

"I know you like her, Russ, but she's always been looking for trouble. And our family has enough trouble going on. Always has. This will get handled." She reached over to brush the hair from his face as he stared at the graffiti-splashed boxcars clattering on the rails. "You stay away."

CHAPTER 2

Meghan had been asleep for about five hours when her cell phone rang. Never a deep sleeper, she snapped awake and snatched the phone from the nightstand. Sunlight blazed white lines around her blackout shades. The digital clock glowed a soft blue 6:44 p.m.

"Shaw speaking," she said.

"Meg, it's me." A bright female voice laughed. "Are you still in bed? I never thought the day would come where you'd be the one running late."

Myra. She pressed her knuckles against her forehead. She'd forgotten dinner plans with her sister.

"Guilty as charged. Sorry, had a hell of a shift."

"You still coming?" Not accusatory. Concerned.

"Yeah, yeah, I'm on my way." She swung her legs over the edge of the bed. "Need me to bring anything?"

"I hoped I could catch you before you passed the IGA. My tomatoes went soft, was wondering if you could pick up a couple for the salad and burgers."

"Of course. Be there in a jiff."

After a quick shower and a trip to the grocery store, she was driving down Whiting Road, the rows of corn flashing by like kinescope frames beneath a cloudless blue sky. Gold stretches of hayfield periodically broke up the flashing green. Turkey vultures circled on the other side of some silos to the east, probably roadkilled deer. Maybe the one over on the 54 from last night. She crested a hill, heading down toward the railway bridge arched over the road. The overpass dropped a patch of night on the asphalt. Darkness pooled beneath the concrete vault, drawing closer, the road beyond only a broken angle of light.

Her pulse quickened as she scanned the bridge. It was wrong to slow her vehicle; it made it an easier target, placed it longer in range of any roadside explosives or overhead fire. She couldn't help easing off the accelerator. There was no one on the bridge. There was nothing here to hurt her. This is what she told herself as she drew deep breaths, palms sweating on the wheel. It had been a while since an overpass triggered anything. When she first got back stateside, she'd go ten miles out of the way just to avoid driving under one. It looked like a giant cement tomb thrown open, her truck rolling into its chilling gloom.

The rectangle of light beyond the bridge expanded as she made her way beneath. She thought of the silver necklace shining in the dead man's red-spattered hand.

The tires shook against the shoulder's rumble strip, and she righted the wheel to swerve back into the lane. The railway bridge shrank in the rearview. She took a breath. She didn't want her sister to see her shaken. Myra gave her a hard enough time about quitting the therapy and refusing the meds already.

Myra, five years older than Meg, was a social worker for the Pike Lake school district. Dad was in Florida these days, something Meghan still couldn't accept, but at least he came up to the cabin for deer season. He was crazy about golf now. Mom passed years ago. Myra lived in a nice little ranch with a garden, just a mile from the Nature Center, where she worked running children's programs over the summer. They had dinner together about once a month. Sometimes Myra invited her to cookouts and things like that, which Meg would usually attend on the condition that Myra wouldn't try to set her up with any of her teacher friends.

She managed to get herself cooled down by the time she stood before her sister, who gave her a hug and complimented the tomatoes she brought. Meg grilled the burgers out on the back deck while Myra made the salad. They ate outside at the glass-topped umbrella table. A bed of orange and yellow tiger lilies bordered the yard, and a serenely smiling Buddha statue sat beneath some blossoming honeysuckle. They made small talk. Myra wore an Indian-print sundress, her hair back in a ponytail, and talked about changes in state funding for the schools and the upcoming millage vote until she asked Meg, "So, what's the matter?"

"Nothing," and then, seeing the doubting angle of Myra's head and pursing of her lips, Meg added, "long night at work. Got a call, found a guy dead out there."

"Oh, my. Car accident?"

"Murdered. Jesse McCreech." Meg shoveled in a forkful of salad, chewing as her sister gaped at her.

"There's a dark cloud over that family. That's awful."

"They don't always make the best choices." Meg shrugged. "And I've seen worse things."

"Still awful. They get the guy?"

"Not yet. That's for Ed to figure out. I just write traffic tickets, run kids out of field parties. I was only out there because he stole someone's lawnmower."

"You've only been with the department for three years. Give it time."

"Four," Meg grunted through a mouthful of burger, then swallowed. "And it's an *office*, not a 'department.' I ran prints on the mower as part of the stolen property case. Maybe someone helped Jesse steal it. If he had an accomplice, maybe that's the shooter. Or maybe he saw something. Surprised Ed didn't bring up the prints. He's a good detective, but I think he's losing his edge a bit as he gets older. Especially since his wife died. He's not a bad guy."

"His son was such a little asshole, though."

"Jeez, sis." Meg clutched at her heart in mock horror. "You're supposed to be the one who stands up for the problem children."

"I know." Myra blushed. "Brad Stoltz was a problem kid, but he made problems for a lot of kids too."

"He had a lot to deal with in high school. You remember how hard it was losing Mom."

"I know. Ed did the best he could with him. But the only reason I'm glad Brad went to college is that it got him out of Pike Lake. He was a bully. I know Ed can be, too."

"Sometimes Ed has to throw his weight around. You don't deal with the nicest people working as a detective."

"You'll end up a detective before you know it. You're probably looking into the murder yourself already. You can't help yourself."

"Hey, I respect the chain of command. But if something comes up, well." Meghan smirked. "We'll see. Anyway, I have a case now, sort of. Ed's tied up with the homicide, so I'm taking over the missing person on Julie Wells's girl."

Myra took a sip of iced tea. "Bree. I know her. She run

away again?"

"I think there might be something more," she searched for the word, "complex to it. Some new evidence came up."

"You think someone," she shifted in her chair, "took her? Sort of like the last time?"

"Can't rule it out. Hasn't been that long, but she just up and vanished."

A pair of chipmunks darted across the yard, and sparrows splashed in the birdbath. The sisters ate, not talking for a while.

"How's Julie doing with all this?"

"She's managing." Meg shrugged. "You deal with Bree Wells, Russell McCreech, or Samantha Wells at school at all? Russell's the dead guy's cousin. He's Leon's kid."

"Is Leon the one who was drunk-driving a tow truck and killed that guy back when?"

"That's Leon's older brother, Duane," Meg said. "Same biker set. Duane's still in prison for that. Leon's the Iron-wolfs guy who runs the Hobble and the gun shop. Oh, and the scrapyard."

"Yeah, that's right. Not surprised Bree got pulled toward that clique. She got into fights pretty often after she ran away. Girls started a rumor that the guy who took her was a pimp."

"Anything to that?"

"I think he was just some internet creep. But she was a pariah after. Had the 'bad girl' rep, not in a good way."

"At fifteen she was no worse than anybody else that age who wandered into one of Dan Hornween's parties. A lot of kids do. Nothing we could nail Dan for. He cooperated with us. Couldn't prove anything happened at his place."

"Well, over the past couple years, she took on a punk

look. Got really, I don't know. Flamboyant. Got prettier, too. She's kind of the leader of her little group. Samantha Black is with her all the time—She's an odd one."

"Odd how?"

"Sam has this zoned-out, apathetic front. She barely turns in any homework but never fails a class. Her test scores are off the charts. She's a borderline genius and doesn't seem to care. Or doesn't want people to know."

"That's a dumb thing for a smart girl to hide."

"She works at the tattoo parlor out on Old 19. Books appointments. That place is bad news."

"Isn't that a Hornween place?"

"Yeah, Ricky Hornween runs it. Dan's little brother. I think Dan runs the whole show since their dad died though."

"Oh, I know," Meg said. "I went on a date with Dan Hornween once, you know. In tenth grade."

"You did? Jesus. I didn't know that."

"You were off with the Peace Corps. Didn't think you'd want to read about it in a letter. He was actually pretty sweet back then, or at least could act like it. Better looking, that's for sure. Took me to go play air hockey and get ice cream. But he was dating like three other girls at the same time, and I told him I wasn't into that."

"Gross. He was in a band back then, right? What were they called?"

"Powerhead." Meghan laughed.

"Powerhead. My God. Yeah. They won the Battle of the Bands one year."

"I bet Dan was crushed that Ricky's band got bigger. Remember sKraYp'D?"

"Ugh. They had that 'Shame You' song on the radio for

a second." Meg grimaced. "What happened to them?"

"A whole lot of nothing. Ricky got sent up on Possession with Intent. So now he runs a skanky tattoo parlor."

"Oh, yeah. Right." Myra took a drink. "Powerhead was actually better than sKraYp'D."

"Not that that's saying much."

"It's not."

Meg chuckled. They both looked out to the sunset.

"I try not to worry about you, you know," Myra said. "How are you?"

"Fine, Myra. Sober, if that's what you're getting at."

"But how are you these days, just, in general?"

"Perfect," Meg said. "Couldn't be better. And you?"

"Oh. You know. Great. Just fantastic."

They both laughed, rocking back in their chairs as night seeped in.

Russell McCreech couldn't focus on the video game enough to make it through a single level without ending up out of ammo and surrounded, so he tossed the controller onto his bedroom floor. He switched off the console and leaned back on the bed to stare up at his masks: a zombie with half its face rotted away to reveal the skull, a blood-spattered Michael Myers, a clown with a mouthful of razor teeth, and twelve more oversaw his room. He'd made them himself. Like empty-eyed guardians, they watched over him from shelves near the rafters. The Big Bad Wolf sat in pieces on the work-table, latex scraps and furry fabric neatly laid out by glue guns, jars of putty, tubes of adhesive, and a tackle box of pins, thread, brushes, and paints. He still needed yellow pearl enamel for the teeth.

A brown-stained Graffix bong stood beside a horn-handled Bowie knife on the nightstand. Piles of dirty clothes and empty cans littered the floor. He reached for the bong but changed his mind. He was practically down to shake and stems already.

Russell dug in his pocket for his smartphone. No new notifications. He pulled up a picture Bree sent him just three weeks ago, one of her nudes, snapped in a spotless mirror. Towels hung neatly on a rack behind her, matching the chrome toothbrush holder and soap dish in the foreground. You could still see brush strokes in her wet hair like tilled rows in a damp field. Her shoulders and the bridge of her nose, lightly sunburned, shone a deeper pink than the honey tan of the rest. She stood to the side, the front leg stepping out slightly to conceal her. Her back arched. Her chin lifted. One hand reached across her body to cover her breasts, the other held out a pink iPhone to the mirror. She smirked, not snottily but with mischief, and her eyes were bright and green. "Thinkin of u" was the message. Russell felt himself stiffen, but then he remembered how things were right now. With a dry mouth, he sucked on his tongue.

He sent her a text:

> Jesse got shot n killed n he had ur necklace. Im
> not mad or NE thing. Just want 2 know ur ok.
> Find a way 2 let me know. Let me help u.

It was the twenty-seventh message sent since he'd last seen her. No replies.

How did Jesse end up with Bree's pedant? Bree could get just about whatever she wanted without having to hit up burnouts like his cousin. Jesse sold weed now and then, and he usually had a mix of pills he traded around, but she had plenty of better connections—her bestie, Sam, for one. And Jesse, while no way on the up-and-up, wasn't a killer or kidnapper—but when your head is all twisted up, who knows what you might do? And, most of all, what was it he wanted to tell Russ before he was shot down?

Russell lay on his back and closed his eyes.

A single knock cracked against the bedroom door. Russell jolted into a sitting position while shoving the phone back into his pocket.

"Little bro, it's Shane. Open up."

Russell rolled his eyes. "Go away," he moaned back.

"It's important." The locked doorknob rattled. "Come on, you beating off in there? I can cuuuuuuum back in a few minutes."

"Dude, leave it alone. I don't need any—"

The door flew open with a splintering crash, Shane's motorcycle-booted foot following close behind.

"*Asshole.*" Russell jumped to his feet. "What the hell, man?"

Shane stepped in, ducking down under the doorframe. He was always breaking shit and then looking confused, even though it was on purpose, and afterward he said the same thing every time. He glanced at the busted frame and said, "I can fix that," before striding into the middle of the room, kicking a couple pop cans. Three years in Jackson Penitentiary hadn't done much to slow him down. If anything, it had made him surer of himself, no matter how clueless he was.

"Sit down, need to talk a sec." Shane fanned the air and grimaced. "Jesus, crack a window. Smells like jizz and bong-water stew in here."

Larry Dodge wandered into the doorway. He scratched at his goatee with a meaty hand. Larry looked like a bald, hulking ogre, even though he was only about five-foot-seven. He rode a Harley with the club, sometimes drove a wrecker for Russell's dad, and worked graveyard shifts at the scrapyard. He was famous for bringing shame to Pike Lake at the wrestling state finals by breaking some kid from South Lyon's arm during a match fifteen years ago. He chose to do that instead of pinning him for first place because, in his words, "The guy just seemed like a dick." Most nights you could find Larry passed out astride his bike in the Hobble's parking lot after closing. Like a kid in a Halloween store, he gaped up at Russell's mask collection.

"Will you morons get out of my room?" Russell flailed his arms. "Please?"

"Sit. Down." Shane's gray eyes glinted. "This is business. Family stuff."

"Larry ain't family." Russell sat down on the edge of the bed. "Unless you two are finally getting married."

Larry pointed at a mask. "One of the Hellraiser dudes!"

"I made that," Russell said. "Made all of them."

"No shit?" Larry whistled. "Damn."

"Hey. Russ." Shane snapped his fingers. "Focus. Need to talk to you about Cousin Jesse. You see anything?"

"You mean other than him dying?"

"I know. It's messed up. But did you see anyone there, anything that—"

"No. Deputy got me as soon as I came in through the back."

"Why you go walking up to a cop?"

"She got the drop on me. Never ran into the law in Jesse's living room before."

"Fair enough." Shane nodded. "Now, I got to know some things, though. That morning—"

"Are those original Transformers?" Larry interrupted, pointing to a shelf across the room.

"Yeah," Shane said. "They used to be mine before Alice gave 'em to this little punk-ass. So, Russ—"

"Can I look at 'em?"

"I don't give a shit," Shane snapped. "Russ, do *you* mind if Larry looks at *my* Transformers?"

"Mom says they're mine now. But, no, I don't."

Larry plodded over to the toys, stomping on clothes and cans.

"Why you going over to Jesse's so early, Russ?"

"Went through this with the cops like five times. Sick of talking about it. He texted me super-late from a blocked number, okay? I didn't tell the cops that, but he said he needed to tell me something important."

"Why the hell would he need to talk to you?"

"How am I supposed to know? He was dead when I got there."

"You think the deputy shot him?"

"Didn't hear no shots walking over there, and she seemed freaked for real." Russ sighed. "Look, I asked Jesse to let me know if he saw Bree around. I ain't seen her for days. He had a necklace of hers on him when he died. Maybe the text I got was about that—where he found the thing."

"Who else does your girl hang out with, besides you and that chubby girl with the bull-ring in her nose? Does she hang out with that prissy kid in your band? Alex?"

"Let me look into it." Russell held up his hand to halt Shane's next question. "I don't need you geniuses kicking my friends' doors down."

"Well, that's the thing, Russ." Shane rubbed the stubble on his chin. "The cops found something having to do with that little girl at Jesse's place. And he's our cousin, and see, you and that girl were a thing."

"So." Russ folded his arms. "What's that gotta do with anything?"

"A couple of things." Shane squatted down to look his brother in the face. "First of all, someone killed our cousin. Now, I know he was a world-class dickbag, but he's family, and we got to take care of our own. Second, if that necklace connects Jesse to that missing girl—and you're her boyfriend—that means cops poking around in our shit."

"Ain't they always?"

Shane ignored him. "But most of all, if anything happened to little Bree—if she was kidnapped, or raped, or chopped up and stuffed into sixteen Hefty bags spread out between Lansing and Detroit—"

"Watch yourself, Shane. I won't win, but I'll make it hurt."

Shane smiled. "I'm just saying: If anything happened to that girl, the first person they're gonna come after ain't poor dead Jesse, or me, or Larry over there. The first one they're gonna pin it on is you, buddy. And since you was the first one to walk onto that scene, you're probably the most likely suspect for killing Jesse. Hell, if I didn't know you so good, I'd be thinking that myself. So, stay out of this shit-storm. Dad has me and Larry on it."

"Check it out." Larry held one of the toys out to them. "Still remember how to transform Grimlock."

Shane winced. "And some other more capable folks. So, don't ask any questions, and keep your mouth shut."

Russell nodded.

"You ain't gonna listen to me." Shane pressed the heel of his hand to his temple and sighed. "Are you?"

"Have I ever?"

Shane stood up and pointed in Russell's face. "Just know that if you go digging around in this, and Dad or Uncle Duane hears—It ain't gonna be a conversation like this one. Even Mom ain't gonna be able to save you. There's something bad going on out there. Let it go."

Russell looked away, up to the masks. Killers and demons, aliens and monsters, made by his own hands, their shadow-filled eyes staring down at the piles of dirty, black T-shirts, rows of horror movie posters, his bongs, knives, and video games. Shane was right. The law wasn't going to be on his side in this, and something bad was going on. Somewhere, Bree was the middle of it. Russ had to find her—before someone else did.

Triple Felony Tattoos hadn't skimped on the red neon, that was for sure. The shop's name, set in an Old West–style font, blazed in the front window. A trucker-girl silhouette sat on top of the letters, holding a pistol emitting flashes of purple gun smoke. The shop shared a strip mall space with a tax preparation office called Taxes-n-More. Meghan wondered exactly how liberal their definition of "more" was. A group of heavy-set boys in jerseys and T-shirts loitered in the lot's corner around a jacked-up truck, eyeing her cruiser as she stepped out and headed toward the parlor.

Samantha was a sleepy-eyed, curvaceous girl with Cleopatra-style eyeliner and bottle-blacked hair, tapping away on her phone and barely looking up when the bell on the door clanged, hardly audible over the music blasting on the shop's speakers. A large framed poster of sKraYp'D, featuring Ricky Hornween at the forefront, hung on the wall behind her.

"Hi, Officer. You hunting for someone, or do you need some ink?" Her voice was flat and nasal, and the ring through her septum glinted as she spoke.

"Think I've got enough tattoos for now. You're Sam Black?"

"Yes, ma'am." The girl nodded and set down her phone.

"Hi, I'm Deputy Meg, in case you don't remember. You're friends with Bree, right?"

"Bree Wells? Yeah, she's my best friend. She in trouble?"

"Well, her mom hasn't seen her lately. Was wondering if you had, or had any ideas of where she might be."

"I haven't been able to get a hold of her either. At first, I was mad. I mean, she had all of our tickets for BlocksFest in Chicago, but she never showed up. Now, I don't know." She leaned over and turned down the music. "It's strange, right?"

"When's the last time you talked to her?"

"Hmmm. Saturday night, I think. Chatted online. Just about regular stuff, you know. What we were watching on TV, what bands we wanted to see at the fest. Nothing weird."

Nothing weird. She felt the need to point that out. Sam's flat affectation made her hard to read; Meghan thought the girl seemed either stoned or medicated. Her pupils were dilated either by drugs or stress, there was no way to tell. But she wasn't talking much and wasn't asking very many questions. Considering the girls were best friends, Meghan found Sam's lack of curiosity unusual. It wasn't the time to pressure her, though.

"Anyone else here I can talk to?"

"The piercer just stepped out to get sandwiches, but he'll be back. Ricky, he's the owner, and he does all the tats. He's out for a bit."

"I thought Dan Hornween was the owner."

"Well, *officially*, yeah. But it's Ricky's shop."

"When will Ricky be back?"

"Dunno. He's out-of-state right now. Flew out on Sunday, heading to Los Angeles."

"Vacation?"

The girl looked around before practically whispering, "I'm not supposed to tell anyone this, but...it's for *Tattoo Kings*. Can you believe it?"

"Tattoo Kings?"

"The reality show." Meghan took the girl's hint of a smile to be approving. "He sent in his portfolio and a tape. They love his work, plus, you know. His story. Famous, then in trouble with the law, now starting a clean new life kind-of-thing."

Meg didn't know if Ricky Hornween qualified as "famous," or if running what was probably a front for the Hornweens' white-trash mafia was exactly a "clean new life."

"Well, that's great for Ricky. Anybody traveling with him?"

"Who knows? Maybe."

"Can you tell me a bit about Bree? What does she want to do after graduation?"

"Bree's creative. Wants to do something with it. Writing books or acting. But, like, she knows she needs another gig to support it while it gets off the ground. Modeling, probably. And she totally looks like a model. Not like a Cosmo type, though. Like an alt-model. You know Shattered Dolls? The website?"

"I'm familiar." It was a porn site of young tattooed girls. They also hosted blogs on which the models talked with the site's fans, which was supposed to make it more sex-positive or something. Meghan didn't get it. "She's not old enough to be on that kind of site."

"Oh, I know." Sam said, a bit quickly. "Shattered Dolls just did an event over at Lil' Angels on Monday night, and Bree was so mad she couldn't go. She's just a month away from being eighteen."

"Did she mention that the last time you two chatted?"

Sam sucked in her lower lip and looked up as if thinking. "I don't think so."

Right. "Could I have one of Ricky's cards?"

Sam gave her one, as well as a pamphlet describing the shop's services and proper aftercare. The girl didn't have much else of use to say. Meg put the card and pamphlet in her pocket and added two underlines beneath the name Ricky Hornween in her notebook before heading out the door.

Russell stood beside the dumpsters near the overgrown lot and watched Jolene step out through the back door of Imperial Dragon Fast Chinese. She dug a pack of Newports from her server's apron. Her red hair, pulled back into a tight bun, accentuated the rouge on her sharp cheekbones and the arches of penciled eyebrows. She shook a joint out of the pack, lit up, and beckoned him over. Dragging on the joint with her weight on one hip as she stood on the strip mall's loading dock, she looked to Russell like one of those women they painted on the side of bombers in World War II, except older, with orthopedic sneakers and a deep suntan.

"Got your text. You searching?" She exhaled, holding the joint out to Russell. "'Cause I got some new green you're really gonna dig."

"I'm searching," Russell said, plucking it from her fingers. "But not for that."

"You need anything else, you've come to the wrong place, darlin', unless it's some almond chicken. They deal that in front." One corner of her mouth pulled into a smile. "But I might be able to send you in the right direction."

Some pots banged and clanged behind the door, followed by muffled yelling. Jolene glanced over her shoulder, then reached out to take the joint back.

"You know Bree, right?" Russell asked. "Hair shaved on the sides. Leather jacket with studs down one sleeve."

"Of course I know your girlfriend, hon. Why?"

"She was supposed to meet up with me and some people to go on a road trip to a fest in Chicago, but she didn't show," Russell said, taking the joint.

"She strike you as the dependable type?"

"This is different. She was really excited about it. And no one's seen or heard from her for days," he said. "No texts, nothing online, silent. Wondering if you had seen her. I'm asking around. Sam's been looking, too. And Bree's mom's got the cops looking for her now," Russ said, "but they ain't taking it serious."

"Well, that's good, in a way. At least she hasn't been busted."

A peach blush glowed in the sky as the sun sank, and the cicadas' songs swelled in the lot beyond the broken asphalt.

"Even if she had, she'd be out by now." Russ reached for the joint, which Jolene hit again before handing back.

"Misdemeanor possession, ain't like they're gonna throw away the key. She don't deal and don't drive around with any Class A's."

"Oh, she doesn't, eh?" Jolene clucked her tongue. "You sure about that? She stopped by my apartment a few days ago. Monday. By herself."

"What for?"

"So, when she came over Monday, she wasn't looking to buy. She was looking to sell. Not the kind of thing I'm looking to move. That girl had big ol' shards of molly. But I'm not into it, believe it or not, and if I sell it once or twice I'll have kids hassling me about it all the time. I got my steady side thing; it gets me by. For now, at least." She grimaced. "So, anyhow, she had that MDMA. Said she had even more, but it was spoken for—said she got herself a regular connection, though. Didn't drop any names."

"We all roll, but I ain't never heard of her dealing. I'm with her almost every day. I would have seen it." Russ rubbed his jaw.

"Well, she might've jumped at an opportunity. Seems like a fest would be a good place to move that. And if anyone around here has a big chunk of MDMA that looks like the damn Dark Crystal, they might've been talking to your girl."

"Thanks, Jolene. Can I get a dime of your new stuff? Got a party at the lake I'm headed to tonight."

"Yeah, don't let the detective work get in the way of a good time, Sherlock," Jolene said. She lowered her voice, adding, "I'm sorry about Jesse, hon. I'm sure that's not easy—with your girl skipping out on the concert, too. Just remember, it's not up to you to sort this out. Bree's a tough girl, she'll turn up."

Russ nodded and took her rough, tan hand, pressing the crumpled money into her palm as she rolled the baggie into his fingers.

"Yeah, well, we all gotta look out for each other," he said.

Uniformed sheriffs and unattended women weren't common visitors at Lil' Angels Gentlemen's Club, and Meghan was both. The doorman waved her through, speaking into his collar-mic before she even stepped from the foyer's grimy light into the bar's pounding noise and multicolored gloom.

The place seemed like a darkened bowling alley retrofitted with a runway stage, some laser lights, and a few disco balls, because that was exactly what it was. What had been an attached pro-shop now sold cheap sex toys and porno. Beneath the sharp citrus air-freshener and dry undercurrent of baby powder, Meg was sure she smelled cheese fries and rented shoes.

She turned the heads of scattered patrons gathered around the tip-rail and lurking in the booths as she passed. All of them averted their gaze, looking back to the topless woman in Lucite platform heels clomping around the runway stage. One man leaned over and said something through cupped hands into his buddy's ear, who slapped his knee and bayed an open-mouthed laugh. A cocktail waitress, wearing a pair of glittery cardboard wings and a feathery halo on a wire, gripped an empty tray and smiled uneasily. Across the room, the bartender's eyes drilled holes into Meghan. She met them with a nod and headed straight to him. The three men standing around the bar dispersed as she approached.

The bartender tilted his shaved head slightly and cracked his knuckles against his palm.

"Help you?" he shouted over the music.

"Tell Dan Hornween the Sheriff's Office is here to talk to him."

"Dan, huh." He looked up as if thinking. "Yeah, he ain't in."

"His Lexus is. Saw it out back."

"How about that. Must've left it here."

"Look—what's your name, sir?"

"Richard," he said. "But they call me Big Dick. You can call me that, too, if y'like."

She rolled her eyes. "Look, Dick. There's a lot of ways this can go, and all of them—except me getting to sit down with Hornween—are a huge pain in everyone's ass. I'll cut to the chase. Get your boss, or I shut this shithole down."

He blinked. "Our licenses are in order, lady."

"Sure. But I could decide all of your dancers need to be interviewed. And you, too. Everyone gets twenty-four hours in a very uncomfortable chair at the station."

"Bullshit. You can't detain for an interview." He sniffed. "Why don't you try again tomorrow?"

"Maybe I'll just spend the evening talking to all of your patrons and dancers, here. I'm sure they'll all be comfortable with that. Nothing the clientele of Lil' Angels enjoys more than an unexpected police encounter, right? I'll park my cruiser right in the middle of your front lot. With the lights on."

She strode toward a table of red-faced boys in baseball caps and college sweatshirts, no doubt home for the summer. A boozy reunion at the titty bar.

"Excuse me, gentlemen, please stay right there." The college kids froze when she called out, one of them holding his beer midway to his face. "Could I see your IDs, please?

I need to ask you some questions."

Panic widened the boys' red-rimmed eyes. A group of shitkickers in the corner stood up from their table and headed toward the door. Meghan glanced back at the bartender, who held two fingers to his earpiece and nodded. He waved over the waitress with the cardboard wings, said a few words, and pointed to Meg. The waitress set her tray down on the bar, walked over to Meghan, and shyly asked that she follow her to Mr. Hornween's office.

They passed through a security door marked STAFF ONLY and went down a cement-brick hallway where two short, tan girls wearing body glitter and terrycloth robes stepped out of the way.

"What's your name?" Meghan asked the waitress.

"Angel Five," she said, then shook her head, blushing. "Sorry, habit. I'm Sara."

"I'm Meghan. Do you like working here?"

"I don't know. It's okay. Do you like being a cop?"

Meg nodded.

"Do you have to go to school to do it?"

"Not as long as you'd think." She pulled her smartphone from her pocket. "Here, take a look at a picture for me."

She displayed the screen with a picture of Jesse McCreech's county jail photo.

"Oh yeah, that's Jesse. Creeper. Used to never tip, always broke, puts his hands on the girls. He's banned from the club—ask any of the door guys."

"When was he banned?

"Year ago, maybe more. Hasn't been in since. Still hangs out in the lot sometimes."

Meg swiped to a picture of Bree in her leather jacket and mohawk. "How about her?"

"I recognize her," Sara said, but Meg's excitement waned when she followed up with, "She's the one from all the missing posters."

"Have you seen her anywhere else?"

Sara screwed up her face for a moment, and then she said, "Just the posters. We should get going, we're not supposed to loiter in the hall."

They arrived at another security door, this one with a camera mounted over it. Meg gave her card to Sara, and then the waitress pressed the buzzer beside the door. The heavy, reinforced steel groaned open. When Meg entered, it boomed shut behind her like a vault. Sara—Angel Five—remained behind. Meg climbed a leopard-print-carpeted staircase, lit by pink neon, and arrived at the office.

Dan Hornween slouched with his snakeskin boots propped up on his desk, backlit by a half-dozen monitors overseeing the club. One hand absently twirled a lock of his long, stringy black hair, the other held a lit cigarette. Orange- and purple-skinned cartoon women copulated with tigers and panthers in a couple of blacklight posters framed above an overstuffed couch opposite the desk. The same leopard-print carpeting from the stairway ran wall-to-wall in the office, and faux torches flickered with electric flame in their sconces to throw shifting light across the dim room

Dan exhaled smoke, a smile splitting his gaunt face. "Evening, Deputy. Looking for a career change?" His gold front tooth flashed beneath his mustache.

"Did you prop your feet up on the desk and light up just so I could walk in and see you looking so goddamn cool, Dan?" She snorted. "Save it. I'm not here to bust your balls."

"Is that a fact, now?" He swung his feet off the desk. "Wish I could say I was happy to see you, Meg. I'm a little bit hurt you never looked me up when you got back state-side.”

“Nothing personal. I figured when I got with the sheriffs, I’d end up seeing you eventually anyway.”

“And here you are.” He sneered. “Now, you know I’m not in the business of talking to cops.”

“You’re not in the business of pissing us off, either.”

“Aw, come on, now. What have I ever done to you? Not that I never tried.” He pointed to the couch, a silver skull-shaped ring glinting on his veiny hand. “Have a seat.”

“I’ll stand, thanks.”

“I make you nervous?”

“That couch makes me nervous. I doubt it’s sanitary.”

“You’d be right. It’s fucking filthy.”

“I’m here to see you about a young lady,” she said, pulling out her smartphone.

“You and everyone else.”

“Here, take a look at this girl.” She handed him her phone. “Recognize her?”

He looked at the screen a couple moments before saying, “I honestly don’t.” He handed back the phone. “But a lot of girls come through here. Who is she?”

“Her name is Brianne Wells. Goes by Bree. Went missing about a week back. Her friend said she aims to work as a dancer.”

“Nice that she has dreams.”

“Was wondering if she had come by.”

“Haven’t hired any new girls in a couple months.” He took a drag. “One’s a Mexican or something. Legal, of course. Other is an oriental. I still hire cheerleader and schoolgirl white chicks but haven’t needed to bring in any more trailer-park-hot ones—even the emo-punk-whatever types like that. Only businessmen are into it, and that's not my clientele. Chicks like that and corn-fed farm girls are all I get, so if anything a bit exotic comes in, I'll bring 'em on. We had this Italian girl pretending to be an Indian—dots not feathers—for a while. Finger cymbals, snake-charmer music—"

"What about your amateur nights?"

He cleared his throat. "First Monday of every month."

"Really, how about that? That's around the last time anyone saw my missing girl."

"Jesus, Meg." He sighed. "What kinda guy do you think I am?"

"The kind of guy who runs three businesses that move a lot of cash with very few verifiable goods involved—self-storage, a strip club, and a tattoo parlor."

"It's a tattoo *studio,* thank you, offering professional body art services."

"That why you called it Triple Felony Tattoos?"

"Marketing, Meg. Everybody loves the outlaw thing. And I know that Lil' Angels isn't exactly a pillar of the community, but teenage girls ain't my business."

"How'd you know she was a teenager?" She placed her hands on his desk and leaned in.

"You showed me a picture." His mustache twitched before he said, "Look at her, for God's sake."

"You have records of all the girls who danced last amateur night? Release forms, ID info, all that?"

"You have a warrant?"

She smiled. "Is that how you want to do this? You really want me to have a judge sign off on a warrant for this place regarding a missing seventeen-year-old?"

Dan swiveled his chair and stood. He stomped over to a

file cabinet in the corner and, after some rummaging and grumbling, yanked out a black binder.

"Here." He dropped the binder onto the desk with a thud. "That's all the amateur nights for the last three months. I run a tight ship, and I'm not so stupid that I'd risk losing a chunk of my enterprise and maybe landing in the joint just to sell a few more watery drinks to hicks who want to ogle an underage girl. We had a sponsor for the last one—an alt-modeling site called Shattered Dolls—so we were double-sure about the performers. Take a look. It's legit."

"Thanks, Dan. You know Jesse McCreech at all?"

"Only by his reputation." Dan sat down and tented his fingers. "And, of course, what they're saying about his recent and not-very-unexpected end."

"Not unexpected how?"

"Jesse McCreech was a drunk, tweaker thief who I wouldn't let through the door here, and that is something of an achievement. Hear he got shot up in some hillbilly deal-gone-bad over a stolen lawnmower. Sounds par for the course on that one."

She smiled thinly. "Your brother around?"

"Ricky's not welcome in the club, either."

"Meaning?"

"Meaning I don't need his bullshit rock star attitude drinking up all my stock for free and trying to pick up my girls when they should be working. He runs the tattoo studio. That's his thing. We haven't been in touch lately. We're not exactly what you'd call close."

"I heard he skipped state."

"Not what I hear. He should be down at the studio. It's what I pay him for."

"Well, he's not." Meghan picked up the binder. "Can I

hang onto this?"

"This is a business. I have a photocopier."

After a couple paper jams and a cold goodbye, Meghan walked out to her cruiser in the back lot with a manila folder of the copied records. Sara, without her halo and wings, stood by a battered red Festiva with a Deadhead decal on the back window, smoking in the moonlight.

"Hey, um, Officer?"

Meghan replied warmly, "Hi, Sara. You off work now?"

"No, just on break. But listen. That girl you showed me—the missing one? I've seen her around. Not here, but you know the tattoo place over on Old 19?"

"Triple Felony? Yeah, I know it."

"Saw her there last time I was in for a piercing. She wasn't getting any work done, just hanging around, talking to the girl up front." Sara looked around the lot. "It wouldn't have stuck with me, but then I saw her again at a party that weekend with an older guy. Like, much older. A couple months ago, maybe more."

"I see." Meghan nodded. "Where was this, and do you remember what he looked like?"

"It was one of the parties at the Hornween place—and she was with Ricky Hornween. The tattoo guy who used to be in that band with that one song. And you didn't hear it from me."

Russell walked toward the party at the lake, heading most of the way through the dirt bike paths, deer trails, and gullies that crisscrossed the sprawling woods from Whiting Road to the 52. Even in the dark, he knew them like a hobo knew the railways. When he moved through them alone, he tried to imagine he was making his way through an undiscovered country. America had once been wilderness from coast to coast. He liked to think about what it would be like if the woods were not some separate place set apart from the world but the entirety of it.

It was hard to do when so many landmarks along the way betrayed his fellow humans: a rusted out old Bronco, deer stands, patches of marijuana that shifted location each season. He steered clear of the plants, figuring they were someone's personal stash—and he admired the work they obviously put into it. They rose like swaying green aliens from the black loam. Sometimes wild strawberries sprouted in the patches of light around them, their tiny fruits like scattered red jewels.

Near one of the gullies in the woods stood a gnarled tree, the trunk wider than a house door, so stooped with age that its boughs spread like a green awning, and the branches' tips brushed the earth. In the daytime, sunlight streaming from between the leaves crocheted the ground beneath. Bree and he would hide there together, laying on the old army blanket he kept rolled in his backpack, smoking joints or sipping vodka and pop, making out until their clothes came off and then pulling them back on when too many mosquitos were drawn to the heat of their blood.

A couple weeks ago, she said, "I'll miss places like this." Still on her back, she picked up her pink top and brushed some leaves from it. "There won't be anything like this when we're in New York."

"Yeah, well, at least we'll be able to find somewhere to go after eight at night." He laughed. "You still hanging out with Ricky?" He tried to make it sound casual, but it was rushed and tense.

"You're still worried about that?" She sat up, revealing the giant black raven inked across her back—which Russell still could not see without thinking of Ricky Hornween leaning over her shirtless body, his gloved hands guiding the needle across her skin. "Jesus. You know, I'm not fucking every dude I hang out with."

"I never said that. But when Sam started working at the shop, I said I didn't want to see her—or you—getting mixed up the shady shit going on around that place."

"Oh, like your uncle's scrapyard and your dad's bar and his gun store are totally legit. They run a motorcycle gang, for godssake."

"It's a riding club. Anyway, I wouldn't want you getting into that, neither." He ran his fingertip down from between her shoulders to the small of her back, softly. "You're amazing—like in every way—and once you get into the bullshit around here, you never get out. You deserve better than Pike Lake."

"You're sweet." She put her head on his shoulder. "Don't you worry. We're going to get out of here. Together. I got plans, babe. Plans in motion."

He raised an eyebrow. "What kind of plans?"

She plucked the cigarette pack from the blanket's folds. "You shouldn't ask questions if you don't want answers."

Something in the way she said it scared him, so he shut up. Now he was alone in the woods, wishing he had those answers. Their tree looked like a misshapen tent, its leaves blue and gray in twilight. He hurried past it, his head bowed as he dragged on his smoke, stomping toward the lake.

On any other night, he would have been excited to be walking on a summer night to a party. He'd be looking forward to a Bluetooth speaker playing on the grass, the bonfire's light spilling across the water, passing bottles and joints until the moon was high and the boys began trying to coax the girls into skinny dipping with them, every time the girls acting reluctant and looking to each other for permission to accept or refuse, every time the boys acting like it was no big deal. Sometimes it happened, and sometimes it didn't. But this wasn't any other night.

He needed to start gathering information. Especially from Samantha Black. If anyone knew what his girlfriend was up to lately, it would be her.

He strode up the slope, greeted by firelight and the lake's murky breeze. He crested the hill and saw the bonfire thrashing and trembling—but no one seemed to be there. Then, sitting on a blanket on the fire's far side, he saw Sam. He smiled and waved, but she didn't wave back. Her oval, red-lipped face looked like a sad-eyed china doll when she saw him. She gave the slightest shake of her head.

His phone buzzed in his pocket. He pulled it out and looked down to read the text without breaking pace. It was a message from his friend Alex, just coming through now that Russell had emerged from the ravine:

Do NOT go to the lake. Bad shit. Call me.

He looked up in time to see a man's lanky shape, backlit by the flames, striding toward him. A large, silver skull ring glinted on his long hand as he snatched the phone from Russell.

"I'll hold on to that for you, kid."

The man's deeply lined face became clearer in the gloom: goateed, sunken-eyed, glaring from beneath a cowl of long black hair. A gold tooth flashed in his smile. Dan Hornween.

Dan slid the phone into his back pocket before clamping his hand on Russell's shoulder. The boy tried to pull away, but the grip held like iron. One of Dan's bony fingertips curled into a pressure point under Russell's collarbone, sending paralyzing pain like an electric shock down his arm. The boy gritted his teeth and tried not to show it. He saw other people moving into the firelight, standing behind Sam, staring like scarecrows.

"Go sit next to your friend," Dan said. "We got some things to talk about."

CHAPTER 3

An electronic dance-pop song with a little-girl-voiced singer blared over the Fat Chef Diner's speakers; Meghan recognized it only as one that seemed to be playing everywhere lately. Years ago, you couldn't see across the restaurant after 7 p.m. because of the cigarette smoke. Now, the air was clear except for the reek of fryer grease and faint murk of dirty mop-water. Detective Stoltz poured three sugars into his coffee and glowered in the direction of the kids hollering over their euchre game in a booth on the opposite side of the diner.

Meghan smirked and said, "Come on, Ed. Not too long ago I would have been over there playing with them."

"Believe me, I know," he said. She caught the barb. Like she was some kid at thirty-four, with two fifteen-month tours of duty under her belt and some damn dark times after it. He must have seen something in her face because he smiled uncomfortably and added, "I hung out here in high school, too. Used to be a place we showed off our hot rods."

Good.

"So," she said, "any movement on the McCreech shooting?"

He shook his head. "None of the snitches know any-thing. None of the ERs had someone come in wanting them to pick buckshot out him, either. No shock there. From the blood out front, it doesn't look like he was tore up too bad. It was an old 20-gauge."

Stoltz usually did a good job covering all the bases. He wasn't a bad detective—a little behind the times, but solid. Meg noticed that he had finally stopped wearing his pistol in that ridiculous *Miami Vice* shoulder rig. It was the kind of tacti-cool bullshit most young cops gave up pretty quickly, but Stoltz had kept it going for decades. He even had his jackets tailored for it. The holster clipped to his belt, that was new.

"You still looking at Russell?" she asked.

"The GSR swabs on him came up negative," Stoltz said. "He wasn't the shooter."

"I didn't figure him to be the type."

"Never know. Anyway, McCreeches as a matter of policy don't talk to police. I get a bunch of shrugs and mumbling. Jesse's known for selling light bags of marijuana and pass-ing off bogus pharmaceuticals, but that doesn't seem like it should lead to this kind of business."

"Folks get killed for less." She sipped her strawberry milkshake.

"True. He was into all kinds of drugs and hung around with that crowd. Who knows what kind of things go through their heads? Medical examiner says he'd been shot with a .38 with a pretty good grouping—guy could use a gun. Waiting on an autopsy with tox-screen still."

Meghan assumed the autopsy would discover that Jesse McCreech's death likely resulted from the five bullets pumped into his body, but she didn't say as much.

A pack of Harleys barreled by on the dark highway outside. She leaned toward the window, peering through the parked cars at the riders' club vests as they passed.

"Ironwolfs out on the hunt?" Stoltz asked. "Imagine the club's worked up with what happened to Jesse. He wasn't a member, but his uncle Leon was. And of course Jesse's dad, too. Duane's still in penitentiary, but—"

"No. They're not local," she said. "What club has a devil with a sword? Couldn't read their rockers."

"Knights of Satan," he said. "Out of Detroit and Windsor, mostly." He raised an eyebrow. "Not usually out here. You want to go catch up with 'em?"

"Nah, but might want to let patrols know to keep an eye out."

"You do that," he said.

She called it in on her radio.

"What about the necklace, Ed?" She was annoyed she had to bring it up herself. "The one Jesse died with—Bree's pendant."

"Who knows? I haven't got anyone who says they saw your missing girl with him. I was hoping you were the one with some info on Brianne Wells."

"As a matter of fact, I do."

She gave him the rundown, and when she was done he said, "So she hangs out with Ricky, huh? What do you think of this reality TV audition story?"

"Honestly, it sounds like bullshit, like the kind of thing a guy like Ricky Hornween would make up to impress a girl like Samantha Black. But as a cover story, it's a bad choice. Too out there, you know? Something a compulsive liar would say, sure, but not something someone sneaking around would make up."

"Well, Sam said he flew out on Sunday, right? And the last time Julie saw her daughter was Sunday, too, right?" He scratched the corner of his mouth. "So…"

"So maybe she's with Ricky? Maybe he brought her along to L.A. with him or wherever it is he actually went?"

"Isn't that something her best friend would know about? Seems like it would be a tough thing for a girl to keep to herself."

"You'd be surprised at the sort of secret lives a girl can construct for herself, even among her friends. Or how far they'll go to cover for each other. I'd like to get Ricky's whereabouts sorted. First of all, I'd like to see if he's even gone. Check his house—for all we know, he's just sitting at home and dodging his work. He and Dan don't seem to get along, and Dan's technically his boss. Or Bree's maybe there, hanging out and laying low for whatever reason, if she knows Ricky's gone."

"And what about this show audition?"

"Rather then try to chase down his credit card info and find out about a flight, I'll just see if I can get confirmation from the network or the show's producers—might have to wait until Monday, but I'll see what contact info I can scare up."

"That'll spook 'em, I bet. I'm sure he'll love that hedging in on his chance at stardom."

"My heart is breaking."

"Mine too. When you gonna do residence check?"

"As soon as I'm done with this." She pointed at her milkshake. "They're not cheap."

* * *

Russell clenched his fists and jaw in the hope that it would hide any trace of his trembling, though he wasn't sure if he shook more with rage or fear. Sam sat beside him on the blanket, her face golden in the bonfire's light, eyes downcast. Five men and two women stood in a circle around them, dragging on cigarettes and passing a bottle, all eerily silent. Dan Hornween rubbed the back of his neck, leaned over, and said through his gritted teeth, "Okay, kids, where is she?"

"Who?" Sam asked.

"You goddamn well know who."

She shot back, "I dunno, Dan! If I did, don't you think I'd be with her? Huh?"

The fire crackled and hissed. Dan hooked his thumbs in his front pants pockets. "This is some shit, girl. And you best figure a way to get it straightened out."

"You're looking for Bree," Russell said. "Ain't you?"

"I hear she's your piece of ass, boy. I know it's hard to keep tabs on her, but I bet you work at it. Now, where's she at?"

"None of your goddamn business."

"Afraid it is." Dan lashed out, tightening one hand around Russ's throat. "Anymore lip out of you, and you'll come up short some teeth."

Russell wheezed, and his head swam. He clawed and pried at Dan's fingers, but the grip was unbelievable. Panic rose as the edges of his vision dimmed.

"Cut it out!" Sam yelled. She tried to stand, but one of Dan's flunkies, a stocky woman in a trucker hat, roughly grabbed her shoulder and shoved her back down. "He doesn't know anything."

"The hell he doesn't." A gust of sour breath from Dan's

snarling lips rasped in Russ's face.

"Goddammit, Dan! Give him a break. His cousin got killed last night."

Dan relented, tossing the boy back onto the ground. Russell laid on his side, hacking and coughing, his head pounding and lungs aflame.

"I am aware," Dan said. "And I had no hand in that."

"Why should I believe that?" Russell managed to say between wheezes.

"Because I couldn't give two shits about your dirtbag cousin. I, being sensible, never had anything to do with him. And I'm not looking to go to war with the McCreech clan, besides. We all had enough of that shit." Dan hunkered down in the dry grass, his face now unnervingly calm, his tone even. "We don't get to choose family. I know how it is. Still a drag when they check out early."

Russell rubbed his throat and gaped at Dan, not sure if he was supposed to answer. Sam looked around at the roughnecks looming in the firelight and said, "Nobody knows where Bree is, okay? She burned us, too."

"How's that?"

"She was supposed to drive us to BlocksFest in Chicago last Thursday. She had the tickets and never showed. And also—" Sam stopped short.

"Also what?" Dan glared hard.

Sam sighed. "She missed some appointments I had booked for her online. High-paying clients. Whales."

"What does that mean?" Russell stared at her, and she gave an uneasy shrug and looked away, into the flames.

"Deputy Meg came by looking for her at the club," Dan said. "Asking if she danced Monday. You send her my way?"

"Bree or the deputy?"

"Either."

"Bree said she wanted to do the last amateur night, to find a way to sneak into it because it was a Shattered Dolls thing. I told her not to, because there was no way she could pull it off to begin with—and even if she did, if Shattered Dolls found out she was underage at one of their events, they'd probably never work with her again."

"Damn straight," Dan said. "When you see Deputy Meg?"

"She came by the shop tonight asking about Bree, and I said she liked to dance and wanted to be a model. An alt-model," Sam said. "That's all."

"Why didn't you have Ricky handle that?"

"She wanted to talk to me, for one. But besides, Ricky's still in L.A."

"What? The cop wasn't bullshitting me?" Dan tilted his head. "What's this about L.A.?"

"Yeah. Since last weekend. You know, auditioning for *Tattoo Kings*—that reality show."

"What the actual fuck?" Dan threw up his hands. "Why the hell didn't he tell me this? Is she with him?"

"I'm the shop girl, Dan, not Ricky's babysitter." Seeing Dan's face harden, she stammered, "I thought you knew. Really, I did. Maybe he thought you'd tell him not to."

"You bet your sweet ass I would have. Like I want that place on TV? That shop's financial aspect isn't meant for motherfuckin' scrutiny. It's not supposed to get that kind of attention."

"You should talk to Ricky," Russell said, the words rushing out. "He was always creeping on Bree."

"Oh, son, Ricky's after any slit that can half-remember he had a song on the radio once upon a time." Dan sniggered. "Believe me, we're gonna talk."

The wind picked up, sending sparks from the fire pit whirling toward the stars. An owl hooted from the woods. Dan's crew stood around like aimless, bored zombies, waiting for a command. He pinched the bridge of his nose and grimaced.

"Look, kids. Your girl has stepped right in a big ol' pile of shit. She might not know just how bad it is or how much deeper she's gonna sink if she doesn't get in touch," Dan said. "If this goes where I think it might be headed—and I know how these things go down—I'm gonna be the least of the pain heading your way. I'm your only chance to sort this out."

"Wow," Sam said. "Thanks, Dan. You're such a great guy."

"No, I'm trash, baby—but not every kind of trash, and not the kind that girl's gotten mixed up in. And those are funny words coming from a pimp."

"I'm not a pimp," Sam mumbled. "I'm a manager."

"Yeah, and I'm a misunderstood businessman. Sucks when the world don't see you the way you see yourself." Dan spit. He gave both of them a hard look. "This is only gonna get worse for y'guys until the girl turns up. You tell her that." As his crew made their way back to their vehicles, Dan spun back on his heel and called out, "Hey, kid." He tossed Russell the phone, which the boy caught in midair. "Be in touch, you hear?"

Meghan's cruiser rolled into Ricky Hornween's driveway to encounter two motorcycles leaning in front of the dark house: a black Triumph with an Iron Cross stenciled on the gas tank, and a Harley with a KoS 1%er patch on one of the saddlebags. These two were probably from the Knights of Satan pack that blew past the Fat Chef Diner earlier—but where were the rest of them? She called for another car and found out that Deputy Mark Williams was the only other one at all nearby, and he was about twenty or thirty minutes away.

"What's his location? Williams, what's your twenty?" Meg radioed, trying to keep the aggravation from her voice.

"Responding to the two-oh-seven at the Edmonds," Darla replied.

"The raccoons in their kitchen? Still?"

"They're being highly resistant," Williams cut in. There was some angry, feral chattering in the background.

"You're telling me that the raccoons are not complying?"

"Roger that. They're some mean ones, over."

"Deputy Williams, tell Mrs. Edmonds we'll come back with some traps. I have a possible burglary in progress and need backup immediately."

"Ten-four, on my way," Williams said.

"Dammit, Mark," she muttered after the confirmation. Meg switched on the car's spotlight and lit up the leaning, clapboard house. A woodpile was stacked against the broken concrete steps. Blinds blocked the windows. The door was closed and appeared undamaged. Behind the house, a ragged field of knee-high corn stretched out into the night. A pasture rolled to the left and woods stood to the right. She stepped from the car, keeping it running. After writing down their tag numbers, she leaned down and held her hand over one of the black motorcycle's pipes. Still hot. She scanned the woods and cornfield, then the house. Her skin prickled.

A muffled shattering and clanging burst from the rear of

the house, like plates and pans being thrown to the floor. She took a step back as her breath hitched, then put a hand on her pistol. She glanced at her watch. Hardly five minutes had passed since she called for another car. Then, there was another sound from inside: a steady, loud, metallic clanging. She crept up the concrete steps and stood to the side of the door in case someone inside decided to shoot through it. Another crashing sound came from inside. Suddenly, the tumult halted. Everything was quiet save for her cruiser's idling engine and the rustle of wind through the corn. A window or sliding glass door rumbled as it opened out back.

She passed the woodpile and rounded the house. The car's spotlight cut the area into sudden and deep shadow, and thinking of the dark under the highway overpass, her insides twisted.

She grabbed her flashlight and lifted its beam to find herself looking into raging blue eyes set in a weathered, blond-bearded face, not even an arm's length away. Her blood leapt.

She swung the light like a club, and it cracked against the man's forearm as he punched her in the eye. She staggered back against the house, the flashlight beam swinging wildly as it fell from her hand. One of the motorcycles behind her roared to life—the other rider was already out front. Meg spun, regaining her footing, and ran after her assailant, drawing her pistol and shouting, "Freeze! Sheriff!" but the biker either ignored her or couldn't hear her over his companion's engine firing up. Nebulas swirled in her vision as he hurried away, clutching his arm.

She ran out to the front yard, now squinting into her own car's spotlight as the black bike tore away down the driveway. The man who had struck her was astride the red

Harley, furiously kicking the engine, looking at her as if she was no more a threat than a squirrel scampering out of the woods. She rushed up with him in her sights. She slowed and crouched in her approach, moving to the side of the bike, keeping the gun leveled at him.

"Hands up! Now! Hands up or get shot!"

He stomped the kick-starter once more and it caught, but as he twisted the throttle, she pivoted and side-kicked him, slamming her boot heel into his thigh. Gravel spat out from the bike's rear tire as it swerved and tipped, dumping onto its side and pinning his leg underneath. He howled—the Harley was certainly heavy enough to break his leg against the ground if her kick hadn't broken the other one. The scream turned to a coughing gurgle when she stood over the biker and blasted pepper spray into his eyes and mouth.

Grunting, she managed to twist his arm behind his back and cuff his wrist. He bellowed and cursed her. As she cuffed the other, a sheriff's cruiser sped into the driveway, lights flashing. Her backup had arrived, but she bet the other biker was already miles away. She stood, wavering, and touched the swollen flesh around her eye socket, her fingertip cool against it. It was going to be one hell of a shiner. It didn't hurt yet, not much. Things usually didn't when they first happened. The real pain, she knew, would take time.

Sam and Russell laid side by side on his bed on top of the rumpled covers, staring up at the rafters of his bedroom where clouds of bong smoke roiled in the soft light as baritone electric guitar riffs droned from his speakers. The terror of Dan's crew ambushing them at the lake had passed. They texted the friends that had been run off, saying it was a misunderstanding about some missing equipment at the tattoo shop, all fine now, but the party was over. Russ floated in a dull haze, feeling as if he and Sam were drifting on a life raft on the open sea rather than lying on his bed. The masks kept their eyeless watch over both of them.

"Sam?"

"Yeah."

"Is she okay?"

After a moment, she said, "Whatever's going on, I think it's bad."

"You think she's dead?"

"I hope not. But I think she's in big trouble. Dan might be right."

"You ever hear of her hanging out with Jesse? Or dealing molly?"

"No. She had no reason to. She had other—" Sam faltered.

"Had other what? What was that shit about clients and her missing appointments? Is Dan right about the rest, too? Are you..." The words sounded so ridiculous and ominous at the same time. "Pimping her?" He remembered Bree, in the woods: *You shouldn't ask questions if you don't want answers.*

"It's not like that," she said. "If I tell you some things, you gotta make some promises first, alright?"

He propped up his head on one elbow to face her, but she stayed flat on her back. "Like what?"

"You can't tell nobody."

"I ain't lived this long by talking."

"And you can't be mad at me."

He huffed. "Now, how the hell can I promise that if I don't know what it is? Getting mad ain't a decision."

"It is if you make it that way. Girls have to do it all the time."

"That ain't the same. And girls just act like they're not mad, anyways."

"Well, you'll have to do that, I guess. But you have to promise—for Bree's sake. I hardly got anyone to help with this mess."

"Fine." He laid back down. "What kind of mess we talking about?"

"You got to tell me what you know about what's going on, too. Why did you ask if she was dealing?"

"You first."

Sam looked up at the masks and rolled one of her earrings between her thumb and forefinger.

"So," she said, "remember Crystal Lewis?"

He did. She was the little red-haired girl with the big laugh. The pretty tomboy who could climb the rope in gym class. She was the one everyone decided was a slut when the boys started sending around pictures of her. They wrote the word on her locker, put it up on her Facebook wall, tweet-stormed her with it. Her parents put her in the hospital, hid her in the house; later, they moved away. But everybody remembered.

"The internet porn star of Chippewa Middle School?"

"That's such bullshit. First of all, they were just nudes. Second, Sean McGuiness took those of her when he came over to her house with some of his friends. She was in eighth grade, and he was in *high school*. And she was the one who got suspended."

"For real? Why?"

"Why the hell you think? He was a popular varsity athlete, his dad is a lawyer, and his best friend—a couple grades ahead of him then—was Brad Stoltz. Their families are close. You know who Brad Stoltz is?"

He remembered the pouch-eyed cop in the wrinkled blazer from that morning, the one who let him go. "Detective Stoltz's son, yeah."

"Right. The Stoltzes and the McGuinesses are tight. Sean's dad and Brad's dad were cops together, before Sean's dad went to law school. So who got in trouble? Not Sean, not any of the boys—Crystal. Her parents made her start seeing a therapist and pretty much wouldn't let her leave the house."

"Why didn't you other girls say something?"

"We were scared."

"So you let them get away with it?"

"Don't even. We saw what was happening to Crystal, and we sure as shit didn't want it to happen to us. You have no idea. We came over to visit her all the time—me and Bree and some of the other girls—her mom and dad let us hang out with her. No boys were allowed, and they took her phone away."

"She wasn't mad at you guys for not backing her up?" He stretched, the body buzz of the smoke feeling more and more at odds with the conversation.

"Oh, she was, but what can you do? She mostly was mad at Sean."

"That guy's an asshole. Was then, probably is now."

"Right? Anyway, this is the thing. Crystal was all pissed that her parents blamed her and locked her away, and in the meantime, those pictures got out on the internet and about a million creeps *obsessed* on them."

"For real?" Russ asked. He had never seen the pictures. But when he heard about it back then, he wanted to—but he wasn't in the crowd sending them around. It never occurred to him that it might be out in the world. Lying next to Samantha no longer felt comfortable, and he squirmed.

"Nasty, I know. So Crystal's all shut in with the whole world saying she's a slut, barely any friends, so she starts camming. Yeah, her parents took her phone but not her internet access. Brilliant, huh? She was just streaming about nothing to whoever would watch and listen when she talked, but most of the time she didn't talk at all. Painted her nails. Read a book."

"And people watched that?"

"All the time. For weeks," she said. "She'd leave it on when we came over, it became like a reality-show thing. And we were all in the cast. People would ask her about us when we weren't there. Bree especially. And then it started to get weird."

"It's already weird."

"There were entire message boards about us, guys scouring the internet for a glimpse of our tits, looking for more shots of Crystal, dudes Photoshopping our heads onto porn stars, writing stories, it was insane. And guys started asking her to show. All the time. Every time. More than she could possibly ban."

Russell clambered out of bed and walked over to his work table. He absently stroked the half-assembled wolf mask. "She learned her lesson after the first time, right?"

"You're damn right she did. She asked for money." Sam rolled on her side to face Russell, leaning on her elbow and propping up her head. "And she got it."

He felt like he was dreaming this conversation, or watching it in a movie, when he asked, "How much?"

She said, "Lots. I bet you could take whatever you're

thinking and triple it, at least. That's how much Crystal made."

"How do you know she wasn't making it up, the part about the money?" Russell asked. "Crystal was pretty crazy."

"No, she wasn't. You remember when all I did was sit in my room online, back when I was all fat?"

"Yeah," he said. "You weren't fat, but yeah."

"Well, it wasn't all just online gaming. I booked Crystal's sessions and was the mod for her channel. For all the channels." She looked at the backs of her hands.

"All the channels." He sat down on the workbench's stool. When he spoke, his tongue felt mossy and thick, and his words sounded strange inside his own head. "How many other girls?"

"Most we ever had was fifty, but usually twenty to thirty," she said. "From all over. Oregon, Florida, Poland, Hungary. Anonymous credit card billing. Cryptocurrency conversion. It was easy."

"Easy?" He stood. "Finding a guy to buy you a six-pack is 'easy.' That ain't."

"It is once you know how. My cousin works in internet security, taught me some things, got me in with a hacker collective. Anyway. All the girls were killing it. But the one who made the most from appointments, that wasn't Crystal. Crystal moved on—she works for Shattered Dolls now. I know you don't want to hear this. It was Bree."

"No. What did you fucking do?" A cold, hateful shudder rattled through his bones. "What did you have her do?"

"What did I have her do? For real? Did Bree ever let anyone tell her what to do?"

"Answer me, goddammit."

"Like you've never seen webcam porn, Russ. I mean, it

was just solo stuff—"

He kicked over a stool and punched the wall. Pain roared in his hand as he stepped toward her and said, "She's my girlfriend."

"It started long before you."

"So, all the stuff we did together, that was nothing? Just some joke, and you both knew the whole time?"

"How the hell does her doing that change anything? She was with you. Only. With. *You.* So some suckers dropped a lot of money to look at her pussy on a screen. That means you're not special anymore, Russ? Because that's the most special thing a girl can do, right? Show you her special pussy?"

"Shut up. I mean it."

"She didn't tell you because she liked you. A lot. She planned on quitting but needed to get enough money for you guys to get to New York somehow. And she thought if she told you about it, you'd freak out and think she was some piece of trash."

He rolled and unrolled his fingers into fists before asking, "Are you still running it?"

"No. I mean, I put it on hold."

"I feel sick." He swallowed before saying, "I could kill you for this."

Her eyes widened, and then she scowled at him through the bedroom's colored haze of smoke.

"Well, I know guys kill girls all the time," she said, "but I didn't think you were one of them."

"Well, I know people pimp high school girls, but I didn't think you—"

"You were mad about her hanging out with Ricky." She pointed at him. "And you clearly got some kind of anger problems. They always say it's the quiet ones. Why shouldn't I think you're the reason she's gone missing?"

"How can you even say that? You're the real psycho here, doing that to your so-called friend."

"She was doing it on her own before me. Remember the guy she took off with a couple years ago? He drove all the way here for her from Colorado to pump and dump her. She was stupid, thought they were, like, in love or something. After that, I came in. Made sure she had no way to exchange info with clients. Everyone's blinded, like a peep show—except me. I give a better split than any of the so-called producers out there. And I keep them safe. No local-to-local, no—"

"So doing this shit got her kidnapped once already and, instead of stopping her, you looked for a better way to do it?"

"She ran off!" Sam took a breath. "I didn't—we didn't—start this. We just wanted to get something back for all this shit we deal with, you know? Just, get some new clothes, a new phone, get high. Get out of here. Something. And we got it."

"You could get sent up for this. You guys are all under-age."

"Nobody treats us like it. Not when it has to do with that. Hell, do you feel 'underage'? Anyway, it was working just fine. I'm not some dumb redneck bitch whoring out passed-out girls for oxies. I'm a manager. It was fair, prof-itable, safe—and I ran it. But then I made a huge mistake."

"The whole thing is a huge mistake."

"Well, whatever. The mistake I'm talking about is telling Ricky Hornween."

He buried his face in his hands. "Is *he* pimping them?"

"Will you stop saying that? It's not prostitution. I never let him near any of the girls if I can help it, besides. Only one local works for me anymore: Bree. I see the way Ricky looks at her. At me. But he's running other things. Without Dan's permission, of course."

"Like what?"

"I don't know what. That shit ain't mine. Dan wants to keep the shop to funnel cash through, I'm sure. He wants Ricky to stay out of it. I think he's trying to keep his little brother out of prison. Or maybe he just thinks he's stupid. Point is, Ricky needs someplace to hide his *own* money from the government—and from his brother. And some way to move it around. Why? For what? Don't care. But I think something's gone wrong. Really wrong."

"What? What did you do?"

"Nothing. But that's the problem. I was supposed to get a money transfer Thursday night, late. We would have been in Chicago for the fest, but I would have done it with my laptop through a proxy. It never came though."

"How much was it supposed to be for?"

"Fifty-thousand dollars, thirty of it that I was supposed to forward to another account. I'd get eight percent. Four thousand."

Russell gaped at her. He had heard of plenty of deals around Pike Lake, and he'd even done a little small-time stuff for friends—but that amount of money was insane.

"Goddammit, Sam. Fucking Hornweens. I warned you. You and Bree both." Russ sat on the edge of the bed and clutched his head. "What's it for?"

"Don't know. I try not to, like I said. But the transfer never came through. And Ricky hasn't answered any calls or texts since he sent me a message two days ago."

Russ's breath shuddered. "Is Bree with him in L.A., doing a—a porn shoot or—or something?"

"I don't think so, Russ. I really don't."

"Why, what'd it say? Ricky's text?"

"All it said was 'Where's Bree?'" She rubbed her eyes. "And now he's gone silent, too. So. Yeah." She sniffed. "Two people we can't find. Your cousin is dead. Fifty-grand that never showed up. Now, what's this about Bree dealing?"

Beneath the tree's whispering canopy, Bree's green eyes sparkled when she said, *I've got plans, babe. Plans in motion.*

Jolene had said Bree had tried to sell her some serious MDMA weight—She might've jumped at an opportunity. Seems like a fest would be a good place to move that.

She needed to get the money for them to head off to New York together somehow…

The money transfer never came through.

"Oh no," he whispered.

Meghan leaned back in the passenger seat of Myra's Subaru wagon as they pulled out from the hospital lot, one hand holding steady a pile of paperwork in her lap as the other set an ice pack in the cupholder. The first pink light of the morning seeped through the night. A soft rain drizzled on the windshield, blurring the roadway before being shrieked away by the wipers. She pulled her knife from her pocket, snapped it open, and cut the hospital bracelet from her wrist.

"You should keep that ice on your eye," Myra said quietly.

"I will when I get back home." She folded the knife closed.

"You're staying at my house, aren't you?"

"Didn't plan on it. I have to feed Mr. Purrs."

"You have Mr. Purrs on a timed food-dispenser. You're

not even supposed to be out of the hospital yet. You might have a concussion."

"I don't. He didn't knock me out or anything. I need to go over this paperwork and work on Bree's case. That means I'm going home."

"It's five in the morning."

"And I usually don't get off till eight."

"Well, I'm not leaving you by yourself. Looks like I'm staying at your place."

"Fine," Meg huffed.

"Will you tell me what happened when we get there?"

"I might, if you stop talking for a little bit and give me a chance."

Myra frowned, and her forehead creased with worry. Just like Mom used to do, and Meghan felt the same twinge of guilt.

"I'm sorry, Myra. It's been a long night, and I've already had to go over it with Stoltz and Cunningham. I just need to relax for a sec. Okay?"

When they got back to Meg's house, after pulling off her boots and placing her gun on the countertop, she put on a pot of coffee and ate a protein bar. Mr. Purrs regarded her and her sister with fluffy indifference from atop the bookshelf.

"You named him Mr. Purrs, but he's never very friendly." Myra reached to pet the cat, who scooted back to stay out of reach.

"That's the joke." Meg threw out the ice pack. "Coffee?"

"No, thanks. I'm just starting to relax after hearing you'd been attacked and hospitalized. And you need sleep."

"I wasn't 'attacked and hospitalized.' A suspect took a swing at me. It happens."

She sat down with her coffee on the couch and surveyed the case notes sprawled across a low table.

"That all for Bree?" Myra settled into a chair across from her.

Meg nodded. "Yeah. Well, some of it's about Jesse. I don't know what the hell is going on with this. She's been seen hanging out with Ricky Hornween at parties, probably met him through Sam Black at the tattoo place. Sam tells me Ricky is in L.A. for some reality TV audition. Flew out on Sunday, supposed to be back today. Which means, if it's true, that he was out of town when Jesse got shot. So he's clear on that. Sunday is the last day Bree's mom saw her, too."

"You think she took off with Ricky?"

"Maybe, if Ricky even went and it's not all bullshit. As much as I'd hate it, at least if she came back with that creep we'd know she was okay. I went to Ricky's place last night to check if he was there, and a couple bikers had broken in. Not local guys. Don't know why or what they were looking for. We got one, the one that hit me, in custody—he's not talking. Still need to call the producers of Tattoo Kings and see if he's really out there in L.A."

Myra pulled her smartphone out of her purse and swiped the screen. "I'll look up the contact info."

"You don't have to do that."

"Well, I'm here, and *Good Morning America* doesn't start for another hour. I need something to do. I know all of this is confidential police business, don't worry."

"Okay. Thanks, Detective."

"Any other leads?"

"Leads, eh? Sure. Fine. Bree also wanted to dance at the amateur night at Lil' Angels—Dan Hornween's club—on Monday."

"Gross. Why?"

"Because she doesn't have a dad?"

"Meg."

"Sorry. Who knows. It was sponsored by some porn site she likes. Nice, huh? Anyway, Sam didn't want her to. Said the last time they spoke was on Saturday. Dan, he's a dirtbag, sure, but he knows how to play within the rules. Guy doesn't even have a record, and he'd kick her ass right out the door if he knew she was underage."

"Maybe she sneaked into it." Myra tapped away on her phone. "Fake ID. Knew somebody inside."

Meg pointed to a thick stack of papers in a manila folder. "That's release forms for all the girls. Still need to go through them."

"So, she might have gone off with Ricky. Or, she might have danced at the club and then disappeared. Any other options?"

"Endless possibilities, but there's one connection that bothers me the most."

"What's that?"

"Don't breathe a word of this. Seriously, Myra."

Her sister gave a solemn nod.

"Okay, remember when I said I'd found Jesse shot dead a couple nights ago? Well, two things. First of all, Russ McCreech showed up at the scene."

"Oh, God." Myra put her hand over her mouth. "You think he did it? I mean, shot Jesse?"

"No, actually, I don't. But I don't know why he was heading over there so early. To warn him? To find something out? To score drugs? Are they both linked to something that happened to Bree? He says it was because he couldn't sleep and Jesse's a fellow insomniac. Whatever. I don't buy it.

And, this is the thing. Jesse died trying to show me—or maybe Russ—a necklace. A pendant that belonged to Bree."

"So Jesse's murder and Bree's vanishing are related."

"Well, I don't think he got killed over a lawnmower. Something bigger is going down. And I can't tell if Stoltz and the sheriff aren't picking it up because they're lazy, or cautious, or if they know something I don't. I feel like—if I don't get a handle on it—more people might end up dead."

"Can you push them a bit more? Reach out for help in some other way?"

Meg sipped her coffee, leaning forward with her elbows on her knees. "I served with a guy who's an inspector with the state police now. He was always legit, but—I don't know. Maybe he'll tell the sheriff I'm making an end-run around him, because they're on the state drug taskforce together, and I'll get shot down. Then Stoltz and Cunningham will find out I'm talking out of school—and that's career suicide. Maybe I'm way off—way, way off. Maybe I'm paranoid and Bree ditched her friends to go off to Chicago and is dancing around in a park there right now." Her cheekbone and head throbbed. "I'm in the dark. I'm supposed to meet with them both tomorrow. Maybe I'll get better intel then, but I'm not counting on it."

"Why don't you trust them? Did something happen?"

"No, but things always do. Whenever you have a command structure, it has to protect itself above all else. If I shake it up, that's the end of this whole thing."

"You don't know that, Meg. You've known these guys for a long time. You always suspect the worst from people. Where did you learn that?"

"Iraq helped."

"It was a war. That's a very different place."

"It was and it wasn't. It wasn't the enemy that got to me. I mean, they did, but they did what was expected."

"What are you talking about?"

"Some shit with my own people. I don't want to get into it."

"Did they—" Myra hesitated. "Did they hurt you?"

In the kitchen, the cat food dispenser buzzed, and Mr. Purrs hopped off the shelf as kibbles clattered into the tray. The clock on the mantle ticked as the rain pattered against the windows.

"It's like this. In the army, you know, if you're a woman—you're either a dyke, a slut, or a bitch, because you either fuck only women, fuck all men, or won't fuck anyone at all—those are the only categories you get to be known by."

"Kind of like when we were in high school."

"Yeah, if our high school was like ninety percent male. Most of them thought I was a lesbian. You deal with the comments. You throw it right back. Anyway. So, we were on base, and I got invited to hang out with the sergeant and some of the other guys. I knew them, they knew me. Brothers and all that shit. They were drinking. Hell, they were drunk before I even got there. We're not supposed to drink on base, not officially, but the sergeant was there, so everyone followed his lead." She folded her hands, and a bad taste blossomed on her tongue. "And as soon as I walked in, Myra, my God, I could feel it. This split-second of silence, it felt like a thousand years with all their eyes on me. Their nasty, smirking smiles, like boys about to do something naughty."

"Oh, God."

"They pour me this huge glass of whiskey. And I know it's a trap. I fucking know it. I'm not stupid. Not about things like this. It's fine for them, but for me—it's not the same. See, if I get drunk, hell if I even take a sip, well, I've violated regulations—and if anything happens to me, well, soldier, why were you drinking? The whole thing becomes about what *you* did. What signals did you give? So, you were fraternizing with personnel on base? Do you have a history of substance abuse? Of not getting along with your superiors? So I refuse. And my heart is breaking because I'm like, no, not this, not from you guys, not after all the shit we've been through. Because I can feel it. And the sergeant's like, 'You're tough, right, Shaw? You worried you won't be able to control yourself or something?' And then he orders me to down it, and they're all laughing, like it's the funniest thing in the world, like he's a comic genius because he ordered me to chug this pint glass of whiskey. And I say it's an illegal order, sir, I would be criminalizing myself by following it, and I refuse again. But now I'm refusing an order. And then they all stop laughing. They're waiting to see what he'll do. He slowly stands up, his jaw working, staring me down, and he's so angry. I can see it. Right then, he hates me. Out of nowhere, or maybe he always did. Who knows? I feel the rest of them turning on me, too. These guys—if we were ambushed and one them got hit I'd be running back to drag him to cover, and they'd all do the same for me, bullets snapping past our heads, we'd do anything to keep each other alive out there— suddenly it's all different. It's all gone. I'm supposed to *be* something for them or *do* something for them, and dammit, they're gonna see that I do it. And I freak out. I kick over the table. I run."

"Did they chase you?"

"I didn't look back. I hid, then sneaked back to my bunk, terrified. As terrified as I was when an IED tore up my convoy under fire. Maybe more. Your training kicks in when things like that happen. They don't train you for shit like this. I slept with a Ka-Bar under my pillow and a screwdriver in my sock for the rest of my time there." Dull pain pulsed deep in her skull, and her jaw clenched. "They spread a rumor that I was a crazy bitch who came in and kicked over their table because I hadn't been asked to hang out with the boys. Headline: Girl Throws Tantrum. They all quit talking to me for the rest of the time I was stationed there, which fortunately wasn't long. I think the incident was part of why I got passed over for promotion. And I never said a thing."

"You didn't report it?"

"The major in charge of handling that and that sergeant had done two tours together. He'd have dived on a grenade for him. Which means he would've thrown me on one for him, too. He wouldn't help me. Not in a million years."

"At least you didn't get…hurt, I mean—"

"I know what you mean. Too bad others weren't so lucky." She cleared her throat. "One did report him, after I was gone. Sounds like she got the same invite, but she took the bait. She was disciplined for drinking, then got a psych evaluation that declared her a borderline personality disorder, and she was sent home with an administrative discharge."

"That's not your fault, Meg."

"Yeah, but there was no record of my complaint when hers was filed, because I didn't make one. Maybe it would have been different if there was. Maybe not." Meg set down her mug, then shrugged. "She checked herself out last year with a painkiller overdose, I heard. And he, well, he's still enlisted. A real hero."

Mr. Purrs crawled into Meg's lap, and she scratched him

behind the ears. Myra set her phone down.

"Have you talked to anyone about this?"

"Not really. The shrink, when I had one. It is what it is."

"It's trauma, Meg. You don't have to deal with it alone."

"What isn't trauma when there's a war on? Eventually, you'll do bad things, and bad things will get done to you." She shrugged. "We just happen to get a different brand of it, and from a different place. And everyone deals with it alone."

"Don't be like this. Just don't. Let me help you."

"I don't need 'help.'"

"Why do you do this? You push everyone away and do nothing to make yourself better."

"I do nothing? Nothing? I'm a deputy sheriff of this county, Myra, and I'm good at my job. I'm sober, and I'm sane, and I did it myself. So please give me some credit here. *Can you do that?*"

Mr. Purrs snapped at Meg's hand, startled by her shouting. She pushed him off her lap.

"Meg. I just want to—"

"To help. I know. You're not Mom, okay? You're not."

"I never said that I was. You," she said, "are being unreasonable."

"*Unreasonable.*" Meg chuckled, the pain in her head like a hammer striking against her temple. Unreasonable. It was a Mom word. She laughed out, "You want to help, huh?"

"Yes. I do. Calm down." Myra looked her dead in the eyes and said, with a hitch in her voice, "I'm your sister."

"Alright. Fine. If you want to fucking help," Meg said, jabbing a finger at the case notes, "then help me find this girl."

CHAPTER 4

Russell had already poured the bowl of Sugar Smacks when he saw there wasn't any milk left. He grabbed a can of Mountain Dew, cracked it open, and slammed the fridge. Motorcycle part catalogs and beer bottles crowded the kitchen table beneath a framed cross-stitch that read "Fuck Housework," bordered by brightly colored flowers. When he shoved some of the crap aside to make room before sitting down, his arm ached from whatever kung-fu bullshit Dan had done to his shoulder the night before. The bong rip he took when he'd woken up that morning had taken the edge off, at least. Between crunching on handfuls of dry cereal washed down with gulps of pop, he scrolled through his phone, seeing if there was any sign of Bree.

"Looks like someone's trying to keep the dentist in business." Alice walked in and half-heartedly straightened up the tabletop.

"We're out of milk," he said, chewing.

"We have eggs."

"Need milk to make scrambled eggs, Mom."

"Not for fried."

"I like scrambled."

"Well, I'm going to the store today. Brush your teeth when you're done, at least. Jesus, boy."

She poured herself some coffee and sat across from him. He continued scrolling the touchscreen.

"You heard from Bree?"

He shook his head.

"How about the cops?"

"Not since you picked me up. Betting they'll be back, though."

She made a noncommittal sound and sipped her coffee. "Heard you had a run-in last night with some Hornween people."

He looked up from his phone, trying his best to keep a stone face. "Not really."

"What do you mean, 'Not really'? Did you or no?"

"Some drama with Sam and the tattoo shop. One of the machines got jacked up. Dan got a bug up his ass about it and came out to the lake. No big whoop."

"Honey, Dan Hornween couldn't give two shits about that shop actually giving tattoos, and you know it as well as I do. He'd have Ricky in there with a ballpoint pen and a lighter if he could. Why the hell would he come out himself for something like that?"

He shrugged. "Guess Ricky's out of town."

"Well, your dad wants to talk to you about this. He's at the clubhouse and expecting you."

"Dammit, Ma." He pushed away his bowl as his heart skipped a beat. "There ain't nothing to talk about."

"He'll decide that. And you best be straighter with him than you are with me. Listening to you bullshit is like watching a one-legged man in an ass-kicking contest."

"Yeah. Well. I'm out of here." He got up from the table,

feeling a burn come into his cheeks.

Shane laughed, leaning in the kitchen doorway with his thumbs hooked in his belt on either side of a massive wolf-head buckle. "You sure are. Get yourself together, we're heading out. Larry's waiting in the van out front."

His protests were useless, and within a few minutes, Russell was sitting beside Shane in his brother's black van, speeding toward the clubhouse, the speakers blaring out Metallica's "Master of Puppets" as Larry Dodge sprawled across the back seat, drinking a forty of Mickey's.

"You always drink this early, Larry?" Russell said, looking over his shoulder.

"Ain't usually awake this early."

Shane grumbled, "You know, Russ, if you get yourself a bike we could ride together."

"I told you," he said, "I don't want a motorcycle."

"A fucking car, so I could ride, then? I'm showing up at the clubhouse in a van because I have to drive your ass." He made a wide left onto Riverbrook Road, narrowly missing a farm's vegetable and egg stand.

"What's Larry's excuse, then?" Russ hitched a thumb at back.

"I'm a fat lazy turd and still drunk from last night." He laughed. "You ain't got no car?"

"He don't even have a license." Shane frowned. "Rides a fucking bicycle around like some kid."

"It's a mountain bike. Half the places I go are off-road, in the woods and stuff."

"Ohhhh, a *mountain* bike. You hear that Larry? He rides *off-road*. What a badass."

Russell rolled his eyes. "What's being a badass ever got you? A stretch in Jackson for punching out your girlfriend before stomping the teeth out of the other guy that was banging her?"

Without looking from the road, Shane punched him in the arm with a force that threw Russell against the door. His head cracked against the window.

"You see?" Russell sneered at him, even though his eyes watered from the ache spreading down his limb and the soreness on his head. Now both of his arms hurt. "You see?"

"You don't know nothing," Shane said. "Don't talk about shit like you got any idea at all. You hear me?"

"Well, gee, Shane." Russell rubbed the cramping muscle in his arm. "Maybe I'd have a better idea if anyone ever talked to me about anything."

"We're going to go talk with Dad now, ain't we?"

"Great. You kidnapped me from breakfast for a ride in your murder-van to get questioned by Dad. Like I ain't had enough of that kind of shit lately. Thanks."

Larry leaned forward, poking his head between the front seats. "You ain't got no driver's license, Russ? Really?"

Russell always liked the clubhouse when he was little—but he'd be damned if he'd admit it now. It was originally built as a party store and canoe rental on the river. It never was much of an attraction, mostly because that part of the river attracted bloodthirsty swarms of mosquitoes from nearby marshlands, as well as poisonous run-off from the (now defunct) mills. It went out of business in the mid-80s, right around the same time Ironwolfs membership had swelled to its highest ever. The Hobble Inn, at that time owned by Russell's granddad, Willie "Snatch" McCreech, was getting too much attention as the local biker bar, and so the rickety, barn-red place on the river was purchased to give them a new hangout. Though the club didn't have the membership it once did, the clubhouse still served its purpose. Bree had always wanted to see inside. Russell told her that getting her in was impossible.

Russell had good memories of barbecues among the roaring motorcycles, of the twangy guitar ballads Mike Morgan used to come down from the woods to sing in the corner, of the hard rock covers his brother Roy's band used to sloppily play in the yard, of the fireworks displays put on by his Uncle Duane, and of the lazy afternoons spent on the dock, sipping Faygo Rockin' Rye and swatting endless mosquitos. But old Mike Morgan had long since lost his mind—what little sanity "Crazy Mike" had left so many years after Vietnam—and rarely came out of the woods anymore except to sell his crop under cover of night. Uncle Duane was in prison and his son gunned down. And Roy, Roy was dead, long before any of that.

The van parked in the muddy lot, and Shane killed the engine. The sun-faded Ironwolfs MC emblem painted on the side of the clubhouse was peeling, along with the rest of the structure. Dad's Harley lurked near the door. Russell clambered out of the van and hurled the door shut behind him. The dirt lot was cratered as if it had been shelled, the largest of the depressions filled with brown water from an early-morning storm. Beyond the roof's peak, Russell saw the old willow's treetop, still leaning over the river as if stooped in mourning. Birds chattered in the trees below a gray sky, and everything felt haunted.

The van's sliding door rumbled open, and Larry belched as he stumbled out. Russell stalked away from the van, Shane calling after him, "Hey, you can't walk in there without a member accompanying you." Russell flipped him off over his shoulder without looking back, shoved open the front door, and strode into the rank odor of sour beer and bad plumbing.

He took four bold steps and then froze. Leon, his dad, sat at the bar facing the wall. Smoke curled from a lit cigarette in the ashtray beside him. The wolf at the center of his three-patch vest glared at Russell with a frozen snarl, set in the middle of a back as wide as a door. A thick Buck knife hung in its snap-sheath on his belt beside a trucker chain. His hair was braided into a ponytail, a deeper red than Russell's own strawberry blond. It's that hair that gave him his nickname "Bloody Leon." At least that was one story.

"Hey, Russ." He did not turn on his stool. When his dad's meaty hand plucked up the cigarette, it looked like a white toothpick between his fingers. "Been a while since you been out here, huh?"

He looked around the club, hoping to point out something new there, just to have something to say. Photos from past rallies, plaques from other allied clubs, and framed newspaper clippings crowded the paneling behind the bar, centered around a giant airbrushed painting of three timber wolves in the snow, howling at the moon. Two crossed axes hung above it. The Black Knight pinball machine stood unplugged and dark in the far corner. The jukebox on the opposite wall was lit, though. Silent and softly glowing, it illuminated the pink and tan bodies of pin-up girls and centerfolds tacked up nearby. Nothing had changed.

Shane and Larry stomped through the door behind Russell.

"I told him he's not allowed to walk in without a member." Shane pointed at Russell then quickly lowered his arm when he saw Leon wasn't looking.

"He's your brother," Leon said. "He's family."

"Yeah, I know, but the club—"

"Did you drive out here in that van? You're not even in your colors, son. Why don't you and Larry wait outside for a bit? I need to talk to Russ."

"Don't you think that me and Larry—"

"Now, Shane."

Shane took a breath to speak, thought better of it, hit Larry on the arm, and said, "You heard him, let's go."

When the front door screeched closed behind the two, Leon called to his youngest son, "Come on over and have a seat."

Russell shoved his bangs out of his face and mumbled, "I'm okay."

"What?"

"I said—" He coughed and tried to speak up. "I said I'll stand."

"Just sit the fuck down, will you?" He patted the stool beside him. "Why's my whole family make me say everything twice?"

He looked over at Russ, the corner of his mouth half-smiling in his long red beard, crinkles deepening around his narrowed blue eyes. Russell's rubber-soled work boots squeaked as he approached and took a stool. His dad patted him on the back. He smelled of stale tobacco and motor oil, and his fingernails were caked with black.

"What's the story, my boy?"

"We're out of milk." It was the first thing that popped into his head, and he regretted it.

"Your mom's going to the store today."

Russell nodded.

"Look, I know you've been through a lot lately. Seeing Jesse like that, well, I bet that was pretty bad."

Russell shrugged. He'd found himself thinking about

seeing his cousin—bloody and then slumping into death—at the strangest times, like when he was pulling on his socks this morning. Jesse's head had lolled over in a way people weren't supposed to move, and his eyes were open and empty. He'd never seen anyone die before, and he wondered if most people had seen something like that—and if so, at what point in life it was the sort of thing folks usually ran into. He supposed it depended on a lot of different things.

Jesse was the third dead body Russell had ever seen, but the other two had been mortician-polished for viewing. Grandpa Willie had been president of the Ironwolfs, so he was buried in denim and leather, sporting club colors in a casket piled with sacks of weed, dirty magazines, pistol cartridges, whiskey bottles, and other offerings. Russell's brother Roy hadn't been an Ironwolf, so it wasn't a full-on biker funeral like Grandpa's had been: no last ride led by the road captain from the funeral home to the cemetery, no final rev of engines by the gravesite. But Roy's dad, "Bloody" Leon, was the club's vice president and younger brother of "Dirty" Duane, the president. And Roy had died on his bike. Confusion regarding funeral traditions and etiquette was apparent.

Russell was twelve, and his tie was a constricting noose that day. He sweat through his dress shirt and jacket. Some club members showed up in suits, others in their colors. Some had brought offerings and tokens (guitar picks, comic books, flasks) but upon seeing the traditional flower arrangements weren't sure if the tributes should be placed in the casket or later tossed into the grave or given at all. They held them uneasily by their sides as they viewed the body before taking their seats. Some set the grave goods beside the casket's platform, others sat with them placed awkwardly in their laps.

When it came time for Russ to approach the coffin, the sight of his older brother's face beneath a sheen of foundation, wearing the same gray suit from his senior photo seven years before, in a black casket surrounded by a chaotic explosion of flowers, overwhelmed him. The thing in the box was no longer Roy, and that meant Roy was no longer anywhere. Russ's bowels churned, and he worried he might lose control, so he fled down the aisle and out the front door into the misty October afternoon. He kept running, yanking off his tie and dashing down Second Street until he could cut through the Salvation Army parking lot and walk on the railroad tracks to sit beneath one of the viaducts and gather himself.

He made it back to the funeral home in time to ride with his mom, dad, and Shane to the cemetery, joining the sullen crowd as they made their way to their cars and bikes. No one ever said anything to him about it other than his mother, who said after the burial, on the way home, "Thanks for coming back, sweetie. I told them all you would."

Now, at the clubhouse, Leon cleared his throat before asking, "You hearing me, son? I asked how you're holding up."

"Fine, I guess," Russ said. "It is what it is."

"You want a pop or something?"

"No. Had one before I got here."

"No milk. Right. Listen. I want you to know that we're all real tore up about Jesse. Uncle Duane was having a hard enough time doing his stretch inside, and now he's lost his boy, too. But you gotta know that there's nothing you gotta do. I hear you handled yourself real well with the cops, though."

"Don't got nothing to hide."

"I know, but listen. Don't you go around looking into this. It's being handled. Tell me you ain't trying to get yourself any more mixed up in this than you already are."

The Pike Lake chapter of the Ironwolfs was down to about fifteen, maybe twenty. There were three other chapters in the state, all of them far-flung in podunk towns. One was in the Upper Peninsula. And none of them, as far as Russell knew, had much of an investigative background. Mechanics. Gunsmiths and locksmiths. B&E, explosives, auto theft, firearms, pot-growing, and lately credit card scams—maybe. But they weren't detectives, and they didn't even know who they were looking for.

"I ain't hunting for that shooter. I'm sure you've got it."

Leon stabbed out his cigarette. "Now, there's another—what do they call it—a wrinkle to this. Look, I'm sure this ain't easy to talk about, but I know Bree's up and gone missing. Hell, her mom's got posters up all over, everyone knows by now." He cleared his throat. "Point is, we lost Jesse right around the time your girl dropped out. Now, why you think that is?"

"I don't know. Could be a—you know—a coincidence."

"You see that?" Leon pointed to a banner with the Ironwolfs emblem on it. "What's our motto?"

"'Fate is a Beast,'" Russell replied.

"That's right. And you know what that means?"

Russell had no idea. He'd thought about it plenty. Any biker he asked gave some half-assed burnout answer like, "It's how we live," or, "That's just a truth you know when you know it." He'd come to decide it was just some scary-ass sounding bullshit they made up to look tough.

"Sorry, I ain't a member."

Leon laughed.

"Well, it means a lot of things to a lot of folks." He leaned over the bar and turned his head to look Russell in the face. The boy saw Shane's cheekbones and his dead brother's eyes. "One thing it means to me is that I don't believe in coincidence." He put his massive palm—rough, cold, and heavy—across the back of Russell's neck. "So, I'm gonna ask you again, and you better think long and hard before you answer me. Why is your girl missing, and does it have anything to do with your cousin being dead?"

"I—" Russell swallowed. "I don't know, Dad. I wish I did. I been asking around about Bree for days now. I'm worried, have been worried since she didn't show for the trip to Chicago. Going kinda crazy about it. What Jesse might have to do with it ain't never crossed my mind, not till I came across him dead a couple nights ago."

"Okay." Leon stroked his beard, still keeping his hand on the back of his son's neck. "Why then?"

Russell shrugged and stared down at the carved-up bar top. He couldn't tell if Dad's hand only felt heavier, or if it was pressing down on his neck. Russell glanced at him, and his dad raised an eyebrow and slowly, deliberately tilted his ear toward Russell.

"It's just, well, I thought I saw—I mean, I saw a necklace there."

"Necklace?"

"Shaped like a 'B,' yeah."

"A bee? What?"

"Not like a beehive bee. Like the letter." He coughed. "It was Bree's necklace, Dad. And Jesse was holding it right up to me when he died. It was like he was trying to show it to me. Or maybe the cop. I don't know. I just—"

"It's alright." He patted Russell on the back. "Calm

yourself down. Why didn't you tell anyone about this?"

Russell stared across the bar, not speaking, and then his dad said, "He didn't kill her, Russ."

"How you know?"

"I guess I don't. But it looks like someone came there with killing Jesse on his mind. If he got taken down from between when he sent you a text—that's what Shane tells me you said—and when you walked over, then they either was there to begin with—which I doubt—or they showed up and got it done without even bothering to say hello." Leon rested his elbows on the bar. "Now, if he got shot down about your girl, that means—what? He kidnapped her with somebody? Why would somebody partner up with Jesse—a guy who couldn't even pull off swiping a goddamn lawnmower without getting a sheriff on his door—to kidnap a girl from a single mom with no money?"

"Because they're stupid." Russ chewed the inside of his cheek. "Or ain't after money. That ain't why most girls get kidnapped, I bet."

"Jesse strike you as that kind of guy?"

"They always say it's the normal ones you have to look out for."

"Well, he sure wasn't normal, so we're clear on that count. And even with a brain full of crank, I don't think he's the kind of guy who would be killing young girls. And I think you feel that way, too."

"I don't know. Yeah. Probably not."

"And if it ain't a kidnapping double-cross with your girl, then it's revenge for something Jesse done to her, and that's right out, ain't it?"

"Why?"

"Because the only one who would be out to revenge

himself for something like that," Leon said, "is you."

"It wasn't me."

"I know, Russ."

His dad tapped out a Marlboro and lit it. With a sigh, he stood up and wandered over behind the bar. The fifth of Jack clanked against its brothers when he lifted it from the shelf and set it on the counter. He placed two shot glasses on the bar and filled them with a short, sweeping pour. When Leon turned away to replace the bottle, he asked, "What did the Hornweens come out to the lake last night for?"

"Something about something going wrong at the tattoo shop." Having said it before to his mom made it easier this time. "I try to keep out of the Hornweens' shit."

"And that's a good plan. We've got some history with them, and it ain't good. So you don't know where Ricky is?"

"He's in L.A., been there since last week. That's what Sam says. Trying to get on some TV show."

"What an asshole." Leon laughed. "Look. I know you want to find out what's going down. We all do. Look at me, boy. I don't want you knocking on doors and asking questions liable to get shit stirred up. But—and I mean this—if you hear anything about Jesse, or anything about your girl, or anything at all, you tell me or Shane. No one else. And that means just what you come across—not what you dig up, because digging ain't your business. I'll make sure this gets taken care of. You got it?"

Russell said, "I got it."

"You goddamn well better. Anything else you need to tell me?"

"Nope. Not now, at least." There was Ricky's dealings with Sam, and the molly that Bree was supposedly running around with, and Bree and Sam's camgirl thing—all of which he guessed his dad would count as "anything else." But Russ wasn't ready to hand that info over yet. He promised Sam he wouldn't tell, and besides, Russ knew that, to Leon, this wasn't about Bree. It was about family. And his youngest son's girlfriend didn't count. If Russell wanted answers, he'd have to be the one asking the questions. "Yeah, can't think of anything."

"Good. You've been through a lot, and we don't know much. Either Bree's okay and just laying low, or off on some adventure, or else—"

"Or else she ain't."

His dad picked up a shot. It looked like a thimble between his thumb and finger. He jerked his head at the remaining one. Russell blinked, then picked it up.

"I always hope for the best, and I prepare for the worst. Either way—" Leon raised the shot glass to his son, "—here's to the bastards getting what they deserve. This time, you can count on it."

Russell didn't drink much but knew better than to turn down a drink from Bloody Leon—president of the Pike Lake Ironwolfs—in his own clubhouse, even if he also happened to be his dad.

Leon said, "Down the hatch," and Russell threw it back. He didn't even shudder. It went down easier than he'd thought.

The police car parked in the sheriff station's vehicle pool was a bright blue Dodge Charger, shiny despite the overcast sky. The vehicle announced the presence of the state police— doubtlessly there to sit in on the questioning of Meghan's assailant from the night before. Maybe someone from the troopers would be joining the meeting she was to have with Cunningham and Stoltz this afternoon too. As she crossed the lot after parking her cruiser, someone called out to her. She turned to see Ryan Russo, impressive in his deep blue trooper's uniform with inspector's bars, stepping out of the state police car and giving her a friendly wave.

"Inspector Russo, nice to see you," she said, extending her hand and smiling. It was no lie—even though they hadn't been in touch much in the past year. Coffee once or twice, the conversation mostly about cop stuff. Her sister had asked if these were supposed to be dates, or preludes to them. She didn't know. It never went anywhere, though she wouldn't necessarily be opposed to it. Cops were never easy to go out with, but it helped if you were one yourself, and Ryan—besides being easy on the eyes—was one of the few who treated her like an equal, even when she was a green deputy on a pretty small patch of country and he was with the state troopers. It came as no surprise; she remembered the same respect from him when she was a PFC and he was a lieutenant in the army, the both of them biding their time on base in Texas before hopping a bird to Iraq.

"You too, Ice." He gestured at her eye, saying, "Even if it looks like that last collar got pretty up close and personal."

No one else called her Ice around here. She and Ryan had been at Fort Hood when she acquired the nickname. It was a reference to the flattop haircut she wore at the time, which the grunts had decided made her look like a certain '90s white rapper. If she was out at the bar with the guys, she could count on "Ice Ice Baby" getting at least one spin from some joker at the jukebox.

"Well, it was definitely up close," she said. "Here for a task force meeting?"

Various county sheriffs and local police had been coordinating with the state troopers on the Narcotics Enforcement and Operations task force over the past five years. Ryan was Stanley County's liaison, and he took it seriously.

"Officially, it's for NEO coordination, but that meeting wasn't for another two weeks. Sheriff Cunningham asked if I could bump up my visit to coincide with…recent events."

"It's been eventful lately, that's for sure. Good news is that I did recover a stolen lawnmower this week. Still waiting to hear back on those prints from you guys."

"Heard you came across a homicide there, too. You're keeping busy."

"Just my good luck, I guess."

He laughed and said, "So, hey, we haven't talked in a while. We'll both be sitting with Stoltz and Cunningham in there, but it's going to be more of a top-down sort of meeting, and I don't think there's going to be a lot of room to hear your take on what's going down."

"And what do you think is 'going down,' Inspector?"

"I don't know what to call it, but it's definitely—"

"Something," she said.

"Something. I'll let you get to your desk and put things in order for the meeting, and then I'll see you in there. But I hope we can follow up one-on-one sometime—sooner rather than later. Meet for coffee?"

She agreed to it because he seemed to mean it. Ryan was one of the good ones, but he was far from a free agent. The task force, his own departmental alliances and investigative needs, and his own career prerogatives all held sway over him. Of course, he had some pull in all of those spheres, too.

She spent about twenty minutes going over the blotter, seeing what calls came in and if any arrests of interest had gone down since her last shift. Nothing much was to be found. It looked like the rest of the Knights of Satan had either high-tailed it out of Stanley County or were laying very, very low. After the blotter, she saw if any tips had come in from the call logs about Bree. Also dry. She read through her case notes and looked over the shift schedules. She noticed she wasn't on the board for patrol tonight or the night after.

The meeting was held in the station's only conference room, and when she entered, Sheriff Cunningham, Detective Stoltz, and Inspector Russo were already seated. Stoltz and Russo sat at the long table's far end, one seat apart, looking like decidedly different cops, but very much cops through and through.

Stoltz's eyes carried even heavier baggage than usual beneath them, and his tie and jacket looked as if he'd put them on after dragging them from underneath his bed. His wife had passed away a few years ago—heart failure—and while Meghan didn't know what damage it had wrought on the man, his wardrobe had definitely taken a hit. That being said, he still knew the county, having been working it for twenty years. Law-abiding locals liked him almost as much as anyone with something to hide hated to find him darkening his doorstep. He sipped black coffee out of a giant Styrofoam cup with the Fat Chef logo on it, then put it back on the table as if the task required the attention and precision of disarming a bomb. Did he have the shakes? Jesus. He'd always been a bit of a drinker, but Meg had never thought it was *that* bad.

Russo still looked military in the way the military wanted

to be seen. Pressed blues and polished boots. Neat, shiny, black hair. Gleaming badge on the left breast, nameplate on the right, and smooth gray tie down the center with a shiny bar holding it in place. For a moment, she was envious of the uniform, remembering her own dress blues and greens—but it quickly passed when she remembered how, and why, she never found herself in the Officer Corps.

Sheriff Cunningham was, well, he was the sheriff. A thick-mustached, big old bear of a guy with the demeanor of a good-hearted rancher. His new laptop, which she knew he was very excited about, sat in front of him.

"Come on in, Meg, and take a seat." As the sheriff waved her in, she saw the slightest wince in his face—it took a moment, but then she remembered her eye. A livid purple swelling had risen up around it, and there was a streak of red like a wet red thread across the eye itself. "Great to see you up and around already. How are you feeling?"

"Just fine, thanks." She sat down and added, "Looks worse than it is."

"Great, great. I just want to say you showed some real mettle out there last night, and we're all impressed and proud to have such a tough young lady with us out there."

She would rather have been called a sheriff, or a cop, but she took the compliment with a nod and a gracious smile.

"Thank you, sir. Just doing the job."

"Well, you really handled yourself out there, hon. Nice work." The sheriff cleared his throat and shuffled some papers. "So, well, Inspector Russo was kind enough to head on over from Lansing to join us. I talked with Ed, and we all decided to loop you in on some info that may have a bearing on some of the incidents over the past couple of days. We're hoping we can all get on the same page."

"I appreciate that, sir."

"Now, what you're about to hear doesn't leave this room. This is all your ears only. Everything with the NEO task force has been on a need-to-know basis."

The sheriff poked at his laptop, and the blue projection screen on the wall flickered before displaying a map of Michigan, divided into the eight NEO task force coordination regions. She didn't know who had taught the sheriff to use PowerPoint—maybe he picked it up himself after noticing it was part of every conference and seminar he attended. These days he made a PowerPoint presentation at every possible opportunity. Her favorite so far had been about procedures for responding to escaped livestock, the overlong bulleted items accompanied by various pictures of cows that slid in from the left and right as a helpful reminder of what cows looked like. The NEO map had been pulled from the state website. It had the official colors and fonts. And no cows.

"Now, it's a slippery thing," Sheriff Cunningham said, "since on one hand we're trying to share information across organizations, departments, you know, across the whole darn state—but on the other hand, you have to make sure that information doesn't get to the wrong people. Leaks, gossip, and—other things."

"Of course," she said.

Like dirty cops, she thought. It's not like Michigan was some failed third-world republic, but there were people on the take. It was one of the only states where lawmakers and state officials weren't required to make personal financial disclosures, so no one knew who owned whom. Plus, law enforcement cutbacks meant less oversight of narc and vice squads, leading some to run hog wild. A few knucklehead cops near Westland had been taken down for helping themselves to thirty grand of seized funds, most of which they spent on strippers and blow—probably tossing it right back to the people it had been snatched from in the first place.

"Now," Cunningham said, "I'll hand it on over to Inspector Russo."

It suddenly struck her that, since Ryan's promotion, his name was dangerously close to that of the detective in the Pink Panther movies, Inspector Clouseau. She would have to remember to ask him to say "Inspector Russo" in a bad French accent later on. She held back a smile, and then, considering the seriousness of the meeting, wondered if maybe the biker's punch had rattled her brains a bit. Maybe she needed sleep. She took a breath and focused.

"I'll second Dale on saying that was some great work last night," Ryan said. "Have you seen the sheet on your assailant yet?"

Meg was relieved that Ryan wasn't following the sheriff's lead and running the meeting like it was a briefing. Maybe it would make conversation easier—less "top-down"—and get her some better intel.

"Not yet," Meg said. "Just a got a name and heard that he had a record."

"Well, as you might expect, Mr. John David Samuels is a charmer. Goes by 'Viking Dave.' Member of the Knights of Satan motorcycle gang, affiliated with one of the Aryan prison outfits, too."

The sheriff clicked on his laptop, changing the slide to a mugshot of Samuels fixing the camera with his best killer stare. He looked much as he did last night, maybe a bit younger with a shorter beard. Next to the mugshot was an arrow pointing to the Knights of Satan MC emblem, pixelated since it was blown up to about four times its original size.

"Double felon, did four years in Ionia for Grievous Bodily Harm, and has a long, long sheet of your standard domestics, drunk and disorderliness, assaults, and so on," Ryan explained. "He's a pro, so he's not talking. Hasn't even made a phone call. Now, from what I understand, you don't get this crew out here. You have a local club, right?"

"We do, the Ironwolfs MC," the sheriff said. "They have a clubhouse on the river, local guy named Leon McCreech is their chapter president—at least in name since his brother Duane got sent up. It was Duane's son, Jesse, who is our homicide. But I don't think the McCreeches and their club are heavies, at least not when it comes to producing or moving drugs. They have a scrapyard, a bar, and a gun shop— sure there's some extra-legal things going on there."

"You can say that again," Stoltz grumbled.

"But nothing we could pin on them," Meg said. "Maybe the IRS could take them down, or a federal case. They're real careful with the gun shop, because they know how hard that could hit them. If I had to guess, they cook their books for the other places, and I bet some cars come in and out of that scrapyard, whole or in pieces, that have owners somewhere who are missing them. Seems like that would be a big hammer for a small bug."

"Maybe. Knights of Satan don't need financiers or accounting tricks on a minor league level like that. And they have plenty of guns. They have some serious backing across the country and in Canada too. They were a meth gang, but meth is on its way out. Now the KoS deal in heroin, euphorics, and things along those lines, mostly."

"We lost a few kids last year to heroin," Stoltz said. "Not an epidemic, but ten years ago it was unheard of in the county."

"Right now, locals drive to the bigger cities to score, bring it back to sell it off, or just pick it up for their friends," Ryan continued. "But it's only a matter of time until someone gets a steady hook-up and sets up shop. And that's exactly the sort of thing the task force wants to prevent. That, and we aim to take down some of the labs and growers you have around the county, too. And what can do a lot to help that along is people undercover—pretty deep—or informants."

"Getting anyone undercover out here would be a job. Everybody knows one another," she said. "Some stranger who rolled in and started asking around would get frozen out pretty quickly."

Or worse, she thought. While the Hornweens and McCreeches didn't get along, she imagined they'd both have the same sort of plans for a narc in their midst, whether they themselves were in the drug game or not. They might actually fight one another for the chance.

"True," Ryan said. "But people will always make mistakes, and those people want to get out of consequences. And so we've been focusing on informants. And, I'm sorry to say, we recently lost one of them. Jesse McCreech."

Oh, that poor dumb bastard, she thought. "Jesse McCreech was a CI?"

"We got him with some heroin on a traffic stop. It would have made him a third-time loser, and he was looking at a long stretch inside. Jesse seemed like a good in-road to the rest of the McCreech folks and some local dealers, so we offered him a deal as a CI."

"And how'd that pan out?" Meghan asked, and then hoped it didn't sound as sharp as she felt.

"Better than you'd think," Stoltz said. "We never got much on the family. But he gave us a meth lab he knew about up over by Woodham, run by a buddy he'd jailed with over in Wayne County."

She'd heard about it a couple months back. It was a rinky-dink, shake-and-bake operation in an apartment complex. Not a major hit against the drug's availability, but at least it wasn't putting the other residents' lives at risk anymore.

"So, that was Jesse's intel. And as a CI, he reported to Detective Stoltz?"

"That's right," Ryan said. "And then Ed brought it to us. Now, those guys were pretty low-end, but it's still manufacturing, and we got them dead to rights. And one of them is the brother of Paul 'Pickaxe' Cross, an enforcer for the Knights of Satan MC."

The slide clicked to Paul Cross's mugshot. Shaved head and thick neck, walrus mustache, tattooed up to his chin with a black dagger inked under his left eye. Maybe the other biker from last night, the one who got away? She never got much of a look.

"Cross is a hitter for the KoS. I'm guessing he's not happy about his brother getting taken down with inside info."

Ryan looked around the table. Stoltz cleared his throat, and the sheriff gave a heavy sigh.

"You think that's what got Jesse killed?" Meg asked. Losing a CI was a big deal. It looked bad, and it sure made it harder to recruit anyone to take his place.

"It's a possibility," Ryan said. "And maybe they're hunting for Ricky, too."

"If, somehow, they got wind of an informer out there," Stoltz said, "they could be doing some house cleaning. Trimming loose ends. Maybe that's why Ricky has skipped town—if he knows something about their business, they might put a hit on him too."

"Huh." She stroked her chin. "Maybe. Can anyone here tell me why I wasn't apprised of the situation?"

Stoltz began, "Part of keeping the CI network secure is—"

"Pardon me, Detective, but the security of Jesse McCreech was no longer a concern after he bled out in his Lay-Z-Boy."

"Meg," the sheriff said, "come on."

"A homicide at which I was the first on the scene," she continued. "Now, I know I'm not the lead on that investigation, but—with respect—I have a missing minor whose mother is very worried about her. That's what brought me out to Ricky Hornween's place last night. Things could have gone much worse than they did. The fact that a dead man with Bree's necklace was a police informant has a clear relevance to my case. Why didn't you tell me?"

"Because task force operations are a bit more important than a missing person case," Stoltz said. "We just found out that the Knights of Satan are connected—"

"*Possibly* connected," Meg said. "I want to talk to him."

"To who?" the sheriff asked.

"The suspect I brought down last night. Samuels. Not about Jesse or that lab out in Woodham. I want to talk to him about Bree. And I think I've earned it."

"Who gets to question who isn't earned on a merit system," Stoltz said.

You got that right, she thought.

"Meg, I don't think that's the best thing right now," the sheriff said. "This perp is our best lead in the homicide, and he could be tied into much bigger things."

"And a there's a young girl who might be deep into it, too." Meg turned up her hands. "I wouldn't be asking if I didn't think it was a real concern."

"We're all as concerned as you are, Meg. Believe me."

Stoltz sounded weary but confident. "I understand your worries, and I take them seriously. But if we're going to find out anything about Bree from that scumbag in holding, it's going to be from something he lets slip. Not by coming at him straight on. We got to keep him in the dark."

"I'm sorry, Detective. I don't mean to push. But how am I supposed to work this thing," Meghan said, "if I'm in the dark, too?"

"We don't want you to be, can't you see that?" the sheriff asked. "That's why we're all meeting here right now. You can keep looking for the girl, and you got some better background now. But we can't let anyone know we're building up an informant network out there. I wanted you to know why we're being so careful. These things take time, but we'll get there."

Time might not be something Bree had on her side. Meg looked to Ryan for help.

He met her eyes and with a slow nod of his head and said, "I'll be sure you get the information you need, Deputy. You can count on that."

She got the message.

She smiled and said, "Thank you, everyone. I appreciate the confidence you've shown in me by sharing this information with me. I'll use my best discretion with it, and I won't let you down."

It had gone as far as it would for now. But that coffee with Ryan had better happen soon.

Russ thought Mike Morgan's cabin looked like something out of a horror movie, the kind of place where teenagers played by twenty-somethings with feathered mullets would have a weekend of skinny dipping and six-packs ruined by a chainsaw-wielding lunatic wearing a burlap sack over his head.

His phone buzzed in his pocket as he coasted his bike up to the gate—if you could call it a gate. Russ hopped off his bicycle and leaned it on a thick timber beam that crossed the road. A NO TRESPASSING sign had been crookedly nailed to it, and a rusty logging chain padlocked it to a massive ironwood on the road's other side. Mike Morgan's cabin lurked in the woods at the end of the overgrown two-track.

He pulled the phone from the pocket of his long, cutoff shorts, glanced at the screen, and answered.

"You heard anything?" Sam asked.

"Nah. Just got put through the ringer by my dad, though."

"What'd you tell him?"

"Just about the necklace. He don't have any idea either, or if he does he ain't showing it."

"Nothing else?"

"Nope." He pulled off his sweat-damp baseball cap and waved away the clouds of gnats. His face was sticky against the phone. "What about you?"

"I'm babysitting at Jolene's, so I can't meet up till this afternoon. She took another shift at the restaurant 'cause her supply's short—her guy didn't show."

Even though Russell didn't think there were feds in white vans cruising the backroads of Pike Lake, he wished Sam would be more careful about what she said on the phone. Especially lately.

"Well, I'm about to go visit her guy right now."

The phone was quiet for a moment.

"You sure that's a good idea?" she asked.

"He was part of the Ironwolfs when I was little. He knows me, my mom and dad, all of us. He was also one of the only people who would hang out with Jesse, too. He'd go over to his house to watch movies, 'cause he ain't got a TV. It'll be fine."

"When's the last time he saw you?"

"It's been—" Longer than he thought. Uncle Duane hadn't been sentenced yet. Years. It might have even been at Roy's funeral. "He'll be cool with me dropping by."

"If you say so."

"He knows what everybody's got. And he's a family friend."

If they could find out who around here had come into a lot of molly lately, then they might have an idea of who Bree had been dealing with.

"Alright. But if anything seems weird there, you get out. All right?"

"Yeah, yeah. Meet you at the bridge around one?"

"Sure. Okay. Bye."

As he approached the cabin, a mosquito whined in his ear. Atop a lean-to shed sheltering a rust-streaked snowmobile and a chaos of junk, crows cawed and flitted, their faces like tiny black knives. Brown pine needles blanketed Mike's long-dead Chevy Blazer, its flat tires half-sunk in the mud. Mike never got another one after it died. Russell hazily remembered it in better days at the clubhouse. Mike's dog— his old one, an Irish setter named Sally—would bound from the tailgate to lick Russell's laughing face. He had a different dog now, a silent and protective Doberman named—

"Vince?" Russell called, hoping that by calling him he could put the animal at ease if it was lurking somewhere on the property.

Then he called for Mike. The cabin was dark and still. A ratty tartan blanket was tacked up over the front window, and the front door's pane had been replaced with plywood. Maybe Mike and Vince were out checking the plants. But Mike tended his crops by night now, mostly, checking the scores of marijuana patches scattered throughout the acres of state forest that backed up onto his land. Russ knocked on the door. There was no response from inside. He thought he heard the creak of hinges from behind the house, though.

"Mike?" He made his way around to the back, his boots squishing on damp leaves. The crows chattered on. A cold dread pooled in his bowels, and every part of his body wanted to run back to the gate, climb on his bike, and pedal away until his legs gave out. But still, he moved forward, rounding the corner and leaping back from a dark heap slouched against the back wall.

It was a hiking pack, its olive canvas stretched to capacity on its frame. A sleeping roll and bagged-up tent, along with two jugs of water, sat next to it. He approached the back door, slowly. His mouth was dry and pasty. The cabin's back door stood open a crack. A pump-action shotgun leaned beside it. Mike always carried a gun in the woods, so it didn't worry him too much. He was probably getting ready to set out.

"Mike?" Russell reached out a single finger and pushed the door open.

He stepped inside to find himself standing in a small kitchen area. An electric hot plate sat on a folding card table with two plastic-backed chairs, one of which lay knocked over on its side. A single dirty plate and fork sat in the basin sink, and a fifty-pound bag of Dog Chow slumped against the wall near a garbage can. The place smelled of sawdust and mildew, and dust motes floated in the shafts of pale light pouring through the rear window's yellowed panes.

He approached a futon mattress on what looked to be a handmade wood frame, a mason jar stuffed with cigarette butts on the plank floor underneath. Two shop lights hung from yellowed cages overhead. A flipped-over crate, piled with books and magazines, served as a low table. Some were author names he'd heard of, even if he hadn't read them: George Orwell, Jack Kerouac. The rest looked like they were mostly about UFOs.

A psychedelic tapestry of Jimi Hendrix tacked to one wall stared coolly across the room at a rack holding three rifles and several boxes of ammunition. A black wood-burning stove squatted in the corner with a few skillets stacked on it. Beside the gun rack, a door stood partway open, revealing a tiled bathroom floor and part of a mildew-spotted wall. The wind blew, and branches scraped against the cabin's metal roof.

"Hello?" he called. Goddamn, this was a bad idea. He stared at the crooked bathroom doorway. A steady dripping came from it.

He took two long strides to the bathroom door and shoved it open with a trembling hand.

On the toilet lid was a brown bottle of rubbing alcohol, a glinting scalpel and hemostat, and a butane welding torch. Blood-soaked towels laid sopping on the floor, and red pools covered the tile. The sink was splattered with it, too. From where he was standing, he could not see inside the claw-foot tub, but shiny red rivers streamed down its side. Russell jackknifed forward, grabbed the doorframe, and dry-heaved.

His first thought was to run away. But he had to know

what, or who, was in the tub. It could be Mike or—

Oh, God, please don't let it be her. Not Bree.

A shadow fell across the bloody room. He spun to see Mike Morgan standing there, head-to-toe in camouflage, his gray beard reaching nearly to his beltline. Before Russell could make a sound, he glimpsed a shotgun butt swinging toward his face. A brilliant flash of pain blinded him, and he was falling. He never felt himself hit the floor.

CHAPTER 5

Meghan was unsurprised to learn, without much digging, that most of the dancers from "amateur" night at Lil' Angels were employed by other clubs. It was a field where the term "amateur" wasn't easy to define in relation to "professional." No one had a state-endorsed certificate in exotic dancing framed on her wall; no one had a full-time position with health insurance and a 401(k). Most of the men watching probably imagined they were seeing college girls struggling to pay tuition or maybe local ladies just looking for a thrill. They were actually seeing women from all across the state with I-9 forms filed in other topless bars, now scooping up tips from a place that hadn't been hosting their routine every weekend for the past five years—if they were on the books at all.

New skin for new eyes. And women looking for new gigs, too. Amateur nights were a chance for clubs to audition talent in front of a crowd—without having to pay them a dime. And, if the event was sponsored by a porn producer—one like Shattered Dolls—it was a chance for those women to be recruited into higher-paying entertainment. Clubs liked sponsors like that—a known porn starlet, mixed with the lure of amateur night, brought in a lot of people—and, since they were hosting, the clubs usually didn't have to worry about the sponsor poaching from their own workers. Megan knew the business better than most.

She had been a bartender at a strip club in Florida after she got out of the service—something no one around here knew, and she hoped to keep it that way. After the army became a dead end, she found herself unwilling to re-enlist but unable to reintegrate into civilian life, either. She could not imagine what sort of work she would do stateside, or where she would go—she hadn't interviewed for a job in years. She hadn't even written a resume since her Life Skills unit in high school. And, more than anything, she didn't feel, for lack of a better word, "normal" anymore. Even if she could get a job smiling as she pointed customers toward the dog food aisle, or cheerfully answering phones and emails, she worried she might lose her cool in a way that might lead to someone else losing teeth. That or she might end up eating her own gun.

So she stayed away from home, away from people she knew, haunting bars all night and sleeping it off all day, drifting southward until she found her way to the Crimson Palace.

It was a stage club in Jacksonville, sleek and sexy like a location from one of those '80s action movies featuring a blow-dried hero, a white Ferrari, and a synthesizer sound-track. A far cry from a hustle club like Dan's shithole out off Deerfield Road, where the girls got most of their cash by going from lap to lap. She shared an apartment with one of the house dancers, a razor-thin, hard-drinking Russian named Valeska, who made most of her cash from her routine. Val got Meg an interview for a security job at the Palace. They offered her a place behind the bar. She was insulted but needed the gig. At least she got to keep her clothes on.

Not all the dancers at the Crimson Palace were a mess by any means, but most had their problems, and Meg had hers. The place took its toll, no matter who you were. Meg always had a few drinks to relax before a shift, a few shots to get through it, a bump of coke to keep the shots from slowing her down, and then the after-hours partying with the girls to shake off the drag of it all. She'd follow it up with a few hours of terror-plagued sleep in her filthy apartment before waking to pound a protein shake and an oxy before hitting the gym and going back to sling drinks, day after day. She busted the customers' balls, talked with them about the girls, poured heavy, and pretended to think they were funny and interesting. She was a "cool chick."

The money was unbelievable. But the stage offered the promise of even more, and she would have been welcome on it. The manager made sure to let her know that every time she clocked out.

The Crimson Palace brought in a ton of cash, unmarked, and the club took more than its fair share from the dancers. After six weeks, Meg had memorized the club's rhythms. Who came in when. Who sat where and liked which girl. Who wanted to talk, who wanted to drink, and who wanted to be left alone. When the cash drops were, where security stood, when the armored car came. And then she started thinking about it. A way out of here. With a bang.

After eight weeks, she bought an unregistered HK .40 caliber from an Albanian drinking buddy. At this point, she began to consider who she should recruit to help her rob the Crimson Palace.

Before she could finish putting her crew together, and she

found herself in the Duval County lock-up.

The charges, stemming from a coked-up brawl with a doorman at some god-awful hip-hop club she didn't even want to get into in the first place, were dropped. After her release, she stood outside the jail's garage door with a split lip and blood caked under her nails. She wore a pair of volleyball shorts and a pink, glittery T-shirt Valeska had dropped off. The sun beat down through the wet heat. Meg stared down into a plastic grocery sack at her torn-up, little blue dress and broken heels. Her feet itched in her flip-flops. Wincing, she looked up to the cloudless sky. Palm fronds crackled in the breeze. She couldn't remember the last time she'd been out during the daytime.

In that crushing moment, the insanity of what her life had become bewildered her. She was an alcoholic, cocaine-addled bartender living with a Russian stripper, and at this moment an unregistered pistol was hidden in her bedroom along with a hand-drawn map of the club she planned to rob—probably with the help of some of the most dangerous people she knew.

Before night fell, she had burned the map, thrown the pistol into a canal, and was on a plane heading to Detroit Metro. One suitcase, no plan. It was Myra who came and got her from the airport. On a school night, too. Meg never talked with her about what happened in Florida. And her dad, well, he never even asked.

The saddest part for her about her father moving down to Satellite Beach was that she refused to set foot in that state ever again. She'd sooner go back to Mosul. Bad times.

Twelve girls had signed up for Dan's amateur night at Lil' Angels. Three were names she recognized—a woman who caught an Uttering and Publishing for trying to cash bad checks at Farmers Credit Union in Pike Lake, another nailed for retail fraud—a case of price tag switching at Walmart—and a young lady she had dealt with personally after her live-in boyfriend pulled a knife on her in a domestic. A few others had citations, a few were clean, and two were out-of-state. At least their IDs were: Kristen Michelle Price, twenty-three-year-old, five-foot-seven blonde from Irvington, Kentucky; and Veronica Anne Cullen, a thirty-four-year-old, five-foot-four brunette from Columbus, Ohio. Both Caucasian. The other ten were scattered across the lower peninsula, but some were close enough that she could meet up with them without losing too many hours, if she needed to. Of course, she had no idea if Bree was even at the club that night. But she had her suspicions.

Julie Wells stood in her front yard, trimming the azaleas beside her mobile home, when Meg's cruiser rolled up. Through the windshield, Meg watched Julie set down the shears and clasp her work-gloved hands. An ache swelled in Meg's chest, imagining the dread that must come in this moment. The missing little girl, the unannounced visit from a sheriff, and all the dark possibilities Julie might imagine as Meg stepped from her cruiser and walked across the yard. Meg grinned and waved, though it seemed strange considering the situation, and Julie smiled back with something like relief—a smiling, waving cop meant it probably wasn't the worst of things.

"Those are really popping, aren't they?" Meg nodded to the bushes.

Julie looked lost in thought for a minute, then nodded and said, "The azaleas? Oh, yeah. Holding up pretty well, too. Fertilized in May."

The two women looked at one another for a moment,

not sure where to go from there, then both spoke over one another.

"I'm sorry," Meg said. "What you were going to say?"

"It's nothing," Julie said, then added, "Sorry, just, you know, noticed something happened to your eye. You okay?"

Of course. Meg made a mental note to wear her aviator sunglasses. Even if it made her look like a stereotypical cop, and tended to make citizens uneasy, it was better than startling them with part of her face beaten to a pulp.

"Oh, yeah. Well, comes with the job sometimes, you know." Meg cleared her throat, looked around. "I just wanted to drop by and check in about Bree. Any news on your side?"

"Not really. Louise—I play cards with her—she says she seen her at the drugstore on Sunday. Or she thought she did."

Meg nodded. "She see her buy anything? Did Louise call it in to the tip line?"

"I don't know. Probably not. She couldn't remember if it was Sunday or not."

"What time on Sunday, or whatever day it was?"

"She didn't say, but I know she goes by there early evening after she's done working at the bakery to get her lottery tickets and stuff."

Meg wrote it down in her notepad and asked for Louise's full name.

"Louise Mitchell. She didn't do anything wrong, not calling in and all, she just thought of it when we were playing cards—"

"No, no, of course not. I just need to keep track of all the info I can, even little things. You never know what might come in handy. I want you to know that if I write things down, or ask lots of questions, not to read too much into it, okay?"

"Sure."

"Alright, then. So, I was wondering if you could look at some pictures for me and see if you recognize any of them. Can we sit down inside and take a look?"

Meg had put together an array of the twelve girls from their DMV photos, all of them except the girl from Ohio, who was scanned from her passport copy in Dan's records. Because of this, Meg had printed them all in black and white so the one photo wouldn't stand out and distract from the rest.

"Who are these girls?" Julie sat in the living room, looking over the sheet.

A clock ticked on a shelf crowded with framed photos, most of them of Bree: smiling in a green jumper and missing a front tooth in an elementary school photo, sitting on a dock making a face at a shiny silver fish she held up on the end of a fishing line, laughing astride a pony at a petting zoo, posing like a pop star in sparkly tights and a sequined top while singing into a hairbrush microphone.

"They're...people of interest for different reasons. Like I said, we're just gathering info now."

"I recognize two, I think, but one doesn't make any sense. One is her." Julie pointed to the woman who had been busted swapping tags at Walmart. "I'm not supposed to say, but she went to my AA group. Maria."

"Does Bree know her?"

"I hope not. She's thirty or something, and, well, I don't think she takes her recovery very seriously. Think she was only going because the court was making her."

"And the other?"

"This girl," she pointed, "is the spitting image of my niece Kristen. But she lives in Kentucky."

That's the one, Meg thought. "Has she been up here lately?"

"No. Haven't seen her since we went down there for a family reunion last summer with Bree. I talked to my sister just a few days ago, and Kristen was talking in the background. She's taking community college down there and working at a grocery store."

"I see." Meg nodded. "Do Kristen and Bree get along? Are they friends?"

"Oh, for sure. They grew up together, text all the time and all that. What's this all about? I—" Julie put her hand over her mouth. "I don't understand."

Meg's friend in high school used to put on a blazer and use her older sister's ID, which—even though it was expired and said she was twenty-five—was good enough to buy them a case of beer a couple towns over. Kristen was blonde, and Bree was not, but the two were about the same size and there was more than a passing resemblance.

"Sometimes when you put together an array like this, you include people that you know would be familiar to the viewer. Just as a baseline check."

Other times, it's because your daughter might have used your niece's driver's license to sign up for a strip show immediately before disappearing. Meg couldn't bring herself to drop that bomb on Julie, not now. There was nothing to be gained. She needed to have another chat with Dan—and he wasn't going to like what she had to say. But there were some other things she had to take care of first.

* * *

The world was a wet smear of color as Russell awakened, blinking back the incredible pain deep in his skull as the face inches from his own came into focus. Vanilla-scented shampoo caressed his senses, and he became aware of warm hands on his cheeks. Gradually, he recognized Sam, her hair pulled back behind a black bandana and her face shining with perspiration, her dark eyes wide as she patted his face and repeated his name over and over in a voice shrill with panic.

He was laying on a couch, feeling as if he had just awakened from a night of pounding beers, and unsure where he was. Gazing down from a wall tapestry across the room was Jimi Hendrix's face rendered in purple and gold. Two images in rapid succession burst like camera flashes in his memory: Mike Morgan head-to-toe in camouflage, dried rivulets of blood streaming down the side of a white tub. Flailing, he choked back a scream when he leapt to his feet, but the floor seemed to rock and toss as he struggled to stand.

"Russ, stop, it's me." Sam hugged him around the waist and forcefully guided him into a sitting position on the couch. He was hyperventilating, one foot tucked under his ass and the other leg outstretched and tense.

"We gotta get out of here," he said, maybe shouted. His ears were ringing, and flashing nebulas pulsed at the edge of his vision.

"What's going on? Are you okay? You were supposed to meet me at the bridge an hour ago. There were cops out there, talking. They didn't see me." She stood. "Came out here to look for you. Where's Mike?"

"The gun—he hit me with—" He clutched his head. "The *bathroom*."

"What? Mike hit you?"

"We gotta go! Did you see the bathroom?" He thrust a

finger at it.

Sam rushed over and leaned through the doorway. Her gasp was almost worse than seeing it again himself. Her sneakers slapping on the floorboards, she ran to him, then dragged him to his feet and pulled him toward the front door. His right arm was slung across her shoulder, his legs unsteady.

"The tub," he mumbled. "Who's in the tub, Sam? Who's in the tub?"

"No one, Russ, come on. Come on." She threw open the front door with her free hand, the sun blinding and cruel. He grabbed the doorframe and tried to pull away from her, back into the house.

"I gotta see who's in there. Is it her? Is it her?"

"*Goddammit, there's nobody in there.* It's just blood—a ton of blood. Let's go, now, now, now, now…"

He broke from her and stumbled to the bathroom, gripping the doorframe as he looked over the red-spattered chamber. Sam cursed.

"Don't track your feet through that shit." She grabbed his arm. "It's bad enough that your fingerprints are probably all over this place now. See? The tub's empty."

When he stood on his tiptoes and craned his head to see into the tub, he saw that she was right. It was smeared and streaked with red, but no one rested inside of it. No clothing was scattered about. Nothing but stained towels and bedding on the floor, along with the razors and the torch.

"Come on," she snapped. "I don't want to be here when Mike comes back, or whoever else, and I don't think you do either."

They hurried to the gate, his head clearing despite the damp heat. Her battered Taurus was parked beyond it. As she dumped him into the passenger seat, he shouted, "My bike!" He pointed to where it leaned on the railing.

"Fuck your fucking bike, we're out of here." She slammed the door, ran around the front of the car, and leapt into the driver's seat.

"I need it," he said. "I don't drive. The tub…"

"We'll come back and get it. With your brother." The car whipped around and then tore down the two-track, spewing gravel and dirt behind it. She hit the main road, tires squealing as she cut a hard turn.

"Turn around. If they find that tub and my bike, *they'll think I did it,*" he shouted.

"We'll get your bike later, Russ, shut up. We're going to go get Shane and Larry."

"*You* shut up. We can't tell my brother."

"What?" Even clutching the wheel, he could see her arms shaking, her whole body trembling. "Why not?"

"Pull over, please."

She pulled her cell from her pocket. "No, you tell me—"

"Pull over, goddamn it, *pull over right now.*"

She yanked the wheel to the right and turned into the weed-choked, broken asphalt lot of a long-abandoned machine shop and threw the car into park. They both sat for a moment, the seatbelt warning bell chiming until she killed the engine.

"Let me at least tell you what happened," he said. She put the phone down.

He tried as best he could, with one hand pressed against the hot swelling left side of his forehead, the massive egg of skin cradled in his palm, to recount the events through a blur of pain and confusion. She listened, never interrupting, until he stopped.

"Well, he could have killed you, and he didn't. You walked into a grower's house, unannounced. You're lucky he didn't blow a hole clean through you."

"Unannounced, my ass," he said. "I was calling out to him the whole time."

"You say who you were?"

"I—" He tried to remember. "I don't think so."

"Well, after he clocked you, he propped you up on the couch with a pillow and your head turned to the side. So, that doesn't sound to me like Mike wanted you dead, or even hurt. He was probably startled as hell when he saw he laid out Leon McCreech's son."

"Not enough to stick around and see if I was gonna live." He rolled down the window as the air grew stifling. A cool breeze drifted in.

"No. My guess is that—"

"He was worried someone else was coming for him," he interrupted. "He was all packed up for the woods. And shit, he's probably out there now, in miles and miles of forest. We got to find him."

"Hell no, we don't." She shook her head. "He's a crazy old 'Nam vet who's lived out there since before we were born, and he's wigged out, with a gun. We'd never find him, and I don't wanna think about what might happen if we did."

"Someone did a lot of bleeding in that tub." Russ swallowed. "We don't know where Bree is."

"Don't even go there." Her lower lip quivered, and then she sucked on her cheek. "Bad shit is going on, for sure. But even if we find Mike, what are we gonna ask? What if he did it? You just think he'll be like, 'Sorry, guys, I know you liked her, but—"

"You think this is funny, Sam? Fuck you."

"No, fuck *you*." She punched the dashboard, and he flinched. "She was my best friend. I grew up playing with dolls and passing notes and catching frogs long, long before you started fucking her."

"It ain't just that." He buried his face in his hands.

Why couldn't this all just stop? He tried to think of something he could do, or something he could have done, to get things back to how they were before or to have kept this from happening. It wasn't perfect before she disappeared, and maybe it had been worse than he imagined at the time, but it seemed like heaven compared to this.

Growing close to her was the best feeling he'd ever had. After they'd been seeing each other for a couple months, Bree finally invited Russell over to her house while her mom was at work. When she walked into her bedroom, he stopped in the doorway and leaned on the frame. He'd never thought about it before, but there was nothing else like walking into a girl's bedroom for the first time. Not because of what you two might do there, but because it was like seeing a whole new part of her, seeing her more completely— the place where she dreamed and where she woke up.

A chaos of lipsticks and cosmetic boxes reflected in a pink dressing table's heart-shaped mirror. Her black leather jacket hung from a post of her tiny twin bed, and her open laptop glowed amid the tangle of unmade blankets. Monster High and My Little Pony dolls crowded a shelf above the headboard. YA fantasy and science fiction novels stood crammed into the bookshelf, side by side with picture books, true crime paperbacks, and autobiographies of porn starlets. A poster of a unicorn galloping down a rainbow was tacked up beside pictures of Slipknot and A Day to Remember pulled from magazines. An old Harmony acoustic guitar, cracked and missing its pickguard, leaned in the corner.

"Here it is." She did a little ballet spin in her purple socks and then spread her arms. "*Ta-da*. My tiny, trailer bedroom. A dump, I know."

"No, it's cool." He pointed to the guitar. "Can you play that?"

"A little," she said. "I've never had lessons. Unless you count YouTube."

"Me neither," he admitted. "Play something."

"No way. It's embarrassing."

"After all the stuff we've done together, you're embarrassed by that?"

"It's not the same."

"You never told me you could play."

"It's not like I'm in a band like you and Alex or anything."

"We play in a barn. Come on."

She folded her arms, bit her lip, and drew a half-circle in the carpet with her toe. "You have to promise not to laugh."

He crossed his heart.

She took the guitar from the case and pinched a guitar pick from the dressing table before sitting down on the edge of the bed. The guitar looked huge in her lap. Her tongue stuck from the corner of her mouth as she strummed a couple of chords and adjusted the tuning pegs.

"Okay. So most of the songs I know are really easy and pretty old."

"You gonna play that thing or ain't you?"

She took a breath, closed her eyes, and began. A simple pattern, plucked: G, C, D, like a million other songs. He'd heard it somewhere but couldn't place it. She started hesitantly, but on the second measure became steadier, and when she started to strum, she sang. And it was beautiful. She wasn't anything fancy, but her voice was clear and strong, right on key and sailing along with the notes. She gently swayed with her eyes closed the whole time, and he thought she could be famous for this, like a real star, if only she could learn to do it with her eyes open.

What was the song? Why couldn't he remember what it was she sang that first time in her room?

"Russ?" Sam snapped her fingers at him, one hand resting on the steering wheel. "You still there?"

"Just thinking about her. She's—I don't know nobody like her. I just wanna know she's okay. I know no one takes the two of us serious, but—"

"I'm not trying to make this a contest over who cares more about Bree, dude." She rubbed her knuckles.

"Twice now I walked into a bloody room." He shuddered. "And everybody keeps hitting me. You almost did, just then. Why does everybody keep hitting me? I ain't done nothing. I'm just looking for my goddamn girlfriend."

"We keep doing this, Russ, I think we're heading toward something worse."

"Maybe…" Locusts buzzed and clacked in the woods outside. "Maybe we should talk to the cops."

"No way. First of all, what am I gonna tell them? 'Hi, I run a cam ring of high school girls and, funny thing, looks like it got caught up in some money laundering or something. Oh, and that missing girl? She worked for it. And is probably moving drugs on the side.'"

"That's on you," he snapped. "Nobody put a gun to your head."

"No, but someone *will* if we go to the cops, can't you see

that?" She stared at him. "You're putting me in prison—and maybe killing me—if you do that, Russ. I'm serious." Her voice was soft, with a slight tremor of anger, or fear, or both. "I'm the only one who's helped you so far, and most of what you know is only because I told you. Think about that."

"Yeah." He took a breath. "But I think Bree needs help, and maybe the cops—"

"You remember what those cops did when Crystal's pictures got out? Nothing. They don't give a shit about people like us. Don't let Deputy Meg's 'I'm just a regular girl on your side' bullshit fool you. It's an act, and even if it's not, there's nothing she can do to help. You know that. She's just a cop."

"Yeah." His eyes stung and misted. "And talking to the cops...with folks like mine? The cops'll put it on us. On me." He blinked. "I don't know what to do, though."

"We should tell your parents. Or Shane and Larry."

"No way, I *can't*. You think any of them give a shit about Bree? Besides, I just told my dad I didn't know nothing and wouldn't be snooping around, and then I get knocked out with a rifle sneaking around Mike Morgan's cabin on the same day? My dad will end me. I'll never know shit. And you gotta remember, we don't know who's into what, you know?"

"You think..." She untied the bandana from around her head and wiped her forehead. "I don't want to piss you off. I just gotta know. You think your dad's people, or Jesse, or whatever, are part of what's going on with Bree?"

He spat out the window, then took a breath, still a bit woozy. Shane wasn't the same since he came out of prison, and though Russ would never admit it, his brother scared the shit out of him. And his mom and dad kept their cards close, at least when it came to Russ and anything illegal. He wasn't afraid of what they might do to him as much as what they might do to anyone else. Bloody Leon and Alice McCreech loved the family and the motorcycle club, and fuck-all to everything else. Bree wasn't a member of either. And neither was Sam.

"All I'm saying is I don't trust nobody. And I mean *nobody*."

She tossed the bandana over her shoulder, into the back seat. "You trust me?"

"A little, I guess—but I'm keeping my eyes on you."

"Good." She started the car. "'Cause I feel the same way about you."

When Meghan was young, the railway bridge over the creek was a hangout isolated from the adult world. It was a place that demanded a half-mile hike down the tracks from any road access, and its accumulation of broken beer bottles, cigarette butts, and rust-gnawed cans made it clear that it had been passed generation-to-generation as a party spot. Twenty years ago, when she was a sophomore, a kid from Meghan's high school named Ted Lawrence went over the side of the bridge. It was about thirty-five feet above a shallow, rocky creek. The fall killed him. Local gossip had lots of conflicting theories about what happened.

Some said he was on acid and tried to fly, others that he was drunk and fell. Most said he was suicidal and jumped. But more than a few locals believed he'd been pushed off by a seventeen-year-old Dan Hornween, who had lured Jake out there for a drug deal and then did him in. Dan was never charged, and there wasn't even any evidence or motive to connect him—the police ruled it an accident—but he never denied it, either. If anything, he made sure people considered it a possibility. Just a year before that happened, when she was fifteen, Dan had taken Meg out for ice cream and air hockey, and they'd briefly made out on that same bridge.

Meg never believed Dan had done it. He wanted people to be scared of him. That was all. It was one of the ways he protected himself, both then and now. Nobody ever grows out of who they were as a kid. Not completely.

Meg watched the sunlight play in the rippling shallows among the rocks far below, then checked her watch. The cloud cover had cleared, and it was shaping up to be a bright and humid afternoon. She looked down the tracks and saw Ryan in his bright blue uniform making his way toward her, holding a plastic sack. Right on time.

"So, is this where the bad kids go?" he asked as he walked up.

"I used to come here. Not as popular now as it was then."

"Where do they go now?"

"Wherever kids go. Online, I guess, wherever the hot spot on there now is. I don't know anymore." She waved it away. "These days, sometimes I'll do a walkthrough when I'm on patrol. If there are kids here, I always let them see me coming at a distance so they can clear out. Makes them think they're getting away, but makes them less inclined to make this a spot to get hammered."

"Don't want the hassle of the MIP busts?"

"Don't want to startle them and have them fall over the side trying to get away."

He laughed. "That ever happen?"

"If it did, they wouldn't survive it. A boy I was in high school with fell down there. They say you can see his ghost on the bridge every Devil's Night."

"Is that a fact?"

"I don't believe in ghosts."

"I meant that they say it, but good to know." He took a deep breath and looked around. "When I said let's meet in a more out-of-the-way place, I thought you'd pick, a mall, maybe?"

"Nearest mall out here has been dead for a decade or more." She shrugged. "Did you bring the coffee?"

"The finest from Citgo. I hope you like mocha." He reached into the crinkling bag and handed her a bottle, then opened one for himself. She took a sip, not exactly thrilled by his choice.

"So, was that meeting the straight dope?" She spat her gum over the side of the bridge, the taste ruined by the coffee.

"More or less. Fact is, though, we haven't been able to make much headway around Pike Lake with the NEO task force. I don't even know how much we need to, but Dale's pretty driven. Partially because he wants to keep himself elected, and partially because I think he sincerely wants to catch bad guys. I have mixed feelings about building up informants out here, honestly."

"Why's that?"

"Because it's risky." He sipped from the bottle. "I've always thought you can get the info you need from good policing without putting civilian lives on the line. You can't protect a snitch, no matter what you do."

She nodded. "Are you guys using any juveniles?"

"No."

"You're that certain? Don't bullshit me, Ryan."

"Your missing girl would never be used as an informant by the task force. There's a temporary moratorium on using anyone under twenty-one after what happened to that girl in Detroit last year."

That case had made national news. A nineteen-year-old woman caught with two-hundred-fifty dollars worth of coke turned informant. They sent her to buy some major weight in heroin for a sting operation. In the car-switching that went along with the deal, the police lost track of her. After a frenzied search, her body was found in an abandoned building the next day. Meghan remembered feeling sickened when she read the article. The informant had been tied to a chair with barbed wire, doused in kerosene, and set on fire—a hell of a price to pay for getting busted as a bottom-rung user.

Of course, Jesse McCreech was a nobody, too. That's who most of the informants were: the junkies, the amateurs, and the kids, all of them terrified and desperate for any way out. And what they were offered was usually only a deeper way in.

"You think the KoS, or someone else, is cleaning house?" she asked. "There was some kind of connection between Jesse and Bree Wells, even if it's once or twice removed. He got that necklace somehow. Maybe someone thought she knew too much."

"Or she happened to be in the wrong place at the wrong time," Ryan said. "We have some questions to answer, for sure. But there's a reason I wanted to talk to you. I pulled some strings to expedite the lab work for the McCreech case."

Getting lab work that quickly was unprecedented. Someone must have owed him something big. She kept her reaction muted. If Ryan was doing it to please her, she wanted to keep him thinking he needed to keep doing more to keep her pleased. If he wasn't doing it for her at all, she didn't want to give the impression that she felt like she had a stake in the homicide investigation—or was trying to snatch it.

"That's not my case, Ryan."

"No, but the stolen lawnmower was. So, officially, I guess I'm talking to you about all of the lab work in the context of that theft."

"The Michigan State Police are in lawnmower recovery now?"

"You sent in the prints on it."

"Well, Jesse's autopsy was no surprise, I bet," she said.

"No. But we ran the blood samples from the porch and the door."

Ryan was really going above and beyond. "And you found?"

"Well, first of all, it's what we didn't find. Most of them were contaminated."

"Are you kidding me? What happened?"

"Ed Stoltz did, and he put it in plastic, for one."

"Jesus. Who puts DNA evidence in plastic?" Procedure was chemically-neutral paper; plastic could wreak havoc with the imprinting.

"Happens more than you know. It's lucky we got anything at all. Not that it matters much, because he either didn't wear a facemask or a hairnet, or he blew on the swab to dry it, or he dirtied his gloves. He fumbled it. His material is in it, it matched from the exclusion profiles. And the other blood we pulled, well, it's inconclusive."

"Animal?"

"That or more contamination. Who knows? Could be a spaceman."

"You're not trying to sell me on aliens, are you?"

"No," he laughed out. "I think the spaceman cases go to the FBI, right?"

"A possum or raccoon Jesse blasted off the porch sometime?"

"Could be a varmint, but if so, it would be recent. But so what? Finding out what kind of critter died on Jesse's porch isn't much use to us."

"Never know. Keep an eye on those samples." She tapped her toe, thinking. "So, we've proven we have a butterfingered, old homicide detective. And if there's an animal or a spaceman nursing a gunshot wound, it might have seen something. Maybe we can show it a photo array. Why did you come to me with this instead of Ed?"

"Because," he said, "I have my doubts about Ed's...acumen. He looks like hell these days, and he botched gathering the evidence. And he overlooked the prints you sent."

"What about the prints?"

"We ran them. On the mower and from the truck's tailgate. And there, we have an interesting match."

She raised an eyebrow. "Who?"

"We have three sets. One unidentified on the mower. I'm guessing that's the owner. Next, the late Mr. McCreech, on the mower and tailgate. And then, a third. On the mower and the tailgate. His prints are in the database, looks like he had a pretty rough time when he came back from 'Nam, a string of arrests in the '70s and early '80s—beat a felony charge once, but just barely. He was either a member or an associate of the Ironwolfs MC. Then he just disappeared, record-wise. Word is that he's off the grid now, probably a grower or a meth cook. His name is Michael Phillip Morgan. They call him Crazy Mike. And I'm betting, unless he has a side-gig doing yard work, he was there that night."

Since Mike Morgan had up and vanished, leaving behind a tubful of blood—and Russ with a mild concussion—finding out what he knew about who was holding wasn't an option. After talking it over that afternoon, Russell and Sam agreed they'd put the word out that the two of them were looking to buy a lot of molly—she had the money if it came down to picking it up, even if he didn't. Calls were made, texts were sent. They'd have to try to score and see who popped up.

A few hours later, they got news from Russ's friend Alex, who said that his girlfriend, Dana, had gotten a bunch of molly yesterday, unground, from a kid they sort of knew named Clint. Dana said Clint was acting like he was some badass dealer, even though he didn't have any capsules for it, wasn't sure how to break down the pricing, and was still figuring out how to use a digital scale. Clint told Dana that if she knew of anyone who needed more, to let him know— or to find him at "Bangin' in tha Woodz," a festival being held on the Hornween property. It was happening tonight.

Shane drove the van down the narrow road, with Russell in the passenger seat and Sam in the back. The sky faded to a pale gray streaked with gold, and the roadway was darkened by the trees' shadows. Shane flicked his cigarette butt out the window and said to Russ, "I don't get it."

"Look. It ain't hard, Shane. Bree is missing, right? And Jolene says Bree was trying to unload a ton of molly."

"So?"

"So this Clint kid has a shitload of it. He might have been in contact with Bree—or at least he gots the same supplier. And if we can find out what he knows, then we'll be that much closer to finding her—and if we do that, then maybe we can find out what happened to Jesse, 'cause he had her necklace."

"I don't get it. People are gonna think we're narcs, man." Shane glanced over at Russ. "You run this by Dad?"

"He told me to go straight to you and have you handle it directly," Russ lied. "And nobody is gonna think we're narcs. We're known to have an interest in this shit. Especially Sam. Right, Sam?"

Sam slouched in her fishnet top and crossed her thigh-high boots at the knees. A score of rainbow-hued, glowing bracelets shone on her wrists. She dragged on a vape, and her free hand fiddled with the candy-necklace around her throat.

"Sam?" Russ asked.

"Huh? What?"

"Nothing. Never mind."

"Great." Shane sighed. "Does this kid know you have to pay a tax to sell at a Hornween party?"

"I don't think Clint knows shit about shit," Russ said. "He's into street racing, skating, skiing, that stuff. Never heard of him dealing."

"Well, he'll be in for a hell of a surprise if the Hornweens get wind of him selling at this thing. Hornweens ain't gonna be thrilled to have us on their property neither."

"Relax," Russ said. "We got nothing to worry about. Find Clint, lead him out, and have a talk. That's all. Nothing heavy."

"If you think this is a good plan," Shane said, "then maybe that fall you took off your bike busted up your head worse than you think."

Blue-and-red lights flashed behind them, illuminating the twilit roadway. Russell's heart skipped when he heard the siren squawk.

"You gotta be kidding me," Shane growled as he snapped off the radio. "Anybody holding? Carrying?"

"I'm clean," Russ said. "You, Sam?"

"I have some dabs and a stun-gun. But I'm not the one driving."

"I'll handle this," Shane said. "It ain't nothing."

Shane pulled over onto the shoulder, and a massive spotter lit up the van. He rolled down the window the rest of the way, clicked on his hazard lights, and killed the engine. He placed his hands on the wheel.

The cop walked up and stood in the window—it was Deputy Meg, wearing a pair of aviator sunglasses and shining a Maglite.

"Evening, Sheriff," Shane said. "How can I help you?"

"Hi, Shane. License and registration, please?"

"Sure." He handed them over.

She looked them over and slid them into her citation book before saying, "Hi, Russ. Anyone else in there with you?"

"Just Sam."

Sam waved and smiled.

Deputy Meg nodded, wrote something in her notebook. "Russ, can you step out of the van for a moment, please?"

His skin crawled. "What? What did I do?"

"Hey, Officer," Shane said, "I'm the one driving, and whatever you gotta—"

"You can wait in your van or in the back of my car, Shane, it's up to you," she said, sharply. "Russ, will you step out of the van and meet me around the back, please? Exit on your side or the back, not on the sliding one by the roadway."

He opened his door and stepped out, then walked around to the back of the van, his pulse pounding. Meg shone her light in his face, then quickly lowered it.

"What happened to your head, Russ?"

"Oh, that?" He cupped his hand to the side of his head. "Fell off my bike."

"Looks like you took a heck of a spill. You see a doctor about that?"

He shook his head.

"Have you seen Mike Morgan around, Russ? Or do you know where he might be?"

He looked away and gave a shrug. "Not really, ma'am."

"Huh. Well, I was just out there." Her voice was even, but he felt her searching his face, looking him over. "Hey, don't you usually wear a cap? A Tigers one, frayed along the brim?"

"Sometimes." His heart raced. He scratched at his neck. He and Sam went back and grabbed his bike, but—where was his hat? He couldn't remember if he'd put it on that morning or not, but—

"Something ugly went down at the Morgan place, Russell. I was worried something happened to you. Among one heck of a mess, I found a hat that looks like the one you were wearing when I picked you up at Jesse's house the other morning. And now a lot of people have questions for you. So let's talk."

CHAPTER 6

The kid looked like he was already on the verge of coming apart, so Meghan wasn't going to push it. The swollen knot on Russell's forehead flickered from purple to blue in her cruiser's flashing lights as he shifted from foot to foot. His pupils were dilated, black with a thread of green around them. He scratched at his neck and looked past Meg, or at some point over her head, when he spoke. Some of his unease was to be expected. The boy wasn't having a good week.

As both a soldier and a sheriff, Meg had never lost sight of the fact that being asked pointed questions, alone, on the side of the road by an armed official empowered to detain, hurt, or kill you if needed is stressful for most civilians. Even when they're in the clear. Powerlessness is always frightening, and sometimes the people you make the most nervous are the least dangerous.

Terrorizing Russell wasn't going to get the answers she needed. She needed him to be *less* afraid of her than he was of everything else happening around him—not more.

"Russ, I don't think you had anything to do with what happened to Jesse. You know that, right?"

He chewed on the inside of his cheek and nodded.

"And I know you want to find Bree as much as I do," she continued. "Maybe more. Now, if we help each other, we might be able to get somewhere with this. First of all, I want you to know that you're not a suspect."

A slight smirk. He didn't believe her. Great. Someone had already put that fear into him. She let it slide, for now.

"But you also need to know that not everybody feels the same way I do on this. I'm not saying what you did and didn't see, or did and didn't do. But a person could get a lot of bad ideas from looking inside Mike's cabin right now."

Russ scuffed the toe of his boot in the dirt and rolled one of his shoulders. If the boy had seen all that blood in the cabin, he'd be thinking the worst. But Meg didn't believe the blood was Bree's. Or Mike's.

"There's some disturbing things in there, Russ. But like I said, I don't think it was you. I have a pretty good idea what happened. I'd like to run it by you."

"Who do you think—" He stopped short, shutting up before the question was done.

"I'd like us to talk about it, Russ. Soon. We're both trying to find Bree. I'm on your side in this. And us not talking with each other, it isn't doing either of us any good. It sure won't help her. Can I come by your place and talk with you sometime tomorrow?"

"Not there." Emphatic. She got it—someone at home didn't want him talking to the police.

"How about we meet somewhere, in the afternoon, then? At Sam's work or a park maybe? Will you give me a call?"

"Yeah," he mumbled. "Meet in the woods or something."

She had him saying yes. Now, she had to close the time gap. She had to get him in *now*.

"Stoltz or one of the other deputies might pick you up

and take you in. They're looking for you. If I can sit down with you first, we can avoid that. Why don't you come with me right now?"

"No." Instant. "And if you take me, I ain't talking. Shane will get Dad, and Dad'll get our lawyer. Can't do it now. And I won't."

Damn it.

"Later tonight?" she pressed.

"No. Gotta be some places tonight. All night."

"Fine. How about I give you a call tomorrow morning and set something up? I know that might be a bit early for a weekend, but it's important, okay? No one has to know."

"Sure, yeah."

She ducked down a bit to seek out his eyes.

"I will, alright?" He looked her in the face. "Damn."

"Okay, one last thing," she said. "Are you in that van by your own free will?"

"What's that now?"

"Are you safe? You want to be riding around in there?" She pointed.

He made a face. "Yeah, I mean, it's just Shane and Sam."

"They're going ask why I brought you out here. Tell them it's because I saw that bump on your head and asked if Shane or your dad have been abusing you. Knocking you around. They won't like it, but it will take the focus off you and put it on me. Got it?"

He nodded.

"Alright, you can head on back—we'll talk more tomorrow. But let's keep this between us for now. Is that okay?"

"Yes, ma'am."

She let Russ go and then walked up to the driver's side and informed Shane that his tags were expired. She let him off with a warning.

"Thanks, Sheriff. Appreciate the head's up." Shane grinned at her, showing surprisingly good teeth. "Pretty sure I got the stickers at home, just forgot to put the dang things on. Don't know what I was thinking. I'll be sure to take care of it first thing."

Shane spoke with the go-along-to-get-along tone that often came with years of negotiating conflicts with authority figures. It was the kind of speaking that rookies took as eager compliance, but she saw it as a brush-off. Or maybe she just didn't like him. He had the predatory, bad-boy swagger and the cool friendliness of an ex-con who felt like he had a one-up on the world—women especially. The sort of vibe Dan had been born with. It looked flashier on a younger guy and scarier on an older one, even though it shouldn't matter. It was all the same bullshit.

The van remained on the side of the road after she pulled away. Time would tell if she played her cards right. It was a risk, for sure—but Stoltz had let the kid walk away after Russ had been at a murder scene, so the detective couldn't be too rough with her letting him go this time. Especially if her hunch about what she'd found at the cabin turned out to be true. Russell was not the one who needed his cage rattled.

She headed through the deepening dark, turning onto Deerfield Road. Her phone buzzed in her pocket, and she answered as she drove. It was Ryan.

"Meg, the troopers are all over Mike Morgan's place. You were right about the blood in the tub."

She grinned. After her meeting with Ryan on the bridge, she headed straight to Mike Morgan's cabin. With the door hanging open (well, unlocked—close enough) she felt she had probable cause to let herself in when no one responded to her knocking—with her weapon drawn this time. She'd had enough surprises for one week. The bathroom was a shock, but what at a glance looked like it could be the aftermath of a torture-murder took on a different appearance with a bit of scrutiny.

It seemed like a panicked, ad-hoc medical procedure. All of the signs pointed to it: bloody blankets and towels, hemostats and forceps, rubbing alcohol, X-acto blades. She bet the injured party had been carried into the bathroom, wrapped in the bedding. Mike Morgan had seen heavy action in 'Nam, and she bet this wasn't his first time removing a bullet or patching a hole. She'd done it herself more than once in the service—though she'd never caught a bullet herself. On the floor, near the couch, she found what looked like Russell's Tigers cap. She hoped the boy hadn't been the one in the tub. She called Ryan. Not Stoltz. She wanted it handled right.

"We dragged a tech in with the mobile crime lab," Ryan said. "We had him look at the blood in the tub. You were right. Not a person."

"It's a dog?" She rolled through a dark crossroads, keeping an eye out for traffic.

"We'll have to run some more tests, but I'm betting on it. Found a shallow grave out back, and exhumation detail dug up a freshly dead Doberman somebody tried to patch up. If we can get a match from it, the tub, and the unidentified sample on the porch—and I bet we can—that lands Mike Morgan at the scene."

"Well, at least his pet. It's circumstantial, but it's strong."

"Right. Now, there's the matter of the baseball hat. We don't have any samples to match it to. A lot of hats look the same. This thing is getting expensive, and right now, even if it is Russell's, we have nothing to charge the kid with. We don't have anything that points to a crime happening at Mike's place, other than maybe practicing veterinary medicine without a license."

"I'll handle Russell. I'd tag the hat as evidence, and keep Stoltz busy with Mike Morgan."

"Sounds like a plan. We'll be in touch."

Lil' Angels was sparsely attended when she slowed down to scope out the lot. The sexpot cartoon woman on the sign gazed out on the roadway with wide, anime-style eyes and a tiny, half-open mouth. Meg supposed the expression was intended to evoke innocence, but it could have just as easily been terror. The neon halo over her head flickered and buzzed at the edge of extinguishment. This time, Meg parked her cruiser in the center of the lot. When she stepped out, she straightened her gun belt and put on her sunglasses.

She needed to find Ricky Hornween. Mike Morgan, too, it seemed. If either of them were still breathing. But now, it was time to see what Dan had to say about how a young lady managed to clock out of her shift at a grocery store in Kentucky and two hours later take the stage at a strip club in Michigan, four hundred miles away.

Russell lifted the joint and drew deeply, its ember a tiny sun-flare just beyond the tip of his nose, before passing it to Samantha. Shane walked on his left, his thumbs hooked in his front pockets, as they made their way toward the music throbbing behind the trees.

At least a hundred cars crowded together in the field, by some wonder parked in orderly rows along orange snow-fencing that had been used to divide the expanse into lanes.

Russ had the feeling he was in a stadium parking lot, other than the trees surrounding it with their leafy boughs like black clouds frozen mid-boil. The stars were bright overhead, and the field was alive with voices. Overlapping hoots and laughter surged and broke with the discordant harmonies and rhythms of a score of car stereos crashing against the rumble and punch of beats emanating through the dark bulwark of the woods. People stood in loose knots between the cars or sat in ragged configurations on the open grass. Here, a barefoot girl in a sundress stood with her arm around her girlfriend as the two shared a cigarette. There, a tank of nitrous oxide propped up beside a pickup truck, the boys inhaling from a black balloon and chortling in a monstrous baritone.

This was Hornween property, but it was a public party. As long as you had the cash for admission (or some other form of desired currency) and your car could make it past the pair of pistol-wearing, sunburned locals in orange T-shirts printed with the words EVENT STAFF at the gate leading to the makeshift lot, you were in. The festivals brought traffic that backed up the roads and were louder than the devil, but they were way out in the country on private property, and neither the sheriffs nor the troopers had the manpower, funds, or inclination to bother fighting the Hornweens anymore, at least on this front. It had been going on for decades.

"So, when Deputy Meg pulled you out of the van, she asked if me and Dad are abusing you," Shane said, staring dead ahead as he stomped along. "That means they're looking for an excuse to take us in. Cops do this all the time. Show up shouting about domestic-abuse-this or child-neglect-that as a way to get inside your place, snatch up everybody, then put the screws on till they can get something to stick."

"I know it," he said, relieved that his brother's hatred of

police trumped any suspicion of Russell's explanation.

"You know what she done, right?"

"What who done?" Russ took the joint back from Sam.

"Bree," Shane said, his voice a low rumble. "Ain't it obvious? She burned somebody bad, and then she took off."

Russ sighed. "You don't know shit about shit."

He took another hit. It was from the bag he'd picked up from Jolene yesterday. More mellow than he expected, red-streaked and sticky.

"She sold off enough of something to get a head start and took the rest with her." Shane spat. "And I wouldn't be surprised if, somehow, Jesse got his dumb-ass self mixed up in it. And that's how he got himself killed."

"Ain't nobody gonna front Jesse any kind of weight." Russ swatted a mosquito on his arm, pulping it to a dark smear of blood. "If they did, shit, they deserve to get taken."

"Maybe Jesse stole it," Shane said. "From, I dunno, someplace."

Russ didn't immediately have anything to say to that. "He might steal a lot, but he's bad at it."

"This seem like it worked out for him? And if you don't think anyone would front Jesse, who would front a goddamn high school girl like Bree?"

"Bree had her own things going on. All I'm saying is there ain't no reason she'd ever run with Jesse."

"Maybe not." Shane shrugged. "But nobody's on their own in this, I'll tell you that. I wonder how much molly your girl was holding when she talked to Jolene."

Russ didn't tell him about the fifty-grand online cash transfer Sam was supposed to have gotten last week—the one that never came through. Sam, unsurprisingly, didn't offer that info either. She wasn't talking, but Russell had come to the conclusion that her blown-out space-case act was usually that. An act. She was always listening and always watching.

"Hey, guys," Sam said. "Check it out."

She pointed a chipped blue nail down the row of parked cars to a black Honda. A boy with spiky blond hair in a tight T-shirt with sunglasses folded over the collar leaned against it, grinning as he chatted up a couple of younger girls. Clint Christiansen. Russ might have just walked by him, listening to Shane yammer and not paying attention to the crowd.

"That him?" Shane asked.

"Yup," Russ said.

"I'll handle this." Shane picked up the pace, striding toward the car and calling out, "Clint?"

"Yeah?" the kid said, lifting his cigarette. The girls backed away as Shane drew nearer.

"Hear you got something we're looking for," Shane said. "Like to talk to you about it."

The cigarette dropped from Clint's fingers, and before it hit the grass, the boy had taken off at a dead run through the lot.

"Shit," Shane barked. "Get him."

Shane and Russ ran after him. Clint broke toward the trees and the wide footpath leading to the DJ and band stages. Russ ran after him, nosing ahead of his brother. He had no idea what to do if he caught up to the kid before Shane did.

"Wait," Russ called out to him, between huffs. "We just want to talk to you!"

"*Help!*" Clint screeched as he made his way into the woods.

Some kids laughed as they dashed by, Clint screaming and flailing his arms, Russ edging closer as Shane fell behind. Strings of colored lights in the trees lit the wooded path. Shadow-forms shifted and embraced, slouching against the trunks or rolling in the leaves beyond the path. Some cursed as Clint and Russ shoved past them, others jeered, and all the while the thunder of distant music and the roaring of an unseen crowd rose as the world bounded and shook in Russell's vision.

He burst out of the woods and into an open field flooded with a sea of humanity rolling as waves in time to a pounding electronic beat. It was cut with streaks of glow sticks and accented by whirling luminous hula hoops. Beyond the sea of roiling bodies, a figure in a hooded sweatshirt hunched over a laptop, sequencers, and consoles, waving his arms like a sorcerer over his cauldron. A girl with a shaved head, wearing nothing but body paint, cavorted around the DJ, holding a flaming torch in one hand and a flask in the other. She dropped onto one knee and blew a giant plume of orange flame over the crowd. For a moment, Russ was mesmerized and lost, but then he spotted Clint pushing into the crowd and ran after him.

The crowd, a crush of sweat-damp bodies, swallowed Russ. His head pounded in rhythmic agony to the baseline. He caught a glimpse of Clint looking over his shoulder at Russ, then hurrying deeper into the throng. Russ struggled, his breath heaving, to keep up with him. From the corner of his eye, he saw a lean girl in a black, sleeveless T-shirt slit from shoulder to waist, half-turned away and gyrating in a clearing among the mob. Her wavy, dark hair was tossed to one side, revealing how it had been shaved to the skin underneath, and both her hands were on the back pockets of her ultra-short cutoffs. Everything seemed to freeze around him as he gaped at her, only her body remaining in motion to the pulse of the music.

"*Bree!*" His scream was nothing more than a twinge felt in the back of his throat over the pulsing noise.

He kept calling her name as he shoved his way toward her. She was here, and even if she no longer loved him, or if she had something going on with Clint, or if she was just having one last blow-out before she skipped town with whatever cash she got from whatever double-crossed deals she'd made, at least she was okay, goddammit, she was alive. She was dancing.

Reaching out, he shouldered his way into the opening where she danced, and clasped her hot, wet shoulder.

"Bree? It's me. It's Russ."

She whirled around, stepping back, and her face seemed to age as he grabbed her arm, the lines deepening around her mouth and creases forming on her shining throat. He said her name again. Dark makeup streaked below her eyes, and then he saw that they were not green but light brown, almost gold, and terrified.

"What do you want?" she shouted, her voice a barely audible screech. "Let go of me! Let go!"

Everything shifted on its axis, and he tried to make sense of it for a moment that seemed to expand like a whirling galaxy. She looked at him as if his next move might be to put his hands around her throat.

She's not who I think she is.

Let go of her.

Let go.

Then he was stumbling backward as she jerked from his grasp and hurried away, and he realized the dancing woman was not Bree. She was thirty if she was a day. A skinny lady with a mohawk. That was all. It had been obvious from the moment she turned around. He staggered into the crowd, colliding with a man built like a wall, Russ's forehead smacking against the man's rough leather vest. Russ slipped in the damp grass and fell hard on his rear.

He stared up at the man, a skinhead-type with a walrus mustache, tattooed up to his jawline, a back dagger inked under his eye. A name patch on the man's cut read "Pick-axe," and below that, "Master-at-Arms."

The man glanced down and stepped over Russell, stalking through the crowd like a hunter, everyone giving him a wide berth. The patch on the back of the man's cut showed a devil with a sword, and Russell recognized the club without even needing to read the rockers: Knights of Satan, Detroit. The music rose into a throbbing, buzzing drone. Then it stopped. The crowd hooted and cheered.

A girl's voice asked, "Are you okay?"

The set had ended. Sam stood over him as the crowd broke up, holding out her hand. He clambered to his feet and said, "I thought I saw Bree. But I was wrong."

"What happened with Clint?"

"I lost him. We can look around, I guess."

"No. It's okay," she said. "It was just a shot in the dark, anyway. But he was scared shitless of Shane for some reason. I mean, more than anyone normally is. Come on, let's go."

"I just saw a Knights of Satan guy in the crowd," he said as they walked down the path. "They're a club that's not supposed to be out here. Something's wrong. I need to tell Shane."

When they were halfway across the lot, they heard Shane's voice saying, "Yeah, be careful you don't party too much like my friend here. He's lucky I found him. God knows what might've happened to him, right?"

The group of kids laughed. Shane had Clint thrown over his shoulder, the boy's arms and legs limp and dangling. His brother saw Russ and Sam and walked over, carrying Clint like a sack of dirt, and said, "Lookee what I got."

"Jesus, Shane. We just needed to talk to him," Sam said.

"Well, he didn't want to have that conversation," Shane said.

Clint snorted and mumbled.

"He passed out?" Russ asked.

"He had a bit of help. Looped back out of the crowd and into the woods. Where he ran into me. All tuckered out, poor little guy. Sleeper hold. Let's take him somewhere a bit more private."

"Goddammit, Shane, you creepy fucker." Russ looked around, then lowered his voice. "This is kidnapping. You want to go back to prison?"

"Nope, so we better hurry and get him to the van, eh?"

Once they were in the van and locked the doors, they propped him up in one of the back seats. Hot, murky air brought out the van's stink of turned food and sour beer and bitter sweat. The kid groaned and scrunched up his face but didn't awaken. Shane patted him down, retrieving Clint's phone, wallet, keys, a pack of Camels, six Jolly Rancher candies, three condoms, and two bags of coarse, amber-colored powder.

"My, my, my," Shane said, holding the baggies up.

"Each of those is a half-ounce. At least," Sam said, peering over the top of the seat behind Clint at Shane and Russ.

Clint took a deep, wheezing breath and opened his eyes. He looked from Shane to Russell then around the van.

"Don't scream. You'll be fine," Sam said, leaning over and speaking softly in his ear.

"Russ? Sam? Look, I know we're not tight." He gestured to Shane. "But you can tell this guy that I never intended to short him. Or his motorcycle gang—"

"It's a riding club," Shane said.

"Sorry." Clint swallowed thickly. "You can have what's on me now, and I'll give you the rest. I swear."

"We ain't trying to rob you, kid," Shane said.

"No, I know, I wasn't saying you were, bro." He nodded rapidly, his blue eyes wide with panic. "I guess this is all just a big mix-up. Now, I know I probably could have handled it better, but—"

"Hold on." Russ raised his hand. "Relax. You know we're not narcs or nothing, but who did you get this from?"

"I—I found it, I guess?"

"Oh, bullshit." Shane cranked back his arm and formed a fist.

"No, for real, bro." Clint squeaked and sheltered his head behind his arms. "It was in the door I got!"

Russ put his hand on his brother's shoulder and shot him a look. "A door?"

"Car door. For my Civic. I sideswiped it against a tree months ago. Doors aren't cheap. Couldn't find one at the junkyard but left my number with a guy there to call me if anything came in. He called me, just a few days ago, right? And sold it to me, cheap. I mean, cheap for a door."

He paused as some people walked by outside the van, one holding up a phone's screen for the other to see. A teen boy ran past them, waving a sparkler. Shane glared at Clint. He took a breath and continued.

"So. Anyway. I really wanted to get it on my car for the

weekend, so I set it up to paint it in my garage. I know, it takes a long time to dry, but I figured if I set up some fans and—whatever, you don't care. Point is that when I took off the inside panels, well, I found the shit." He threw his hands up. "I swear. I thought I got lucky, yo. That's all. Thought someone stole and scrapped a smuggler's car. You gotta believe me."

"What color?" Russ asked, a cold pit forming in his stomach.

"The door? I painted it black like the rest of my car."

"Not now, goddammit." Russ rolled his eyes. "When you got it."

"It was purple."

Sam and Russell locked eyes. Bree drove a purple Civic.

"What scrapyard?" Shane leaned in.

"McCreech Salvage, your place, I swear. And the guy who set me up with the door had a vest just like yours."

"A club vest?" Russ asked. "Did it have a devil with a sword on the back?"

"Knights of Satan don't ride out here," Shane said.

"Tell that to the guy I ran into in the crowd. Dude named Pickaxe."

Shane did a double-take. "That ain't good. But right now we need to get a handle on who was at the yard."

"He had a vest just like that." He pointed to Shane. "With the wolf on the back, the diamond right there, and everything. That's why I ran when I saw you. Guy who called me was named Larry. Seriously, that's all I know."

"What the hell?" Russ's skin crawled with horror. Larry Dodge? His brother's tag-along, the goofy, bald biker who drove tow trucks for his dad? "Shane, you know anything about this?"

Shane took a breath, the tendons on his neck rising through his skin as a deep crease formed between his eyebrows. "No. And I ain't sure I believe it."

"I swear it. God strike me down and shit." Clint held his hand over his heart as if pledging allegiance to the flag. "Dude had the whole car. He'd already taken the engine out. I can show you where it is. It was just a couple days ago."

"Yeah." Shane patted him on the arm. "I'd like that. But first, I'll take what's left of the goods you came across. And then, if we get this sorted, you might just end this night all in one piece."

Meghan gave a stiff nod to the hulking bouncer as she pushed past him into the club. She strode straight across the floor, a hip-hop bass-line rattling her bones. A wire-haloed cocktail waitress, three skimpily-clad dancers, and a throng of beer-drinking locals stepped out of her path. When Dick the Bartender called out and waved her over, she ignored him, making her way toward the door in the back of the club. She jabbed the buzzer box beside it and glared up into the black camera orb overhead.

"Excuse me, Officer." A guy with a shaved head and a line-beard that looked as if it had been stenciled on with an airbrush approached. His pumped pecs stretched the white letters of the word SECURITY printed across his black T-shirt. "Can I help you?" he roared over the music.

"I'm not looking for someone to move a piano or spot me at the gym, so I doubt it."

"What? You're moving a piano to a gym?"

"I'm on the job." She pressed the buzzer again and kept

it depressed. "I need a word with your boss."

"Mr. Hornween isn't in there, Officer." He folded his arms and stood at his full height. "And you're disturbing the guests. You should go."

"Look, sir." She turned to face him, her hands on her hips. "I know you're only trying to do your job. But so am I. And I'm a sheriff and you're—you're not, okay? So I advise you to back off." She saw the button on the intercom labeled TALK and pressed it before leaning toward the console and shouting, "Dan, it's Deputy Shaw with the Stanley County Sheriff's Office. Open the door, now."

"This is harassment, lady." He took a step forward. "I'm going to file a complaint—"

"You better disengage from this right now, or you'll be making that complaint from a hospital bed."

Baldy blinked and stepped back. He placed his finger on his earpiece. Two more goons were making their way across the club floor—one who was previously posted to the right of the runway stage, and another that emerged from the door leading to the attached video and sex toy shop near the entrance. One looked like an ox, the other a greyhound, both wearing the same black security shirts. For once, she wished she had brought Deputy Williams with her—even if he was the sort of man who had trouble dealing with unruly raccoons, at least she wouldn't be alone. Baldy was sizing her up, too. She glanced over at the bar. Dick wasn't there anymore. Someone grabbed her shoulder from behind.

She drove her elbow back into the man's solar plexus, then pivoted to strike the heel of her hand under his chin. Dick crashed backward and landed hard on his ass. A woman screamed. Meg stepped away from Dick, who struggled to breathe, and used her left hand to snap out her collapsible baton an inch from Baldy's face. Her right settled on her holstered sidearm.

"Back off," she commanded. "Now."

Baldy lifted his hands and backed away.

The two other goons froze in their tracks, and the dancers stopped their gyrations onstage. The song ended, and the blue-mohawked DJ did not play another. He gaped at the scene with both of his hands clasped in shock. Dick wheezed and hacked on the stained carpet. Someone sniffled, and a glass clinked against a table. Everyone in the club stared at her.

Dan Hornween appeared in the entrance across the club, wearing a black cowboy hat and lowering a cell phone from his ear. He looked around the club in bewilderment for a moment, then waved his hand dismissively at his security staff.

"Sorry, folks, just a little misunderstanding," He called out to the crowd. "Everybody gets a free beer and a shot. Once my bartender gets his ass back behind the bar. Where it belongs."

Dick had found his way onto one knee and steadied himself against the wall. "Right away, Dan," he croaked before heading back the way he'd come from.

"Everybody get back to having fun. That's what we're all paying for." He clapped his hands once, flashing a gold-toothed smile. He jabbed a finger at the DJ and yelled, "Music!"

The flustered DJ ducked behind his laptop, and a decades-old Marilyn Manson track blared out. The goons returned to their posts as Dick began lining up plastic cups of beer and thimble-sized whiskey shots on the bar, and the small crowd made its way over to claim them, the altercation forgotten. Meg collapsed her baton and returned it to her belt.

Dan shook his head at Meg and then ran his keycard through the console's slot. He opened the steel door and bowed. "After you, Deputy."

She looked through him. He sighed and walked up, leaving the door open behind him, and she followed.

"Too bright in here for you?" he asked as they walked up the leopard-print stairs.

She snapped off her sunglasses. He gave a low whistle at the sight of her black eye.

"Bet there's a story there." When she didn't answer, he added, "All due respect, Meg, but have you lost your goddamn mind?"

"I'm looking for Bree, and I'm not putting up with any bullshit this time."

"Well, great. I'll have you know I was heading out to my property to see how the event there was going. Dick called to let me know you were here as soon as you showed up, you know that? I turned the car right around."

"Your point?"

"Dick was only trying to tell you I was on my way, and he caught a beating for it. Thought you were one of the good ones."

"He got knocked down, so what? Dick should know better than to walk up and grab a cop from behind."

"I didn't hire him for his smarts, I'll give you that." They made their way into the office. He tossed his cowboy hat on the couch as he passed, then sat down behind his desk. "But you could have just asked for me when you came in. I don't live in this lair all the time like a dragon, sleeping on a mountain of golden panties. You've made everyone in this bar think you're a ball-crushing fascist."

"You're telling me I've lost the esteem of folks who hang around a run-down strip club in a failed bowling alley?" She stood with her arms folded.

"Hearts and minds, Meg, hearts and minds. Didn't they teach you anything in the service?"

She had taken about enough of this, but after that scrap out front she couldn't lose her cool now—she already had narrowly dodged a brutality complaint hardly a year before. "One of your dancers last amateur night wasn't legit, Dan."

"I got you all the paperwork. No one gets on that stage without a legal ID, and we know what we're doing."

"In order for an ID to be legal, it has to be presented by its owner." She pulled a copy of the offending driver's license from the breast pocket of her coat, unfolded it, and slapped it on his desk. "You had a girl from out-of-state on the roster that I have verified was working a shift at a Piggly Wiggly in Kentucky when she was supposedly on stage here."

"What do you want from me?" He turned his palms up. "I do the best I can here, but ID theft happens all the time. It's a whole industry. Maybe an illegal immigrant is dancing under a stolen identity. Hell, maybe someone with a stolen ID is working at the Piggly Wiggly in Shitsberg, Kentucky, and the real one was on my stage Monday."

"That," she said, pointing at the paper, "is the ID Bree Wells danced under."

"Oh no, don't even try to go there. That lady is blonde," he said. "Bree isn't even close."

"Bree was seen at the drugstore on Sunday night by one of her mother's friends. I checked out the store video. You know what she bought?"

"A pregnancy test and a copy of *Seventeen*?"

"A bleaching kit. Oh, and there's something else. The girl

in this ID? That's Bree's cousin."

"Well." He grimaced and scratched at his goatee. "Ain't that a kick in the balls." He folded his hands and sighed. "Where do you want to go with this? Because I know you think the worst of me, and of this place—but honestly, this is all news to me."

She looked him over. Dan was a hard read—he seemed as if he could flip through his emotions like TV channels, and she wasn't sure if it was by choice or just because of some bad wiring in his head.

"I need to talk to some people. Ricky, to start with."

"And I wish I could tell you where to find him. Maybe he's still out in LA. You and me aren't the only ones looking for my little brother." He glanced up at the security monitors behind his desk for a moment. "Had some dudes come by here yesterday hunting for him, too. I wasn't in at the time, but they didn't seem to be very cheery about it, from what the staff tells me. Dick and the crew sent them packing, but they were some hard customers."

"Bikers, I'm betting. Knights of Satan guys, right?"

"How'd you know?"

"I came across a couple of them breaking into Ricky's house last night. One of them is sitting in a cell right now." She pointed at the screens. "You got tape of the guys from when they came in?"

"As a matter of fact, I do." He opened up a laptop.

"Well, if you have tape from that," she added, "you must have footage from the amateur night on Monday."

He hissed. "I know this isn't what you want to hear, but—"

"Don't even try to withhold it," she snapped. "Bree danced here. I could bring the walls of this place down around your ears if you don't cooperate."

"And don't I know it. But the feeds are digital, right? I got six feeds." He pointed to the security screens. "And I got one hard drive. It fills up quick. And it resets every Friday morning. Automatically."

She took a deep breath. Frankly, she was surprised he kept any archive at all—but she supposed it was to cover his ass if something went south with an unruly customer, or to keep an eye on the dancers getting payment without kicking up the club's share. Still, it seemed like a pretty convenient way out.

"Anyway, here are the chuckleheads from yesterday." He spun the laptop, which showed two burly guys, shot in sharp black and white footage from an overhead angle, trundling in the front door. She took a step forward and leaned in to look at the screen.

"Pause it." She pointed to the screen.

He tapped the spacebar and the image froze. One of them, the blond, looked right up into the camera. The one they called Viking Dave, who was currently eating bologna sandwiches and farting into a plastic mattress in the Stanley County Jail. The other one, in profile, had a shaved head, a tattooed neck, and a thick mustache. Paul "Pickaxe" Cross.

"Them the ones you nailed busting into Ricky's house?" he asked.

"One of them, at least," she said. "I can't tell you more than that. Ongoing investigations and all."

"I don't have any business with these guys," Dan said. "The Knights of Satan are, well, unpredictable. One minute they're buying a round for the whole bar, the next, they're trying to kill everyone there. More importantly, they're also under federal scrutiny."

"Ricky into anything with them?"

"If he is, I'm going to beat him so bad that his kids'll come out retarded. I mean, if he ever has kids. Not that retarded kids don't deserve love." Dan stared off into the distance and pursed his lips. He looked like he'd forgotten what he was talking about. Out of nowhere, he snapped his fingers and pointed at her. "Ricky and I didn't have the best parental role models. You know? Since he got out of the joint, I've tried to keep him away from guys like that. But, you know, our business assets attract a certain kind of guys."

"If these guys have it out for your brother, he's in some serious danger. They're no joke. You need to send Ricky in to us. I know you want to keep him safe."

Dan snapped open a gold Zippo and lit a cigarette. He blew a couple smoke rings and watched them drift to the ceiling. His chair creaked, and the drumming of the sound system downstairs boomed through the floor.

"I hear your brother's been seen with Bree, out and around," Meg said, after Dan began another round of smoke rings. "And they're both missing. We both know Ricky has an interest in young girls."

"From my experience, that isn't an unusual interest." He set the cigarette in a chrome skull ashtray and laced his fingers behind his head. "You gotta point here?"

"Somebody's woven quite a web. And I think your brother and Bree Wells are caught up in it. People are going to end up dead, Dan, if we don't do something. People we care about. Maybe some already have."

"Humph. A web, eh?" He plucked up the cigarette and took a drag. "So, who do you think is the spider, then? Ricky?" He pointed at Viking and Pickaxe, frozen on the laptop screen. "These dirtbags? The very dead and never-too-bright Jesse McCreech?" He rolled up the sleeve of his cowboy shirt, revealing a sun-blasted tattoo of a spider with eight red eyes fixed on the nude woman struggling in the web wrapped around his forearm. The sight of it made her feel ill. "My dad always used to tell me you're either predator or prey."

"Your dad sounds like a creep."

"He was a lot of things, like everybody is. Who do you think is the spider in this web? Someone right under your nose?"

"I don't know." She glared into his dark, vein-netted eyes. "Not yet."

"A few years ago, swarms of spiders overran a whole village in India. You hear about this?" He gazed down at the tattoo on his arm as he spoke, working his fingers. "Millions of the things swept in like a crawling, biting flood, covering every living thing. Like something out of a horror movie or the Bible, right? Then the spiders were gone—*poof*—they just went to wherever spiders go. Nothing left behind but bites. People died, so stuck full of venom their hearts gave out. Nobody ever even figured out what kind of spiders they were."

Meg realized her hands had balled into fists, and she unclenched them. Dan rolled his sleeve back down and clicked its pearl-snap cuff.

"I'll be talking to all the staff that worked last Monday," Meghan said. "Get me a list, with addresses. And tell them to be cooperative."

"They're not predisposed to be forthcoming with cops, especially cops who barge in and beat on them for no good reason. But I'll see what I can do."

"And charge records," she said, flatly. "From the bar. And

the ATM. Idiots always come to places like this with cash, but they always end up spending more than they brought."

"You'd know all about that, right?"

Was that a jab about her past? Did he know something, or was he just taking shots in the dark? Or was he just saying that as a cop, she dealt with a lot of idiots? He twisted his head and cracked his neck. It sounded like someone snapping a head of celery in half.

"Charge records," she said.

He swiveled in his chair, dragged open a file cabinet drawer, and plucked out a manila folder. He spun back and held it out flat to her. Written across the top in black marker was RECEIPTS with Monday's date. One corner of his mouth pulled into a sneer.

"Thought you'd never ask," he said. "Good luck with the spider hunt, Deputy."

Russell used to like walking through the junkyard and imagining how every crumpled, bent wreck, with its leaking fluids and broken glass, was once someone's brand new car. He pictured them rolling off the lots with the stickers still on the windows, their drivers puffed up with pride behind their wheels as they breathed deeply of fresh upholstery and plastic. He tried to picture the scrapyard as a kind of vehicle Valhalla, a place where all the wrecks could share their gasoline-powered memories and tales of the road behind. But that's not how he saw it tonight, in the dark. Tonight it seemed like nothing other than acres piled with dead machines.

They'd collected two more sacks of molly from Clint, who retrieved them from his bedroom, under Russell's supervision. Sam and Shane waited in the van out front, parked in the cracked driveway of the two-car garage ranch where a Red Wings flag proudly fluttered in mid-June. Russ handed the drugs off to Shane, who shoved them under the dash. Then they began the long drive to McCreech Salvage.

On the way, Shane made a call to their dad, making sure that Larry was called away from the scrapyard and held at the clubhouse until they could get things sorted. When they got to the scrapyard, it was unattended save for three mastiffs pacing the grounds. After Shane entered the gate code, the dogs trotted alongside the van as it crawled through the headlight-illuminated labyrinth of ruined cars and rusty appliances, around the mountains of tires and piles of shopping carts.

With a shaky voice, Clint directed them to one of the cement-block storage garages at the far side of the grounds. The structures occasionally served as repair shops for the family or for other Ironwolfs, and they were never locked. But the rolling metal door of the one Clint pointed to was secured with a thick padlock visible from the van. Shane parked and killed the engine, but he kept the headlights trained on the garage door. Outside, the dogs circled. Russ watched Shane reach down and pull a thick crowbar from under the driver's seat.

"Let's go," Shane said.

"Um, can I stay here?" Clint watched the mastiffs from the window, who watched him back.

"Yeah," Russ said. "You too, Sam. The dogs know us, but I ain't sure how they feel about you guys. They get aggressive at night."

Sam looked up and nodded, her face ghostly in the light of her phone's screen, as the two brothers climbed from the van into the damp heat of the night. Moths and gnats swarmed around them. With the headlights at their backs, their massive shadows came into sharp focus against the garage door as they approached. Russell's legs felt unsteady. Shane knelt to work the crowbar into the lock. He planted his feet and, after three full-body yanks on the bar, the lock gave out with a sharp crack. Its pieces caught the light as they sprang through the air.

Shane nearly fell when the lock snapped, but after a step backward he regained his balance. Russ squatted to grip the door's handle, its metal cold and gritty in his palm. He took a breath, gave the handle a twist, and rolled the door open.

There, in the stark glare and deep shadows of the headlamps, was a purple Honda Civic—or what was left of one. It had been backed into the garage and, now without wheels, sat on blocks. The hood was gone altogether, revealing a gutted engine compartment. One of the doors was completely missing and the other was removed, leaning against the wall beside a workbench. The bumper had been detached and now rested on a plastic tarp across the garage floor. There was a wide scuff on the bumper's lower right from the time Bree and Russell were a bit buzzed and she'd misjudged a turn at the Burger King drive-thru. It was all Russ could do not to scream.

"Goddammit." Shane slapped his forehead. "Larry, you idiot, what are you thinking?" He pulled his cell phone from his pocket and began texting.

Russell hurried over to the doorless driver's side and leaned in. The interior had been cleaned out. There wasn't even change in the center console. He pulled the trunk release, and a dull click came from the car's rear.

"Russ." Shane spoke more softly than usual. "You might not want to look in there."

But he was already in the depths of the garage. Spider webs hung like white drapes in the headlight beams, and the trunk cracked open like a wide, dark mouth. Russell gripped its upper jaw and threw back the trunk lid. Empty. Purged, more like it. The trunk's floor panel and spare were gone, leaving nothing but a hollow space.

A dry, splitting noise startled Russ. He jolted back from the trunk and hurried around the passenger side as the wrenching and snapping continued.

Russ squinted through the van's beams to see Shane standing over the car door that leaned against the wall, the crowbar in his hand. He'd crudely forced the interior panel from the frame, breaking it and pulling it back. The resulting hole had disgorged a few brick-sized packages. They were piled around Shane's feet. The dogs stood backlit in the garage doorway, hulking and indistinct animal shapes, their eyes aglow.

Shane slowly turned his head to look at Russ, his expression chillingly blank, and he said, "Dad's on his way."

The night shift sergeant at the county jail made some noise about having to pull two deputies off their rounds—after lights out—to bring a high-risk inmate like Jon "Viking Dave" Samuels to an interview room, but Meghan showed the picture of Bree and claimed (falsely) that an Amber Alert was going to be put out for her soon. The prisoner, she explained, might have info about the girl's whereabouts. Time was of the essence, minor in peril, all that. He begrudgingly agreed. She was taken to an interview room, where she took a seat at the table and waited.

After thirty minutes alone in a windowless, beige chamber,

she started to worry that something was wrong. Was the sergeant calling the office? Or, worse, Cunningham or Stoltz directly? She hoped that by coming late at night, she would get less-connected staff who would be unwilling to call someone from the office personally at such an hour. Maybe she'd made a bad move—she still had the records from Dan to go through. Maybe her time would have been better spent on that. She could try again in the morning to get Cunningham or Stoltz to give their blessing for her to interview the prisoner. Not that she should have to ask in the first place. As it was, she decided that from here on out she would be asking for forgiveness rather than permission.

At last, two officers brought in Samuels. Handcuffed, stuffed into an orange jumpsuit so small it could only accommodate him by being unsnapped to the waist, and limping along with his head bowed, he looked not like a violent outlaw but a sad, tranquilized circus bear. Maybe they had sedated him—she didn't think to ask. He slumped in a chair, his elbows on the table to support his cuffed hands. One of the officers stood in the corner, the other took a post by the door. Samuels lifted his head, and his blue eyes stared at her through the tangles of his long, blond hair. For the first time, she saw how his lower lip was split, his nose was broken, both of his eyes were swollen, and his face had been pummeled to a livid purple and red.

"So now you get a turn beating on me while I'm cuffed too?" His voice was deep and dull. "Give it the best you got. Come on."

She shot a glare at the officer behind him, who smirked.

"No, Mr. Samuels. We already had our fight, and you had your hands free then. I've put that behind us. I'd like to ask you a few questions, though. Your most serious charges are connected to an incident you had with me. It could help you quite a bit to have me make a positive statement to the prosecutor and judge about you."

"Right," he grunted. "Talk to my lawyer."

"Hear me out, at least." From a folder on the table, she produced a photo of Bree Wells and placed it in front of him. "You see this girl? That's all I care about. Whatever you—or your buddies—are up to in my county? Nothing to me. Why you were out at Ricky Hornween's place last night? Not my problem. I am looking out for her." She pointed to the photo. "And I think you might know where I can find her."

"Why the hell would you think that?"

"Call it a hunch. It's usually pretty quiet around here. But it was no accident you ended up at Ricky Hornween's place last night. He knew my missing girl, and what do you know, right before she vanished, this gentleman got a surprise visit."

She presented a picture of Jesse McCreech, blood-soaked and dead in his recliner in a crime scene photo. Samuels was unmoved.

"Right around the time the Knights of Satan came riding in, how about that?" Meg clucked her tongue. "Like I said, not my case, not my business. I'm not looking for names or confessions. Only this girl. She's just a kid, and I want to keep her safe. You do that, and maybe I can help you have a better time with, well, with whatever other kinds of issues you might be dealing with soon."

"Look, lady." Samuels shook his big, shaggy head and sighed. "As a rule, I don't make statements without a lawyer. You can beat on me all you want, but that's not gonna change."

"So, you're saying if we get a lawyer in here, you'd be willing to talk to me about the girl?"

"Lemme finish. What's between me and Ricky is between me and Ricky." He pointed a cuffed hand at the pictures. "But I have no idea who that missing jailbait or this dead shitkicker are. You wanna try to railroad me, go for it. I've never seen these fuckers before in my life. Good luck."

She held his eyes—he was a pro, so there was no telling what his game was, but there was no defiance or slickness to him. Samuels just seemed like a beat-up, dog-tired, defeated convict.

"Don't stonewall me, Dave," she said, "you're not doing yourself any favors. I'm not asking for you to give me names, to inform, anything like that. I'm only asking for info about the girl."

"Jesus H. Christ." He closed his eyes and took a breath. "I—don't—know. Okay? I'd love a chance to help straighten some shit out at no cost to me. I'm pretty short on friends in this bumblefuck hick county. But you're barking up the wrong tree, lady." After a moment's silence, he added, "Can I go back to my cell, or do you want to ask me who killed JFK while you got me here?"

"That was Lee Harvey Oswald," she said.

"Keep telling yourself that. We done?"

"I hope for your sake you're not lying." She nodded and stood. "Let me know if you think of anything."

He grunted. "Sorry about your eye."

On the drive back to her house, a thick fog of depression swallowed her. Mike Morgan was a solid suspect or witness for Jesse's murder, but he was in the wind. Though she doubted he'd gone far, there were over four thousand acres of land around his place, much of it densely forested.

Flushing him out would mean mustering local cops, sheriffs, and the DNR, and even then it was unlikely they'd get themselves much more than some tick bites and twisted ankles. Ricky Hornween was God-knows-where. Myra had tracked down contact info for Ricky's former agent and for the producers of Tattoo Kings, but neither had returned Meg's calls or emails. All Meg had for her work was a sighting of Bree at a drug store, and a list of names of patrons and dancers of a strip club she probably danced at on Monday night. Most of them would be evasive or outright hostile to questioning. At least she knew the girl was probably blonde now, whatever that was worth. And she had her boyfriend, Russ, willing to talk about whatever he knew tomorrow morning. Still, it felt like the case was treading water in an ocean of sharks—and she had the churning, dreadful feeling that time was running out.

Mr. Purrs greeted her with an angry meow as she hung up her coat and took off her equipment. He nuzzled her ankles and then, inspired by nothing, took off at a dead run across the house. She tossed the folder of the club's records and other case notes onto the sprawl of investigative material already covering the coffee table.

Her phone buzzed—one new text, an hour or so old, from Myra:

> Everything ok, sis? Let's meet up tomorrow, love you. Call anytime.

Exhaustion settled on her like a lead blanket. She muted her phone but kept her radio on as it charged in the corner. After a shower, she changed into sweats and set her laptop to play songs at random.

The music helped, but as tired as she was, her thoughts bounced and banged around in her head like shoes in a tumble dryer. It was a chaos of images and sounds: bullets snapping by her head, Dan's gold tooth glinting as he threw back his head and smiled, Myra pouring a glass of lemonade, Mom rolling dough on the kitchen counter and then lying wan and shriveled on a hospital bed, Bree sullen and silent at fifteen in the back of Meg's cruiser, Meg's dad's hands on her own as he helped her aim a rifle, a half-forgotten boyfriend from middle school crying, the dead cat from her past, snorting blow off a key in a Jacksonville restroom, lifting a dripping bottle of bourbon from its hiding place in the toilet tank, an explosion ripping through her convoy, Russell raising his hands in her Maglite beam, the rising fear as the soldiers in her unit all stared her down, bloody paw prints in the tub, the redolent sting of drinking from a tumbler of whiskey, and at last the shining pendant shaped like a B in a dead man's red hand.

A banging at her front door jolted her awake. She was disoriented. A mostly drained bottle of whiskey was on her kitchen table, along with a glass of melted ice. The faintest blue of morning glowed in the windows. Her temples throbbed and her mouth was dry. Music still drifted from her speakers, the playlist looping through for the first or fifth time, the singer going on about how everything hits at once. The banging on the door, again. It hurt her head. She glanced at the stove clock: five fifty-three in the morning. Panic. On your feet, soldier—who could it be? Better get the pistol, you can never be too ready. The banging, Jesus, what the hell?

She yanked open the door, leaning from around the side of the frame, her pistol gripped and held flat against the wall. Outside, birds twittered and chattered. Deputy Mark Williams stepped back with his hand still raised to hammer on the door one more time. She blearily gaped at him and asked, "Mark? What's going on?"

"Sorry for all the noise, but I could hear the music in there, so I figured you were home. We've been trying to raise you on the phone and the radio but got nothing." He gave her a quizzical look. "You alright, Meg?"

"I'm fine." Shit, could he smell it? When did she get the whiskey out? She couldn't remember what time she got home. "I was asleep. Been pulling some long hours."

"I know you have. Well, when Cunningham and Stoltz couldn't get a hold of you, I came over to tell you myself. Bree's been found."

Her breath caught in her chest. "Is she safe?"

Deputy Williams looked down. "A fisherman found her body in the creek down from the railway bridge. I thought you'd want to get to the scene right away."

"I'll be right out." Her ears rang as if a bomb had just detonated. "Just give me a sec to get ready, alright?"

"Sure. I'll be in my car. I can drive us if, um, you need that."

She closed the door and pressed her back against it. The same songs kept on playing. She slid down the door and sat on the carpet, her knees even with her shoulders. She absently set the pistol on the floor beside her before clasping both hands over her mouth, keeping her scream caged inside.

CHAPTER 7

Leon rolled into the scrapyard just after midnight, driving his blood-red Plymouth and tailed by a cycle ridden by a one-eyed gun-dealer named Wink. They parked behind the van. Neither of them looked happy to see Russell and Shane, who leaned side-by-side against the garage door. A creeping numbness had overtaken Russell since witnessing the incomplete remains of Bree's Honda.

The mastiffs came trotting up to Leon, wagging their tails and surrounding him. Wink dismounted his motorcycle and ambled over. When the one-eyed man reached out to pat one of the dogs, it gave a ferocious snarl. Leon snatched Wink's wrist to yank his hand away. The mastiff's jaws snapped together, a hair's breadth from Wink's fingertips.

"Did you just try to pet an actual junkyard dog?" Leon glowered at him. "How have you lived this long?"

Wink wiped the dog slobber on his pant leg as Leon walked over to his sons. He looked the brothers over, folded his arms, and said, "Car's in there, along with the other shit?"

He was quick, direct, as if he was there to give an estimate on some bodywork. Shane nodded.

"You take any of it, either you?" Leon asked. "If you did, you better hand it over."

"We got some off Clint, the kid who bought the car door," Russell said. "It's up under the van's dashboard."

Shane glared at his brother and huffed.

"Wink." Leon jerked a thumb at Shane's black E-series. "Get it out of there." As Wink headed to the van, Leon looked back to his sons. "The girl and the kid still in the van? Samantha and what's-his-nuts? Clint?"

Russell nodded. His dad frowned. Wink came back, holding up the sacks of molly. Leon waved him away before saying, "Shane. Get rid of those kids."

"On it." He flicked his cigarette butt, a streak of orange in the dark. "So, what do you want done with them?"

"Dad, please," Russ burst out, the shock now hitting him, "they didn't—"

Leon winced and raised a finger. "I meant, take them home. That's *all*. But make it clear that they're gonna keep their traps shut about this."

Shane said, "What about the—"

"Wink is gonna hold this place down. I've got Skeev and Huckleberry up by the front gates. Get on out of here. I'll call when I need to see you again, and you better come running."

Russell followed Shane toward the van. Leon reached out and gripped his younger son above the elbow, his hand tightly wrapping around his bicep as he passed. Russell turned to stone.

"Not you, Russell." He rolled his tongue around in his mouth. "You, my boy, are coming with me. Get in the car."

There was no point in arguing it. The Plymouth's door felt as massive as it did when he was five years old, like the lid of an enameled steel coffin he had to drag open to climb inside. He slammed it shut as the velvety bucket seat ensconced him. Hanging from the rearview, a rabbit's foot gently swayed on a brass chain. Its dry, yellowed claws poked from its furry toes. Through the windshield, Russ watched a silver-haired man with an eye patch stand like a sentinel before a garage sheltering the remains of Bree's car and the forbidden cargo it had contained. Russell remembered giving her a pink teddy bear for Valentine's Day, so long ago, almost five months—she'd kept it on the Honda's dash. Gone. Whoever had thrown it away probably never even considered that it had meant something to somebody. Leon ducked into the car, eased the door shut, and slid in the key. Under the hood, the Hemi came to life with a clattering roar. Russell stared out the window as the muscle car crept out of the scrapyard's ruin.

The roads were dark and there was no music. After a thousand years, Leon said, "Talk."

"She's dead," Russell said, careful to steady his voice. "Ain't she?"

"I got my suspicions," he said. "But I give you my word—as your dad—that I don't know. And neither do you."

"Did you—"

"Irregardless, there is one thing I do *not* want to hear from you right now—and that is you asking me about shit you don't know about. That ain't a privilege you got right now. I want to hear what you *do* know about." A vein throbbed in his neck. "It ain't a request, son. Talk."

"I don't know where I'm supposed to start."

The wheel creaked when Leon's hand tightened on it. "Start at the start. And fill in what you left out last time."

"All right. Fine." Russell sniffled. "So, like I said, I ain't seen Bree since a couple Sundays ago. She'd just gotten in a fight with her mom about the Chicago trip…"

Leon kept his eyes ahead, his face lit only by the dashboard's glow, now and then interjecting "go on," or "uh-huh," or "right," as his son recounted it as best he could. The wheels droned on, rolling against the road. Russell told him about Samantha's camgirl ring, the plan to launder Ricky Horn-ween's money through her accounts, the fifty-grand transfer she never got, the shard of molly Bree had tried to sell to Jolene, the bloody discovery he'd made at Mike Morgan's cabin—and how the cops had found Russell's hat on the scene after he'd fled. He told it right up to them snatching up Clint and ending up at the junkyard.

When Russell finished, he feigned exhaustion from the tale, rubbing his eyes with the heels of his hands to surrep-titiously wipe away tears.

"That's all I can tell you," he croaked.

"Huh. Well." His dad cleared his throat. "I know what it's like to fall so hard for a woman that you'd follow her down to Hell. You got some balls, and some brains to go with them, kid. You managed to sniff out a trail, keep on it, and track it back to your girl's car. Which, unfortunately, is on our property. Now, I know that it ain't your doing that it's there. And it sure as shit ain't mine. But it ain't good for us. That, and you got yourself placed at some cluster-fuck at Crazy Mike's, who, by the way, could have just as easily gotten spooked and blown your guts out as cold-cocked you. Now I have to see if anyone can track down my crazy ex-Green Beret friend in the state forest—which ain't likely—and my youngest might be sitting in county lockup within the week. Do you know," he asked as he rolled the wheel to drive onto the highway, "why I told you to stay out of this?"

Russell turned away and looked out his window, seeing nothing but his own face reflected like a mask, his eyes hollowed out against the night.

"You think I'm weak," he said.

"Nope," Leon said. "That ain't it."

"I know you do. Like you said, I ain't dumb. I know I ain't like Roy was, or Shane. I can't hardly change a tire, still ain't got no driver's license, don't ride with the club. Till I was with Bree, you probably thought—"

"Shut up." Leon rolled one of his shoulders, then leaned back in his seat. "No, you ain't like Roy. Shane neither. And you know what? Shane's hardly got the stink of penitentiary off him. Roy's dead and gone. Know what it feels like to be a dad who can't keep his sons out of prison or the graveyard?"

"No," Russ said, his voice hardly more than a whisper.

"You're goddamn right you don't. I made promises. Things were supposed to go different with you. *And that's why I told you to keep your nose out of this.*" His fist smashed like a hammer against the dash, and Russell recoiled in terror, cowering against the door. "You are up to your neck now, sonny. All of us are. That's the end of that."

"Why does—" Russell faltered, then took a breath, and with a shake in his voice asked, "Why does Larry have Bree's car? And where the fuck is she? Huh, Dad?"

"I done told you: *I don't know.* But you can ask Larry yourself. He's being put on review by the Ironwolfs. The board's meeting at the clubhouse in a few hours, so first you and me are gonna work out *exactly* how to explain all this. And then there's the matter of the cops." Leon reached out and patted him on the shoulder. "You wanted in? Well, congrats, my boy. Don't say I never warned you."

"You got that wrong," Russell said.

"Got what wrong?"

"I never wanted in."

A tent enclosed the crime scene on the creek's shoulder. Surrounded by swaying reeds and cattails, it seemed to breathe like a pale, living temple as a gentle wind billowed its walls. Flies droned and buzzed, alighting on its stark, white surface as it swelled and constricted. Their blue carapaces glinted in the morning sunlight. Meg stepped out from the tent, feeling hollowed-out and feverish in the corpse-fragrant humidity. She tied the flaps closed and put on her sunglasses. A single drop of sweat trickled from the nape of her neck and trailed down her spine. A knot of sheriffs and state troopers gathered in the shade of a dogwood. They all watched her approach.

Detective Stoltz and Inspector Russo flanked Sheriff Cunningham, who said, "What do you think?"

"Brianne Wells," Meg said. "The tattoo on her back looks pretty new; her mom probably doesn't know about it. Hair's been bleached. The body jewelry, haircut, birthmark on her hip all match up. The body is hers. I'd like to volunteer to be the liaison with the family," Meg said.

"Thank you for that," the sheriff said. "I'm sorry things had to go this way. You did the best you could."

"Thank you, sir."

"Think she jumped from the trestle, or fell, maybe?" Cunningham pointed down the creek to the railway bridge arcing over the water about a mile down.

"I could see her as a jumper," Stoltz said. "She's clothed.

Looks busted up pretty bad."

"Her vehicle is still missing, though," Meg cut in. "I think she was dumped, maybe over the side of the bridge, maybe further up the creek," Meg said. "The water levels swelled after the rain yesterday and washed her down here. She was killed somewhere else."

"I'm sure the medical examiner will give us a better idea," Ryan said. "The State Police are handling the evidence gathering and forensics on this—unless you have any issues with that, Ed."

Meghan hoped she could conceal her relief; the last thing they needed was Stoltz's doddering ass stumbling on that part.

"I should work the scene and direct it." Stoltz grimaced. "This is going to be my investigation, isn't it?"

"Of course, Detective," Ryan said. "But the sheriff reached out to us about the McCreech shooting, so we're kind of in this already."

"That was a different case." Stoltz looked to the sheriff. "Dale, what's going on here?"

"This is going to be a joint investigation," Cunningham said, raising his hands to calm things. "We can't do the lab work in-house, for one thing. We still have to recover the victim's vehicle. With both Ricky McCreech and Mike Morgan in the wind, we're out two persons of interest who might—or might not—be connected. We need some reach across counties. So, we'll coordinate with the troopers."

"Fine," Stoltz grumbled. "As long as you're not pushing me out, that's fine."

"And what about Deputy Shaw?" Ryan asked. "She's done a good deal of work looking into the victim's circumstances."

"Meg, can you hand over your case notes and debrief

Detective Stoltz and Inspector Russo this afternoon? Then I suppose you can move on."

"Sir?" She felt as if a bucket of water had been thrown in her face. "I've been working the Wells girl's case for days. If I may—"

"When you were working it, she was a Missing Person." Sheriff Cunningham pointed to the crime scene enclosure. "Well, it's a damn shame, but we found her. Homicides and suspicious deaths go to senior investigators. You know how this works."

Stoltz blithely looked past her, to the troopers and deputies searching the underbrush edging the woods, eager to get back to the scene. Her lip curled back, and just as her tongue curled to spit out a dagger, Ryan met her eyes and gave her the slightest shake of his head.

"Don't worry, Deputy, we'll be consulting with you, of course," he said.

"Of course," Stoltz echoed, looking out across the creek. "We're all set here, then?"

The wet morning air was suffocating, and a chill slithered across her skin. She could still smell the dead girl, could taste the rancid bloat of her body softening on the creek's shoulder. Bree had probably been killed before anyone even noticed she was gone.

Meghan gave a stiff-lipped nod and said, "Of course, sir."

The windowless clubhouse was dark, save for a light behind the bar and the colored glow of the jukebox in the corner. The floor had been cleared, leaving a jetsam of tables and chairs shoved against the walls and piled in the corners. Russell sat among the haphazardly arranged furniture as if he too had been pushed out of the way into the room's furthest reaches.

They stood in a ring, shoulder-to-shoulder, gathered like a pack surrounding its prey. Some had their scalps shaved to the skin, others grew their hair long and wild, some had the thick, bushy beards of pirates and moonshiners while others sported neat goatees and sideburns. They wore greasy sneakers and banged-up boots. Some were young. Most were not. All wore the three-patch vest with the face of a wolf on its back. Russell knew all of them and shared blood with many more than a few.

Larry Dodge stood with his arms folded and his chin up in the circle. Just a few days ago, Larry had been staring up at the masks in Russell's bedroom like a kid in a Halloween shop, and slouching in the back of Shane's van, chugging on a forty and air-drumming to Metallica when they all drove out to the clubhouse. Did he know Bree's car was at the scrapyard from the start? Had he only been pretending to be Shane's lackey the whole time?

Leon McCreech cleared his throat and stroked his beard, and somehow the room became yet more silent.

"Y'guys did right by coming in. I know most of you ain't slept yet, and even more are still drunk. Alice is making another pot of coffee in the back. We can get to that after, and of course we'll have Injun pouring drinks at the bar here if you'd rather get back to it. But we got some serious discussing to do. Before we get to the matter at hand, I gotta ask, firstly, anyone seen Mike Morgan?"

"Ain't nobody seen Crazy Mike." It was Hound, a pipefitter who spent his evenings as the king of the Hobble Inn's pool tables. "Some people would like to, that's for damn sure. A lot of folks were counting on re-upping from him, the town's pretty dry right now."

"If anyone hears anything about Mike's whereabouts," Leon said, "you get word to me or Cowboy." It was Shane's road name, because of some old movie. He didn't like it, but in a club with guys who went by Pukey Lou or Cock Stain, he couldn't complain too much. "But there's another thing we got to take care of tonight. Our brother Larry Dodge, also called Digger, an elected officer of the Ironwolfs, is accused. Stand and face the board."

Larry walked into the center of the ring, which tightened to fill the space he left behind.

"Digger, you are accused of using Ironwolfs' garage property for criminal activity without board's permission, for trafficking narcotics, and for—aw, hell. Fuck it." He clapped his hands together, then cracked his knuckles. "Where's the girl?"

"What girl?"

"Fuck you, Larry." Leon took a deep breath and exhaled through his nose. "You got exactly five seconds to start explaining why you put a missing girl's car full of drugs in my goddamn garage, what you know about the bloodbath at Crazy Mike's, and what it has to do with my nephew being shot dead or—"

Larry looked down and said, "You're gonna take my colors."

Leon took one long step forward and smashed his fist down between Larry's eyes. With a wet crunch, blood sprayed from his nostrils and spattered across the floor. He stumbled back before dropping to one knee. Russell felt lightheaded, watching it.

"Don't interrupt the acting president." Leon flexed his fingers. "If you don't tell me everything you know, right now, I'm gonna take more than your colors. I'm gonna take you apart."

Larry dragged himself to his feet. His goatee and the front of his shirt glistened with slick, dark blood. It dripped from his chin and patted steadily against the floorboards. When he spoke, his words were slurred by injury.

"I was working overnight at the scrapyard, hoping someone might call for a wrecker, even though it was a Monday. Summer. Maybe some kids would get in a smash-up or not know how to change a tire. You never know. Spent the whole time working on my bike and watching TV. Nothing came in. Then somebody starts honking at the front gate. I mean, he's laying on it, and it's about three, four in the morning. Dogs are going nuts." Larry spat a red gob into his hand. "So I grab up a pipe wrench from the office and then head out. And it's Jesse at the gate, driving this girly, purple Honda I ain't never seen him in before."

Russell buried his face in his hands.

"And then what?" Leon folded his arms.

"I open the gate and let him drive in. And he gets out and he says he's gotta get rid of the car. And that I gotta help him. He's all jumpy and weird. And I'm thinking, aw, shit, he stole this car. Like maybe some dumb Birch Hills girl out getting drunk on the trails left her keys in it and Jesse just took the thing. And I'm about to tell him to just dump it on the road somewhere—hell, I'll come pick him up, and then he reaches in his pocket and hands me a wad of cash. About twelve-hundred."

"No way," Injun scoffed. "Jesse ain't never had twelve-hundred dollars in his whole life. Not at once, at least."

"If he did, he'd shoot it, drink it, or smoke it," Skeev said.

"Shut up," Leon said.

"I swear." Larry held out his open hands. "He hands me the money and tells me to crush the car. Get it gone and don't say nothing to nobody. I say I'm supposed to tell Leon if we disappear a car, but he's begging me not to, so I finally, I cave, okay? And like that, he's gone. Has me buzz him out, and he just straight up walks away into the dark."

"It's fifteen miles from the scrapyard to his place, at least," Leon said. "He didn't walk that."

"Someone probably picked him up." Larry sniffed, then gingerly wiped his nose, turning the back of his hand a glistening red. "Dunno."

"Mike Morgan?"

"I really don't know, Leon. Honest."

"You didn't shred the car, though. Even though you took the cash."

"Naw. I shoulda. I been hurting for cash. My roof is leaking, worse than I can fix. Fridge is going, too. Plus, put some money on the wrong teams lately. Can't win. Anyway. I knew this kid who had been looking for a door, same model, same year as the Honda. Know some other guys who are always looking for ricer parts, too. With the cash Jesse gave me, and selling some of the parts, I could get my head above water again. Didn't want to take the car out on the road, figuring it was scorching hot. Locked it up in one of them garages in back, half of them are empty most the time anyhow. Planned to part it out, then use one of the flatbeds to haul the rest over to the shredder when it had been stripped, and still hold up my end."

"Did you know about the drugs?" Wildcat asked.

"You think he'd sold that door if he did?" Shane glanced at Wildcat. "Gave it away like a prize in a Cracker Jack box?"

Russell chewed his nails. He called out from the corner, "Who cleaned it out and wiped it down?"

"Shut up, Russ," Leon barked. "Only members can talk during a meeting. Don't make me say it twice." He hitched up his jeans and asked, "Who cleaned it up and wiped it down?"

"It was like that when I got it. I swear. So clean I thought it might've been taken off a used lot. Seems real stupid now." Larry hung his head, and blood dribbled from his nostrils. "After Jesse got killed, I got real nervous. Like, maybe he got killed over some deal with the car. I thought maybe I might be next, since I'd seen the thing. And then when I found out that missing girl drove the same kind of car too, well, I figured the less everybody knew about this, the better. I wanted to shred it, but I ain't had a shift at the scrapyard since shit went south, and Shane's around all the time besides. Until tonight. I was just heading out to fire up the flatbed and drag the car to the shredder when Injun and Wildcat showed up and told me to saddle up and head to the clubhouse. And I figured they was gonna kill me on the road. But what could I do? At least I'd die riding. Surprised I've lived through this much of the night."

"Don't get too used to it." Leon held out his hand, palm up. "Key to your ride. Hand it over."

Larry dug in his jeans pocket and retrieved the key. His puffy eyes brimmed with sadness as he handed it over to Bloody Leon, like a child forced to surrender a beloved pet. Leon's giant hand rolled into a fist around the key. Without a word, he slowly turned his back.

From the far corner, Russ saw his dad standing with his hands on his hips, the light cutting his red-bearded face with black fissures of shadow. The rest of the ring of men faced inward around the accused. Larry didn't defend himself when they all fell upon him, nor did he make a sound. A blow to the side of the stout man's head sent him reeling, and the immediate barrage of smashing fists and stomping boots brought him to the floor. As the beating continued, Leon ambled slowly across the barroom, his boot heels clacking against the creaking floorboards, a rolling chaos of concussive and bone-splitting strikes echoing out behind him, and Bloody Leon seemed not to be drawing nearer as much as swelling in size until he threatened to fill the room with his presence. With a curl of his hand, he motioned for Russell to stand, and the boy was on his feet before his mind was aware of it.

Leon looked down at him with dull blue eyes and said, "You've always been the quiet one. But silence is what keeps us strong, boy. You keep that in mind going forward. I talked to the board. You're a prospect for the club. Con-gratulations."

Russell's throat constricted and he choked back an acidic gurgle.

"Ain't got a motorcycle, Dad."

Leon grabbed his son's right wrist with his left hand, twisting and pulling Russell's arm so he could hold the boy's hand open. Leon, with red-smeared knuckles, reached out and pressed a glinting key into Russell's palm. Lines crin-kled around his eyes as he smiled. "Yes, you do."

"This is for Larry's bike—"

"Larry ain't got a bike. Not anymore. Shane will get you set up with a cut and your prospect patches. I'm sure you'll give them respect. You've done real good so far."

Terror and exhilaration commingled, the way he'd felt adrenaline surge when he first encountered the pleasures of slasher movies, liquor store shoplifting, and midnight vandalism. The light shifted and Russell looked up to see his brother standing beside his dad. Blood was spattered across his face, and it gleamed in coppery droplets on his blond hair. Shane leaned forward and squeezed Russell's shoulder.

Leon said, "I'll take you back to the house, Russ. The guys will clean up this mess." He jerked his head to the bikers standing over their fallen former comrade. "And Shane'll ride out to the scrapyard so him and Wink can shred that car."

"But, Dad," Russell stammered. "It's Bree's car. It's evidence."

"You got that right." He looked to Shane and said, "Crush it."

Russell, searching for words he could not find, watched his brother walk across the bar and out the front door.

"Don't worry, my boy. This ain't done by a damn sight. It's being handled, like I said." He slapped Russell on the back, nearly knocking him a step forward. "Welcome to the club. We're all real proud of you."

Time and forgetfulness had obscured the old McCreech place's history just as clinging vines had overwhelmed the orchards that once surrounded it. In the late morning heat, Meghan felt as if she was broiling inside her Kevlar vest, and her gun belt felt like an iron girdle digging into her hips.

She pounded on the front door. Russell had not called this morning as he had promised he would. He had not answered Meghan's calls, either. She tapped her foot against the porch planks. Crows cawed in the yard's unkempt apple trees, and a train whistle moaned in the distance. Again, she hammered two reddened knuckles against the door. No answer. The unmistakable blatting of a Harley engine revved in the near distance.

She looked out across an expanse of crabgrass, beyond the gnarled trees and past a bare clothesline's posts, to the outbuildings. The motorcycle revved again, the hammering of its engine tearing from one of the structures. It wouldn't be the boy out there. But it would be one of his clan, and she might as well pay whoever it was a visit. Maybe it would be Shane. She felt in the mood to push some buttons, and he might be dumb enough to let her get a rise out of him, to let something slip.

A fallen apple, bursting and sweet with decay, ruptured beneath her boot as she crossed the grass. What remained of Brianne Wells washed up in her mind. Glossy black nail polish on swollen, mud-caked hands. Arms and legs as soft and white as grubs. A blackbird spread its wings in inky scars between her shoulder blades. Her face turned to the side, one cheek pressed into the mud, her little black skirt smeared with algae and hiked up to her waist, her body left to shed its flesh until it lay naked down to the bones—the sort of thing that happens when you come across the wrong man.

She unsnapped her holster as she walked toward the stone outbuilding where the motorcycle barked and growled, an old wagon house wrapped in creeping ivy. As she rounded the front, she was surprised to find Russell McCreech crouched inside. He squatted next to a midnight blue Softail Harley, peering at the engine with a small spanner in his hand. Another, smaller motocross bike leaned against the back wall. When she called his name, he jumped to his feet with a start.

"You ain't supposed to be here," he said, setting a

spanner beside a toolbox on a tarp.

"That Larry's bike?" she asked.

"Mine now."

She blinked and canted her head. The bike was low enough for the boy, but starting him off with a cruiser that heavy seemed like a way to have him in a body cast the first time he dumped it. She couldn't believe that Leon and Alice McCreech, who had already lost one son in a motorcycle wreck, would put him on a machine like that. Then again, the two of them were never going to be up for any parenting awards. But why would Larry let his ride go? Something was not right about it.

"I thought we agreed to talk, Russ."

He wiped his oily hands on his shorts, leaving black smears across the denim. "Don't got nothing to say."

"Sorry to hear that. I was counting on your help. There've been some...developments. Can you tell me something about Bree? Did she have a raven-type design tattooed on her back, pretty recently? Her mom didn't know about it, but I thought you might be able to confirm."

He knelt down and peered into the engine again, as if his gaze had become lost in its tiny labyrinth.

"Russell, I'm sorry, but I don't know the best way to tell you this. *Look at me,* please."

It was a command, and he did, the point of his chin and edges of his cheekbones barely defined in the otherwise smooth and lineless upturned face of a child, strands of his coppery hair sweat-soaked across his forehead, his eyes defiant.

"We found a body by Grass Creek, Russ. Earlobes gauged up with black acrylic plugs, navel and tongue piercing. We think it's her, but—"

He broke in, his voice cracking as he asked, "Is it her or ain't it? You know what she looks like."

"A face gets harder to recognize the longer it's been since the time of death. Things happen to a body, especially when it's been left outside. Everything else seems to line up, but we'll need a medical examiner to confirm it."

She silently reprimanded herself as the boy's eyes widened. He paled. Dammit, she wished she hadn't put it that way. Too late now.

"So," she continued, "that's why I'm asking about the tattoo. Did Bree have one like what I described?"

"Yeah." His voice shook as he spoke. "Got it from Ricky Hornween about a month ago."

"So she *did* spend time with Ricky, then?"

"I told her not to. Hornweens..." He trailed off, staring off into nothing.

"I'm so sorry for you, Russ. I know you loved her. Samantha did, too, and her mom, and a whole lot of other people. I want you to remember—look at me, hon—that I've been out every night trying to find out what happened to her—"

"Lot of good *that* did, huh?" Hate crystalized in his eyes.

"It's awful. And you might not believe it, but I hate it every bit as much as you do. We need to find out what happened to her. The real, no-bullshit truth. You aren't going to find anyone else who wants that more than I do."

"So what?"

"You're a smart guy, Russ. I've got nothing to hide. No angle. This is my job and I care about it. I take care of people in this town. I want this solved. And that's all. Who else do you know who can say that?"

He was quiet for a moment. Confused, brow knitted, he said, "Ironwolfs don't talk to cops."

Leon McCreech, you evil son of a bitch, she thought. That's what was up with the new motorcycle. The poor kid wanted his dad to love him, to respect him—and the boy was probably a bit terrified of him, too—so when he got the call to join, he took it. As if he had a choice. It was just to get him to keep his mouth shut, and Russell was too dumb or too sweet to get it. Here he was, a goddamn mess with a dead cousin and dead girlfriend, tinkering with a bike he hardly knew the first thing about, to show he was a good little outlaw like his daddy and big brother.

"Russ, the Ironwolfs aren't going to take care of this, and you know it. For one, I don't think any of them care as much as you. Or me. For another, they're not detectives, alright? This isn't what they do."

"Oh, and you guys got all that down, huh? Who killed Jesse, then?" he snapped back. "And what about those pictures of Crystal Lewis? You didn't do shit about that one, did you?"

He was shaking. She remembered hearing some buzz about the case, a local girl who had some nude selfies of her sent around, but that was a few years before she joined the sheriffs, when she was still lost in the Florida nights.

"Russ, it's not always easy to handle things when a girl takes pictures of herself and—"

"See, that's what I'm talking about. You're looking for the 'no-bullshit truth'? Right."

"What are you getting at?"

"Crystal didn't take those pictures. Sean McGuiness and Brad Stoltz did. And probably did more than that. She was what, twelve, maybe? One's dad is a lawyer and the other one's a cop. Funny how nothing happened to them."

Inward, she recoiled. That had to be a rumor. Sean and

Brad were a couple of hard-partying athletes in high school, and she'd heard they'd had a few MIPs and maybe a DUI squashed—the fringe benefits of being connected in a small town—but that was light years away from what Russ was suggesting.

"Is that true? Because—no, *look at me*, Russ—that was before I was back in town. And I've never heard that before. If that's what occurred, we could do something about it, you and me. I would never allow something like that to happen, or keep quiet about it." *Except when I did,* she thought. But that was a long time ago. "You believe me, don't you?"

"It don't matter. It's too late now. For everybody." He swiped a wrist across his eye and swallowed. "I—my dad's gonna be back soon. You should go."

"Someone else is going to take over the case. Soon. This is serious, Russell. Don't you want to know what happened at Mike Morgan's? Don't you know that they're going to make you the prime suspect? We're getting close to something here." A pleading timbre rose in her voice. "There's not much time before—"

From behind her, a woman's husky voice interrupted, "Russ is right. Time to hit the road, Deputy."

Alice McCreech stood beneath one of the weird, vine-choked apple trees. A lean, tanned woman. Pretty but rough, a life measured out in bad tattoos and worse decisions. She coolly dragged on her cigarette and stared Meghan down. Russ leaned over the side of the Harley, one elbow propping him up, chin resting in a hand wrapped over his mouth. He looked like his mother's boy.

"You know how to get ahold of me," Meghan said to him. "Again, I'm so sorry to have to tell you the bad news."

He stared ahead, silent, tears welling up. When Meghan walked past his mom, Alice followed just a couple steps behind, like a guard escorting her off the property. Meg kept her eyes ahead and her pace steady—there was nothing to be gained in going nose-to-nose with her. She didn't even want to give the woman the satisfaction of a cursory over-the-shoulder glance.

"I know what you think of us," Alice said as they passed under the crooked branches.

Meg kicked her way through the fallen apples. "That so?"

"Cops all think the same thing about McCreeches. That we're rough folks. And that my husband is a bad man. And you know what? You bet your ass he is."

"You're proud of that?"

"Proud of him. You never been in the places I been in. It takes a bad man to keep other bad men from the door."

"Yeah?" Meg stopped short and spun to face Alice.

The other woman leaned back, then placed her hands on her hips. "That's right."

"I've been a lot of places, Alice. Every bad man will tell you the same thing, everywhere: that he's the one keeping the others away. And that's why the world's full of bad men and we keep getting more." By her side, she rolled her fingers into fists and then unclenched them again, adding, "Make sure Russ is careful on that bike. A single wreck on one of those can kill a kid. But you know that."

Meghan saw the flash of pain in Alice's face, and it felt good for half a moment before it felt sickening. She turned away from Alice before the woman could respond, and then hurried to her car. She was nauseated the whole way driving over to see Julie Wells, rehearsing in her mind what to say, how to say it, hoping it would go better than it did with Russell.

Julie was out front, sweeping the seedpods off of her driveway when Megan pulled up. Mauve azaleas burst in the golden sunlight, and a squirrel chattered from atop a maple tree at a cat stalking across the lawn. A crow, perched on the mobile home's deck railing, cawed to spread the warning. Julie watched Meg approach. Her boots felt heavier with every step. The deputy removed her sunglasses and gave a slow shake of her head as she took a breath to speak. Before Meghan could say a word, Julie knew. The broom handle clattered against the asphalt, and then it felt as if Meghan and the other woman had been pulled together by a river current. Julie clung to her and wailed, her cries muffled against the deputy's shoulder. Meg held her as her own tears flowed, whispering, "You'll be okay," knowing that she wouldn't, not in the same way, ever again.

CHAPTER 8

Russell crested the hill on his dirt bike, taking air before landing hard on the railway trail. Gravel spat from the rear tire as he swerved. He hadn't ridden anything with an engine since he was twelve—since his brother Roy died in a wreck on that wet October night five years ago. The motor screamed as his heart hammered. When the abandoned trestle came into view, it was crowded with kids. He seized the brakes and skidded to a halt.

The sight of it momentarily terrified him, as if he had come across a horde of zombies in the depths of the woods, all of them gazing over the side of the bridge and down the meandering creek in the evening's bronze light. Some kids sat on the edge, their legs dangling over the side, while others held hands in pairs or gathered in clutches. Here and there, candles glowed in mason jar lanterns on the concrete abutments or among scattered bundles of wildflowers. The bike chattered and muttered as he rolled up.

He looked out from the bridge, down the creek banks far below, to a distant white tent cordoned off with yellow tape. A couple of white vans and a scattering of police cars surrounded it. Tan- or blue-uniformed figures walked in lines through the brush or paced the shallows in hip waders. A couple of men in coveralls were setting up a generator near the vans. Russell killed the motor, swung down the kickstand, and made his way toward Samantha. His friend Alex stood nearby. Conversations hushed as he passed.

Sam stared through him.

"Hey," Russ said.

"Hey." Alex looked down and scuffed his sneaker toe in the gravel.

Alex's bangs were combed in a swoop across his forehead, and his yellow T-shirt, printed with a pattern of green skulls, made him look jaundiced and sick. His delicate fingers fluttered together like moth wings as he searched for something to say. Russ tried to remember the last time he'd hung out with Alex—just the two of them. He'd somehow lost track of him in the blur of months since Bree and his lives had become intertwined.

Bree had noticed it too. Weeks before, when they were sitting at a picnic table on the patch of crabgrass next to the Dairy Queen's parking lot, Russell's phone buzzed. He looked at the message and rolled his eyes before shoving the phone back in his pocket.

"What was that?" Bree said after swallowing a spoonful of her banana split.

"Just Alex, complaining about how the band isn't practicing enough, and he's worried I ain't 'committed' to it."

"Well," she said as she tried to scoop the cherry from the half-melted ice cream, "you can't blame him for that. When's the last time you practiced?"

"Don't have it in me to tell him that I'm not sticking around this shit town." Russell popped the bottom of his cone into his mouth and said, still chewing, "If he had a girlfriend, he wouldn't complain half as much."

"Doesn't mean he doesn't miss you."

A jeep boomed rap music as it rolled into the parking lot, and sparrows flitted in the dust around a fly-swarmed trash barrel.

"Why you sticking up for him? If you knew the way he talks about you, you wouldn't, believe me."

"Oh, whatever." She dropped the plastic spoon into the ice cream sludge and tossed back her hair. "Everybody does. I've heard it all. I'm a skank, I'm a psycho, a headcase—"

"Hey, don't—"

"Look, I know. My life was hell at school till I started knocking girls on their asses. Still isn't great. But did Alex say any of that stuff before we started going out?"

He thought about it. "Not really."

"He doesn't want to lose you, that's all."

"Just because he—you know—he sounds like he does, don't mean he's like that."

"So what if it does? But I don't think so. All I'm saying is that nobody wants to lose anybody. People compete for people. It sucks. Doesn't have to be that way."

"What're you getting at? Just because I ask you about Ricky Hornween, or text you when you're out with Sam Black—"

"Jesus." She sighed. "I just think you should remember that we both need friends. They were there for us before. And if something happens, if things go wrong, they'll be the ones there for us after."

"I don't want there to be no 'after' for us."

"Me neither," she said. "For real. But you need to keep your friends around. We don't always get to pick how things work out, and you got to think about who you'll be left with if something goes bad, you know?"

Now, standing on the bridge and looking at Alex, Russell couldn't think of a thing to say to him.

He turned away from Alex and Sam. Looking out across the creek at the white tent, Russell heard himself ask, "Is she in there?"

Sam hooked her arm around his and said, "Come on." She marched him away from the crowd. He stepped over a bundle of lilacs and black-eyed susans, the ground spinning as he asked again, "Is she in there?"

"She was, yeah," Sam said. "Keep walking."

"Who found her?"

"Kyle Price's uncle. Fishing, I guess."

He looked around at the crowd as the twosome made their way through it, and he asked, "Why are they all here? Half of them never talked to her or nothing."

"Some just because it's something to do. But Bree meant a lot to people. More than she thought. More than any of us thought, maybe." She closed her eyes for a moment. "You remember what happened when Dakota Wilson dumped paint in Bree's hair in art class?"

He did. It was before he had started dating her, but he'd seen it happen.

"Bree hooked her in the jaw and dropped her like a sack of shit. Kicked her stomach when she was on the ground, too."

He'd never heard the sound of a woman taking a boot to the stomach before, the timbre of her retching cry. His mom and dad had their screaming matches, fueled by hours of whiskey and darkness, and though their clashing voices were frightening among the toppling furniture and breaking glass, they had always turned their violence on their surroundings but not on one another.

Seeing Bree kick the shit out of Dakota had seemed savage and strange. He had never seen girls hurt one another in that way, though he knew they got hurt like that all the time. He instinctively wanted to stop it, but it was so intense he could only listen. It paralyzed the room, and he found himself drawn to Bree in that moment for reasons he could never explain. He wondered if something like that had been done to her before she died, and a cold and slimy feeling slithered across him.

"Better than that cunt deserved," Sam said. "You know, Bree was terrified after that happened. She beat the hell out of a pretty, popular bitch. Girls don't get to do that to each other. Not to girls like Dakota, at least. Bree thought she was going to be expelled, or put in juvie, or hunted every day of her life at school. She was already labeled and tracked as 'emotionally impaired.' Like it was some sort of impairment that she acted like that, when everyone treated her the way they did. It worked in her favor in the end. They couldn't expel her for behavior consistent with her 'diagnosis.'"

He smirked. "Right. And Dakota couldn't press charges because she started it. Bree shaved off the part of her hair with the paint on it, was back in school with a mohawk three days later. Smoking a cigarette on the corner like some badass bitch."

"And, deep down, everybody wanted to see someone put Dakota in her place. Everybody. The fact that someone laid her out, and then came back untouchable, just doubled-down on the fuck you. It meant a lot to girls who were—I don't know. Not the right kind of girls."

He glanced over his shoulder at the crowd. Their eyes swarmed him like hornets.

"They're staring at us. All of them." He swallowed. "They think I did it, don't they?"

She unlooped her arm from his and took a drag on her vaporizer. "You were her boyfriend. That's who usually does it."

"I didn't." They moved into the woods, where its cool shadows were abuzz with winged things.

"Well, who did, then, Russ? You and I both know she didn't jump off that bridge. That mess in Mike's tub? Your cousin shot dead?" Anger darkened her eyes. "And we both know where her car ended up. Some coincidence that your people are all over this, isn't it?"

"Keep your voice down, goddamn it."

"Keep my voice down? Are you kidding me? You don't tell me what to do. Ever."

"You're gonna get high and mighty with me, for real? You pimped your own best friend—"

"It's wasn't like that."

"—and laundered money for your shitbag boss, who was probably using her as a mule for drugs. That's you. All you. You got her killed."

"By who? Your family's dirt-ass, white-trash biker gang?"

"No. I..." He trailed off.

"How do you know?"

"I—I don't. I guess I don't feel it. Could be other things." He rubbed his temples and squinted. "You could say it looks like my people. But I could just as easily say it was yours, and you know it."

"Hornweens are not my people. Don't say that."

"Whatever. That don't matter. What matters is that whoever is responsible for killing Bree pays for it. And I swear to God, that's all I want."

"What if you found out it was your family, Russ? If it was Shane, or Jesse, or your dad?"

He looked her dead in the eye and with a flat, assured voice said, "If that's what it came down to, I would do what needed to be done."

"You don't mean that."

"I do. They think they can hold this family bullshit over me. They have no idea what I can do. Nobody does. I guarantee somebody's in for a big motherfucking surprise."

"Same here." She took a drag. "You'll help me find who did this? And hit them back? Hard?"

"I'll make sure they don't get back up again. I mean ever. But I can't do it without you." He stammered out, "I need you for this, Sam."

She hugged him, suddenly and tightly, her heat-dampened body pressed against his own. The tang of perspiration cut through her vanilla-scented perfume, and her tears soaked into his collar. He held her and kissed the top her head and rubbed between her shoulders, unsure what to do, and she sniffled once more before pulling away and wiping her eyes and saying, "Whoever did it, I want them dead. If you won't do it, I will. I promise. And don't you dare fuck me over."

"You neither. Hear anything lately? Since—since they found her?"

"One of those biker guys, a Knights of Satan dude, came into the shop. I was out, but Skunky, the piercer, he was working. Guy was asking where Ricky was. And then, when Skunky said he was out, he asked for me. By name. What if they come to my mom and dad's house? Or come back when I'm working and I'm there by myself?" She took a deep drag on the vape, and Russell caught the whiff of hash oil when she exhaled. "It's gotten out of control. I'm thinking I should run, but then they'll put it all on me for sure. Maybe the cops can help us—"

"We can't. You said yourself that you'd be dead if you go the cops."

"It all leads to somebody dead, doesn't it? I'm scared, okay? What if I'm next? If I go in, I'll do time, sure. Whatever. I'll get out and start again. At least I wouldn't be wandering around out here with a target on my big white ass."

"A lot of people could get sent up if you squeal," he said, working hard to keep the quaver of panic from his voice, "but not because of anything that has to do with Bree. Cops and prosecutors have a hard-on for arrests and convictions. They'd be happy to put away my people and the Hornweens for whatever they can. Stripping cars. Drugs and dirt. Bullshit and nothing. Bree'd just be collateral damage to the cops, another girl dead for doing shit she wasn't supposed to. Plus, more people might get snuffed to keep it all quiet. Maybe not the ones we would want, neither."

She sat down on a fallen log beside the trail, looking in the brittle light as if the blood had drained from her, and threw up her hands. "What am I supposed to do, then?"

"Give me a chance. My dad is mad as hell to hear about the Knights of Satan out here. They're not with us, but my Uncle Duane is in prison, and I guess he's connected with some of them inside. I'll feel it out. And you and I both know Ricky has something to do with this."

"He's gone. Might be dead, too. Wouldn't be surprised. He's real dumb."

"Maybe. Dan will try to protect him if he's still alive, though. He won't give up that scumbag if he killed Bree or Jesse. But Dan don't want his brother getting wiped out by KoS people, either. He told me to give him a call, back at the lake the other night. I might just do that. See what he has to say."

"Be careful." She nodded, thinking. "Jolene is close with Mike Morgan—they have some history—and she's pretty tight with a few girls at Dan's club. I babysit for her, I'm sure she'll let me crash and lay low at her place. I'll tell my mom and dad I'm going camping with some of my girl-friends. Maybe I can get a better handle on what she knows. She gets talky when she's drunk, and she likes to drink. And I'll see if she can set me up with some of the dancers—I'll act like I'm looking for new camgirls."

"*Jolene* knows you do that?"

"She thinks I work as a contractor for a company that does that. Doesn't know it's all my thing."

"So," Russ said, "just to be clear, we agree, no cops? Deputy Meg came by, trying to buddy up with me. We're keeping her out, right?"

"For now."

"What do you mean, for now?"

"I want whoever killed Bree to pay for it. I also want to live through this. I don't care how it gets done. Right now, I don't think that the cops are our best option. But that could change."

"Give it time for us to work it out," he said.

"How long?"

"A week."

"Three days," she countered.

"Five," he said. "Five, and we talk about it first before going to any cops. I need to know you're a hundred percent on board with that."

"All right." She stood and brushed the leaves from the seat of her pants. They shook hands, silhouetted in the wooded gloom, and walked together toward a swarm of white faces made spectral by the light of tiny screens. Some kids knelt beside candles or stood with arms draped around one another, gazing up into their phones' camera lenses to snap pictures in remembrance of one who died. Russ moved like an invisible boy among them, the dead girl's lover's presence merely background noise in the ongoing documentation of their lives, a specter who could not grieve, or commiserate, consumed with lethal and silent wrath as he kicked the dirt bike's engine to snarling life and rode.

Deputy Mark Williams, sandy-haired and square-jawed, sat with his elbows on the booth's tabletop and thanked the waitress who brought his order. Meghan sipped her iced tea and smiled. His open, gentle face seemed at odds with his massive shoulders and narrow waist. Mark lifted the glass of milk and finished half of it in two gulps, then delicately placed it back on the diner's paper placemat. He noticed her watching him from across the table and said, softly, "You never get too old for protein and calcium."

"That's right," she said. "I'm a fan of milkshakes, myself."

"What flavor?"

"Strawberry."

Mark had technically been on the job longer than Meghan, but as a part-timer splitting his hours with the fire department. He spent the bulk of his off-hours handcrafting birdhouses and furniture that he and his wife sold at craft fairs. Mark never treated Meghan with a bit of resentment when she was promoted above him; he was helpful, even-tempered, devoutly Lutheran, and honest to a fault, all of which made his sometimes-soft-headed policing a bit more forgivable.

Mark picked up his grilled cheese sandwich and looked at it forlornly, then put it back down. Pop country twanged over the sound system, and a dish-sprayer blasted beyond the swinging kitchen doors.

"Something wrong?" Meghan asked.

"By the creek." Mark batted toward the darkening windows and shook his head. "I saw the victim today."

"It was only her body. And her name is Brianne Wells."

"I know that, Meg. It's easier not to say it."

"But less accurate."

"I guess. I saw her by the creek—"

"Her body."

"There's a difference?"

"When it comes to accuracy, there is. Bree Wells was a high school junior. She collected key chains and read novels about young people saving the world. She wanted to be a model. She drew pictures of imaginary animals. She tried to run away from here, but we brought her back. She loved to dance. And sing. She stayed out too late, and she made her mother worry all night. She liked to push limits, to break rules. She was a fighter. She wanted to live, to do something important, or—I don't know—do something exciting at least." Meghan folded her hands on the table. "That was Bree Wells. And what we saw down there by the water, well." She turned up her hands and was unnerved by how empty they felt. "That was awful."

Mark nodded, looking down at his sandwich.

"But that was her body. That's all it was," Meghan said. "Bree's gone. Don't confuse the two. It's an easy thing to do, and it's—"

"Inaccurate?" Mark looked up, his voice hollow.

"Right." She sipped from her glass, swallowed.

"Inaccurate."

"You're not working the case?" Mark said.

"It was a missing persons case. We found her. Well, she was found."

"Just her body," he said.

"More accurately, yes."

"You should be working the case. You put in the time on this. And the work."

"I'm not a detective. Handed over all my notes to Stoltz and the State boys a few hours ago. When it comes down to it, Ed's put in a lot more years than both of us put together. But it's a nice thing to say, thank you."

"Not saying it to be nice. Saying it because it's true. And honestly, I want to find out what happened to the victim—to Bree. And I tell you what." He looked around the diner, finding it empty in the purgatory between the dinner hour and the late-night rush. With a lowered voice, he added, "Ed's lost his edge a bit since Gladys passed on, if you ask me."

"Well, I'm sure that was a heck of a blow for that whole family. With Brad off at college now, and the oldest—what's her name?"

"Fay. The one in Arkansas."

"Right, with his boy at school and her out there, he's all by himself at the house. Has to be lonely."

"Yup. I can't imagine what I'd do if I didn't have Donna," Mark said. "Don't get me wrong. Ed's still a heck of a cop. But I'm worried about him. Just between you and me, he's been real irritable and a bit slow on the uptake. You know, he's got some real bad back problems."

"I did not know that. You think that's what's been getting to him? Being all alone and having a bad back?"

"Dunno." Mark shrugged. "He quit wearing the shoulder rig for his sidearm. You notice that?"

"I did," she said.

"That's because of his back. Says the imbalanced weight on his shoulder makes it worse."

Or caused it, Meghan thought. Hanging a weighty .45 and holster under your arm for twenty-five years might do that.

"I wondered why he'd switched," she said. "He's been wearing that thing since I was a kid. Sounds like it's pretty bad."

"Yup. So, between you and me." Mark leaned in. "Me and him were at the Donut King a few days ago, just talking about the goings on and all. I got up to wash my hands before I had my fritter, because, you know, you should."

"Always."

"Yup, for sure. But when I came back, I was walking up over his shoulder, and I saw him shaking out two oxycodones— I know them on sight now, since we've had so many problems with them. He tossed it back with his coffee. Now, I don't know how strong they were, but I think a couple of those could make you real foggy."

Maybe that's why his evidence collection at Jesse's crime scene had been so sloppy. Could have been that he was doped up. Or drunk. Or both. She thought back to the meeting yesterday—how he'd struggled to set his coffee cup evenly on the table. Maybe Stoltz had developed some habits that were mucking up an already messy case. Good luck getting him to step aside, though.

"Could be." Meg swirled her straw in her iced tea. "But he's got a history of good work in this town, and kept up even as it's gotten a bit rougher. You've been here a long time, you've seen it. Speaking of, I was wondering if you remembered a case from before I joined up. About four years ago."

"I was part-time then." He took a bite of his sandwich and, chewing, added, "Wasn't too involved with many investigation-type things."

"Oh, this wasn't a bigger thing, but I hear it got people pretty stirred up at the time. Crystal Lewis, over at Chippewa Middle School? Family's not in town anymore, but I guess there were some pictures of her getting sent around, online and such, that, well, weren't the sort of thing a girl her age should be doing."

"Oh. That." Meg thought she saw his cheeks flush. "Yes. I remember. Crazy, what kids will do these days."

"Can you give me a rundown of what you remember? I only ask because one of Bree's friends mentioned it."

"Which one?"

"Oh, I'd have to look at my notes. You talk to so many people, you know, I can't just place everyone off the top of my head." She made a goofy face and tapped her noggin. "Anyhow, it seemed like a sore spot to the kid. Why do you think that might be?"

"If you ask me, you can't do things like that and not expect consequences. The girl I mean."

"The girl?"

"Right. I mean, of course boys shouldn't send around pictures like that, but really, what would you expect them to do?"

"She was twelve, Mark."

"Oh, I know, it's terrible," he stammered. "But the boys are curious at that age. And if a young girl doesn't want that sort of attention, well, then, she shouldn't go looking for it."

"That's one way to think about it." Meg pursed her lips and did her best thoughtful nod. "Who took the pictures, though? There's talk that she was pressured into it."

"Girls always get pressured to do things, don't they?" He sheepishly ate a french fry. "I mean, I don't know. I just assume it's like that."

She noticed his non-answer to her question. Bringing up Ed Stoltz's son, Brad, and his friend Sean McGuiness—that would shut it down right here.

"I suppose," she said. "But that doesn't make it right."

"Sure, I guess. But you don't need a whole lot of brains to know that if you take your clothes off in front of a camera, well." He wagged his finger once. "That's obviously the sort of thing that can come back and bite you on the behind."

"I'm confused." She scratched behind her ear. "Because really, Mark, if some boy was involved in taking those pictures, or somehow intimidated her into it, that would be a pretty serious charge."

"Right. It could really mess up a kid's life. His college prospects, work opportunities. So, why push it, you know? Why make this thing even more damaging than it already was?" Mark sipped his milk. "It seemed like that was the thinking then."

"So you guys just let it go?" Meg crunched on the ice from her drink, the cold a satisfying jolt through her molars.

"Not just let it go. I mean, there were some people given talkings to and all, probably. The school handled it, I think. Like I said, I was part-time then." Mark looked away for a moment. "But, like I said, girls got to expect these sort of things to happen if they act a certain way. It's not like Crystal Lewis was some kind of angel, we all know that. And boys, they're going to get a bit out of hand sometimes."

She changed tack. "Do you think that's what happened to Bree Wells?"

"Do I think what happened, now?"

"That she was a girl—no angel, mind you—who acted a certain way, and a boy got out of hand with her?"

"Aw, sheesh, Meg. That's terrible. You can't compare kids playing you-show-me-yours-I'll-show-you-mine with—what happened to Bree." He ran his thick fingers through his hair. "That Lewis thing. I know it could have been handled better. But that was years ago, and there's nothing to gain by dredging that up again. This thing with Bree, it's going to go a lot better."

"Is it? I hope you're right."'

"We already got a suspect, don't we? That's a start, and a good one if Ed can keep his head in the game."

"We do?" She blinked. She'd handed over her notes not even three hours ago, which seemed to her like a pretty short time to review them and pick a suspect.

"Sure. Ed likes Mike Morgan. I mean, at first he thought she might have been a jumper, but now he thinks Morgan's a good bet."

"Crazy Mike? He's a person of interest, for sure. Solid ties placing him at the scene of Jesse's murder. But that makes him a suspect for Bree's?"

"The county's had about how many murders in the past ten years? Six?" He pointed his fork at her. She frowned at it, so he put it on his plate. "Almost all of them cut and dried. Then we get two in the same month, hell maybe the same week. Doesn't it make sense that there's a connection?"

"Connection, maybe. But I wouldn't call Mike a suspect. I'll agree he's important. If we can collar him, it could go a long way to sorting out what happened."

"If we can do it and not have to shoot him."

Meg's brow knitted. "What makes you think it will come to that?"

"Mike Morgan is an ex-Green Beret gun-nut. Probably a grower or a cooker. A paranoid PTSD type. Ed makes him sound like a real terror. Says to remember it's better to be stuck doing deadly force paperwork than to be stuck in a graveyard."

Wonderful.

"Mark. You say you want to help this case? You want it to go better than the thing with the Lewis girl did?"

"I do. Like I said, I wish you were handling it."

"Well, you said Ed is slowing down, and a bit foggy. I don't think that sounds like he's the right guy to be bringing in Mike Morgan, especially if he's scared of him."

"No. Probably not."

"Listen to me. I've dealt with Mike before. We're both vets, and we have a certain mutual respect, in a way. For the experience. If you hear anything about his whereabouts, can you let me know first? And if Ed is going to snatch him up, can you make sure I get the call, so I can be there? I think I can talk Mike down and bring him in without it getting deadly."

"Okay. If you think so, Meg. And I'll keep you posted if I hear anything more."

"That's great. I'll do the same for you. We have to bring Mike Morgan in alive. If we can work together to do that, I think it will go a long way to solving this thing."

They shook hands, and she wondered if Mark was as simple as he seemed at first glance. He was wrongheaded, but well-intentioned, if that mattered. And he seemed to know as well as she did that if Mike Morgan died, then everything he knew about two cases would be buried along with him, forever.

The Hornween house exuded a lonely menace that reminded Russell of Castle Dracula, without the majesty. It leaned, an ashen and turreted shape razor-cut from the silvery twilight, atop a hill jutting from the surrounding woods and rolling fields. A crumbling fieldstone wall, topped with coils of rusty barbed wire, surrounded the property. Russell stood astride the dirt bike, its headlamp shining through the gate's towering bars and casting long, striped shadows up the winding drive.

He jumped when a static-tinged voice to his left crackled, "What do you need, kid?"

He noticed a metal access box, nearly concealed by weeds, with a speaker and a keypad. After walking his murmuring bike over to the panel, he leaned over and called out, "Yeah, it's Russ. I'm here to see Dan. He's expecting me."

"This is Dan. You don't have to yell at the box. It's right in front of you," the voice crackled. "Come all the way up the hill and to the right. Don't leave the driveway. You'll come to a storage lot. Park your bike at the clown, someone will meet you there."

"Did you say 'clown'?"

With an ear-rending screech, the gate rolled open. He twisted the throttle and crept through it. Clattering and clacking, the gate shut behind him as he motored up the hill. In the knee-high grass, beneath the scattered pines, various animal statues along the route peered at him. A gorilla with arms raised, Kong-like, among the goldenrod. Near the hulk of a rusted Packard towered a pink tyrannosaurus. A listing rooster the size of a woodshed had partially sunken into the soft ground a few yards from a purple rhino. Each of these briefly came into vivid focus in the headlamp's glow before fading back into shadow as Russell passed, drawing nearer to the crooked house on the hill.

He'd heard the creatures were from miniature golf courses the Hornweens used to own. "The House on the Hill" was a bit of a local legend, and kids from his high school often talked about going up there to see the strangeness it held. No one ever tried to sneak in. Rumor had it that the property was laden with traps: spring-loaded steel jaws or pits full of barbed stakes hidden in the tangled weeds. And then there were the people who hung around there, too.

The drive forked, the left path snaking up the hill to the house, the right leveling off and curving around the hill. In the crotch of the fork stood a gallows-like post from which a narrow, domed cage hung overhead. A life-sized green skeleton slumped inside, its arms crossed to point in either direction. As instructed, he turned right, his curiosity about the property tempering his unease.

The drive opened up into a plateau on the slope, surrounded by a tall plank fence. Flatbed trailers held disassembled carnival rides. His light fell across a line of carousel horses, their faces pressed up between their trailer's slats like livestock on the way to slaughter. Russell laughed despite the creepiness of it. Ivy crept across the garish surface of a concession stand adorned with hot dogs and ice cream cones possessing manically grinning faces. He passed what seemed to be a giant iron octopus folded inward upon itself. There were shuttered shooting galleries and a bone-dry dunk tank. A Viking ship's streaked dragon-prow stood frozen mid-roar as it leaned from the back of its trailer, dead orange bulbs in its eyes. All of the attractions seemed to have been placed haphazardly in the field, as if they'd been dropped there by a tornado.

Then he saw the clown, and he recoiled. The giant white face laughed with a red-lipped mouth that gaped wide enough to swallow a person whole. Propped up against the trunk of a massive oak, it seemed like some kind of weird idol hungering for a sacrifice, the tree's branches spreading above like a leafy mane hissing in the breeze. To its left, scores of railroad-tie stairs had been cut into the hill to make a steep climb toward the turreted house.

Just beyond the laughing face, a dilapidated trailer stood at the plank fence's end, the sheer bluff dropping beyond it. Russell could see stenciled on it, faintly, "Hornween Amusements—Detroit, MI." Its grimy windows shone with lantern light.

When Russell parked and shut off his bike, the door creaked open, and a bone-thin man, shirtless in his overalls, emerged. He was bald save for a fringe of straggly silver hair hanging down to his shoulders. A walkie-talkie was clipped to his hip pocket, and an inverted cross was tattooed between his eyes.

As the man approached, Russell noticed that one side of the stranger's face was smooth and featureless, and there was only a misshapen hole where his ear should be. The overalls revealed that much of that side of his body shared similar scarring. Burns. Bad ones. Russell looked down as to not stare, glancing at the man's bat-like feet, dirty and bare with long yellowed nails. Russell felt ill when he smelled him, a reek like spoiled meat.

"Turn around," the man said through his jagged teeth.

"Hell no," Russell said, backing away.

"Ain't gonna hurt you, boy. Just need to search you before y'go up to the house. No wires, no weapons. Either that or hop back on your motorbike and head on back down."

Russell turned around, trying to conceal his revulsion as the man's icy hands swept down his legs, grasped his crotch, and smoothed over his chest and back, gagging from the man's overpowering reek.

"All done. Head on up the steps. Someone will let you in the back."

Russell stepped away and trudged up the steps, the burned guard's smell lingering on him. He glanced over his shoulder to see the skeletal man hunched over and muttering into his walkie-talkie. A mild ache throbbed in his calves when he reached the top of the steps. From the hilltop, he looked out across the rolling woods. Here and there he spotted a gleaming porch light or outdoor flood lamp illuminating part of a home or barn. To the west, the lights of Main Street glowed in the distance, a weak luminance fanning across the purple sky before being swallowed by the star-flecked blackness. The lake stretched to the east, droplets of glowing windows bordering what looked to be a smear of nothingness, like God's thumb had accidentally brushed the canvas and rubbed out part of the world.

A woman said, "The view's better up here on the balcony."

She leaned over the railing high above him, the black turrets rising behind. Tank top, hemp necklace, smoking a cigarette—Sara Van Dorne. She'd gone to Pike Lake High, and then was sent over to the alternative program. He'd heard that she dropped out after getting arrested for something or other.

"I'm looking for Dan," Russell called up. "He up there?"

"Yeah. He sent me out here to get you." She pointed at a

wood ladder running up the side of the house to the balcony. "Come on, he's waiting."

He climbed up and walked onto the wooden deck. Sara leaned on the railing. Another woman, wearing tiny cut-offs that barely covered her ample behind, sprawled facedown, her legs to the side and making slow rotations as if pedaling a bicycle. She laughed incessantly, her giggles muffled by the beanbag she'd collapsed onto. A baby-faced girl wearing a ragged, patched-up denim vest over a slinky bra sat with her tiny bare feet propped up on a glass-topped patio table, across from a dark-skinned boy with what looked like elvish runes tattooed around his neck. They were sharing a foot-long vaporizer that glowed like a lightsaber when they hit it. Hip-hop played softly from a Bluetooth speaker in the corner, its beat a quiet compulsion.

Upon seeing Russell, the guy gave a slight nod and held out the vaporizer to him, smoke coiling out from his nostrils. Russell took it, fiddling with it for a moment before he found the button for the coil. He took a small hit, holding it to his lips and swelling his chest to look like he was indulging more—he didn't want to look intimidated, but also didn't want to end up like the girl on the beanbag.

"You're Bree's boyfriend," Sara said. "Ain't you?"

The girl on the beanbag continued to giggle. Her muffled hoots made it sound as if she was suffocating.

"Yeah, I am." He exhaled as he spoke—the vapor tasted like honey and hops, with a slightly fuel-like aftertaste and he was glad he had taken it easy with it. He passed the vape back and added, "Or, I was her boyfriend, now, I guess."

It took him a moment to remember what they called it: past tense. Everything about Bree was past tense now. Everything that Bree was…was. Maybe his love, maybe that was still there, but what sense was there in loving in the present what was only in the past? And sadness settled like a fallen leaf on his heart, and its rhythm seemed to stop for a moment—as if he'd passed away in the space between its beats and become a dead boy, standing before the two robots propped up in patio chairs and a girl giggling and rolling on the beanbag like a broken toy while an overlooked song played in the background and a woman leaning on the railing asked who it was that he had loved.

"I heard that they found her. I'm so sorry," Sara said.

His brow furrowed. "Me too."

The girl in the vest wordlessly held out the vaporizer in consolation. He waved it off, and Sara asked, "What are you doing here?"

"I need to talk to Dan." He took a breath, then shook up his thoughts and shoved them into a semblance of order. "Is he here or not?"

"Sure, of course. You can go through that sliding glass door. Pass through that room and make a left. He's in his office, first door on the right."

The darkened room he stepped into from the balcony was some kind of music room that had fallen into disuse. A Marshall stack stood in the corner, and cases of guitars lined up like coffins beside it. Recording equipment crowded a long table, most of it ancient—reel-to-reels and four-tracks, drum machines and equalizers, microphones and effects pedals, all held together by a snake nest of patch cords and frosted with dust. On one of the walls, a mural depicted a horned silver skull at the conjunction of two crossed lightning bolts, the word POWERHEAD written in angular block lettering over it.

The hall beyond was long and creaky, lined with thick

doors of dark wood and decorated with dreary, crookedly hung watercolors. Only one door, to the right, stood open. Light spilled into the hall, and he heard a low voice talking in the room to which it led.

Russell poked his head in and saw Dan Hornween, dressed in a purple kimono and carving up cocaine with a pearl-handled switchblade on a slab of jade atop a desk that looked like it should belong to an admiral. A black velvet portrait of a dramatically posed Bruce Lee took up much of the wall behind him. Dan chatted on the phone and occasionally glanced at a computer monitor as he laid out a few lines, but he stopped a moment and beckoned Russell, then pointed to one of the threadbare claw-footed chairs across from him.

The boy walked in, dazed. Whatever they were vaping on the balcony was creeping up on him. Volumes about Eastern martial arts and mysticism crowded the office's bookcase, lumped in with a generous helping of business inspiration and nude photography books. A framed Japanese battle flag stood out among the scattering of signed rock tour posters, carnival playbills, and some movie lobby cards for old exploitation trash like *Love Camp* and *Kidnapped Cuties*. Russell sat down and noticed another black velvet rendering, this one beside the door and depicting a smiling and hogtied Bettie Page, winking. Russell thought of the selfies Bree used to send him, flirty and sweet, and then of the white forensic tent beside the creek. The room tilted under his chair, his belly churned, and a cold film of sweat rose up on his forehead.

"I gotta go, got a visitor. Yeah—be in touch—for sure." Dan set his cellphone down and then snapped his knife closed before tucking it away in his robe. "You okay, kid? You look like you're going to be sick."

Things whirled into place, and he said, "No, I ain't gonna be sick. But, no. I ain't okay."

"I dig." Dan picked up a short, wide straw, its bottom cut at an angle. "Not much is okay lately. Bump?" He gestured at the jade slab and offered the straw.

"No. Got any whiskey?"

He pulled a mostly-drained fifth of Wild Turkey and a shot glass from a desk drawer. "Help yourself."

Dan snorted up a line.

"Now," he said, rubbing a knuckle on his nostril, "you said you wanted to talk business when you called. And I just want to kick that bullshit to the curb right now, because you and I both know this visit is personal. And I don't blame you for it."

Russell stared at him, the shot's heat still in his belly. "What's with the nosferatu-looking motherfucker down there?"

"You mean Finch? He had an accident doing some work for my dad, long time ago. He lives on the property now."

"Blew up a lab?"

"He wasn't baking cookies."

"Did you build an abandoned carnival just to have a place for your freak?"

"That's not nice, kid. And that carnival is what built this family. Three generations, till we got into pinball machines and mini-golf shit. And the bowling alley. Amusements. Hornweens have always dealt in amusements."

Russ poured another shot and downed it. A bolt of fire struck him in the gut.

"Take it easy, being angry doesn't raise your tolerance," Dan warned. "If you puke in here, you're scrubbing it up."

"Did you kill her, Dan?"

"Why the hell would I do something like that?"

"Dunno. Why does anybody?"

"I never killed any girls. A dead girl is of no use to anybody. I was the one who warned you guys about Bree being out of her depth. Beware of mad dogs lurking, amigo, because lurking they will bite. And mad dogs abound this summer. It's a bad one for it."

"Ricky?"

"You think it was my brother?"

"Was it?"

"I don't think so."

"Don't fuck with me, Hornween."

"Ha! Really? You come here, some freaked out kid trying to look like a hardass, to what? Drink my whiskey and pump me for info like you're a goddamn PI? I'm being nice, and I'm playing along, because I feel for you, kid. You remind me of myself, once upon a time."

"That supposed to be a compliment?"

"An observation." Dan leaned back in his chair and laced his fingers behind his head. "Look. If Leon was here, or Shane, or Alice, even, that would be something. But you? People are getting killed. Say your piece and go home. You aren't the type to get involved in that sort of business."

"It became my business when someone killed Bree. Like you said, you can't blame me. And I'm here because I got a—what do you call it—"

"A theory?"

"Right."

"Enlighten me."

"You run things, and Ricky wants to be more involved. He was a rock star—a half-assed one in a pretty shitty band—"

"Be fair, sKraYp'D was worse than 'pretty shitty.'"

"—and he still wants to be a big deal, right? So when he got out of prison and found out the whole nu-metal thing is a big joke now, the next best thing would be to become a player in the family business. And I don't mean tatting kitty-cats onto girls' asses like you have him doing now."

"Hornween Amusements Inc. is entirely legitimate." Dan hunched over and snorted up another rail of coke. "But please go on."

"You don't want Ricky hedging in, so you tuck him away at the tattoo shop."

"Or maybe I care about my brother and would like to see him stay out of the joint."

"Or maybe you think he's a loser who ain't cut out for your kind of work. Anyway, he ain't happy about it. He wants in on the game, bigger money, better outlaw cred. So he sets up his own thing, on the side. Gets a good line on some MDMA and some H, probably through the Knights of Satan MC, who Ricky knows from either giving them tattoos or from prison."

"Or from giving them tattoos in prison." Dan, gacked out weirdo that he was, seemed vaguely amused. He tented his fingers and said, "And you know this how?"

"The Knights of Satan MC are cruising around looking for Ricky, and it ain't because they need more tattoos. I'm guessing they want something from Ricky that he don't have. Either money or drugs."

"Let's say you're onto something." The switchblade appeared in Dan's hand. He spun the closed knife through his fingers as he spoke. "Say Ricky and those Detroit dirtbags had some strained relations. How's that your business?"

"From what you said at the lake, I guess you know about

the camgirl thing Sam has running. Well, Ricky knows, too. Sam bragged about it to him, and it got his attention. If Ricky sells a shipment, he knows he can't come into that much cash without drawing attention, and he can't use the shop's accounts to hide it, neither. He ain't gonna put it in his mattress. He wanted Samantha to run a deposit through the accounts she has set up for her cam shows—some off-shore-Bitcoin-whatever, I don't know, but what matters is this: The money never showed up. So either someone got dicked over, or something went real bad."

"If what you're saying is true, that is indeed what that suggests." The blade popped from the knife, and Dan tapped its flat on the edge of the desk as he stroked his chin. "But that would still be Ricky's problem. Again, how's that your business?"

"Because Ricky got a call about an audition for *Tattoo Kings*—right when he was supposed to deliver to his buyer. He ain't gonna pass up a chance to be famous again, to get his dumb ass on TV. But he can't do both. And he's already made promises."

"He shouldn't be doing any of these things." Dan leaned forward, scowling. "He has a hell of a nice tattoo studio. I know, I paid for it."

"Right. You ain't down with this plan, and almost any-one Ricky knows well enough to deliver for him is tied to you. I think the shit was supposed to go to Chicago. Ricky knew through Sam about us planning to head out there for Blocksfest. I bet his buyer planned on unloading a ton of it while the festival was in town. Ricky tattoos Bree, he knows her, knows she wants money to get out of this shit town, knows she has tickets to the fest—a perfect cover to go there. Sam would've told him to go to hell. She's not gonna move that kind of weight, stick her neck out for him like that. He makes a deal with Bree and loads up her car to be his mule to Chicago while he's in L.A."

"That would be a stupid plan."

"Ricky ain't smart, and Bree thinks she can do anything. Or thought, now, I guess. Bree delivers, the buyer transfers the cash to Sam's accounts, she forwards the supplier their cut, takes hers, and the rest will find its way to Ricky through however Sam sets it up. That's what was supposed to go down." Russell poured himself a shot. "Bree was seen with a lot of molly last week, either she was skimming or maybe it was her advance. Then she disappeared. Nobody went to Chicago. I bet you got a pretty panicked call from Ricky. He's out a ton of product. And the Knights of Satan are looking to get paid. He keeps it vague but tells you to find out what happened to Bree."

"So, you think we killed her because she tried to burn Ricky and make off with the goods?" Dan folded his arms. "Is that what you're telling me?"

"I don't know who killed her. Just like I don't know who killed Jesse. Jesse died holding up Bree's necklace, saying 'Wasn't me,' so he was trying to tell me something. I watched him go. He was family, but he lived the kind of life that ends like that. That's done and done. But he said he wanted to talk to me, before he died. Something got all fucked up, man. And I can help you manage this mess. But if you want help from me, you got to help me get who killed Bree."

"I *got* to, eh? Is that it?" Dan wagged the blade at Russell. "And you'll help 'manage' it for me." Dan's eyes grew darker, glinting, like a vampire's, and Russell felt a pain in his guts and his legs weaken. "What makes you think you're walking out of here?"

"I don't walk out of here, then all my family is coming for you. Hard. You think I'd come here without telling nobody? So don't bother with that threat—I ain't the dumb hick you make me for."

"All you've done is proven that you're a different kind of dumb. Your girlfriend was a camwhore slut, and if what you're saying is true, got killed trafficking drugs. And you're out trying to avenge her honor, you stupid little shit."

"Avenge her murder, asshole. Not her honor. And who else is gonna do it?"

"You're gonna get yourself killed, too."

"You think I ain't thought of that? Listen up. Fact is, the Knights of Satan will get their payment one way or another. Even if they kill your brother, they're gonna want a slice from your pie. My family can help you with that. My Uncle Duane knows some Knights of Satan leadership, can get a sit-down for you."

"I don't make deals with children, and you're not in any position to arrange them, anyhow. You can go play on the balcony, though." Dan jabbed a finger at Russ. "If I hear from your dad and some other grown-ups, I might consider it."

"I'll make that happen." Russell surprised himself with how quickly and assuredly it came out. "Dad and Duane aren't going to quit hunting for who done Jesse, but I'm going to insist on one thing. Ricky got Bree killed doing what he should have done himself, I want y'guys to help make that right. You do that, and I can tell you what you really want to know." Dan's bloodshot eyes widened when Russell hitched a thumb at himself and said, "I know where Ricky's shipment is. All I want in exchange ain't nothing but revenge."

* * *

Meghan walked in her front door and was startled to find someone standing in her kitchenette. Myra looked over her shoulder from doing dishes at the sink. The empty whiskey bottle had been moved to the center of the counter.

"I can't deal with any more surprises today, Sis," Meghan said.

"Sorry, I have a key. I dropped by your work to give you a cassoulet I baked. They said you're not on patrol tonight."

"They took me off for a couple days after the incident with the biker at Ricky's house. So I can 'recover.'"

"I heard about Bree." Myra set a dish on the drying rack and turned to face her sister. "I thought maybe you needed to eat. I don't know. I guess I wanted an excuse to check in on you. I came by to drop it off. And I found that." She pointed at the bottle.

"Yeah. Well, that was a mistake." Meg pulled off her boots. "I slipped."

"Before or after they found her?"

"Before. Hit a dead end. Exhausted. Crashed hard and woke up to news of a dead girl." Meg sat down heavily on the couch, and Mr. Purrs growled at her from the armrest. "So, that's how the missing person case was solved. I couldn't get to her in time. Or, hell, maybe she was like that before I even started."

Myra sat down and put her arm around her. Meghan tensed, then sighed out, "I already cried about this."

Myra hugged her and stood. "You probably need to eat."

"In a bit."

Myra busied herself straightening and picking up around the house as she spoke, a nervous habit their mother had also shared. "Do you want to talk about what happened?"

"To Bree? Or about my relapse? Or what?"

"Whatever you want." She straightened the shoes by the door into a neat line.

"She was dead in the creek down from the railway bridge. I saw her. Had to tell Julie today." Meg leaned forward, putting her face in her hands, speaking from between her palms. "Last place I can put her was at Dan Hornween's club that Monday night. I assume that now it's a matter of finding out everyone who was there, and where she went after. Her vehicle is still missing. Dan isn't going to like the visit he's gonna get soon from Stoltz."

"You think someone killed her?"

"I'm sure of it. Only other possibility is that she over-dosed, and whoever gave it to her panicked and scrambled to cover the tracks. Waiting on toxicology and all the rest from the medical examiner."

"Is that a list of charge records you have from the strip club, there on the table?"

"I had one," Meg said, confused, "How did you know? I gave all my notes to Ed and the State Police earlier today—"

Myra pointed to a manila folder on the coffee table. Meghan flipped it over and saw, written in black marker, RECEIPTS.

"It was under the table when I came in. I found it straightening up."

"Damn," Meghan said. "I was supposed to hand this over. I must have knocked it off the table stumbling around last night. God. What a mess."

"Can we talk about the relapse sometime? Later?"

"Yeah, all right." Much later, Meghan thought. "I grabbed a bite today with Deputy Williams. He's pretty torn up, says he wishes I was still on the case. Worried Stoltz is getting soft." Meg rubbed her temples. "Say, that reminds me. You worked for the schools when that kerfuffle happened with Crystal Lewis, the nude pics?"

"Ugh, yeah. It nearly made me quit. Poor girl."

"Russell McCreech had some words about it when I tried to interview him. Said something about Brad Stoltz and Sean McGuiness being the ones who took them, or spread them around, and nothing happened to them."

"That's what I heard, too." She shook her head. "But by the time I got wind of it, McGuiness's dad had already started legal action against the district, the cops were dropping it, and Crystal's parents had taken her out of school. I wasn't allowed any access to any of the kids involved. When things had settled enough that I could look into it, well, none of the kids trusted the school anymore—that included me. It took me years to get that back."

"Did you talk to any of the parents?"

"I tried, with the boys' folks. Ed and Gladys were good people, but they thought their son could do no wrong. Blamed it all on Sean being a bad influence. And Sean's parents blamed Brad. But most people blamed Crystal for causing problems." Myra looked like she wanted to spit. "Real 'hometown heroes,' those two." Myra wiped down the counter with a paper towel. "You better make copies of your own before you hand over those charge records. Ed's going to be embarrassed."

Meghan blinked. "What do you mean? Was he at amateur night? I know he's lonely, but I never thought—"

"Haven't you looked through that folder yet? Sorry, I'm nosy, couldn't help myself. Anyway. Ed's son, Brad, was having quite a time at Lil' Angels that night with guess who—Sean McGuiness. The dynamic duo was back in town that night."

Meg snatched up the folder and ran her finger down the columns. Their names were all over it: S MCGUINESS and B STOLTZ. The paper trembled in her hand.

It was mid-morning, and the Hobble Inn probably would have been empty even if the front door hadn't been locked, and if there hadn't been the sign with an angry hornet reading "Buzz Off! We're Closed!" in its diamond-shaped window. Dust motes floated like plankton over the narrow trapezoids of light cast on the floor from the glass-block windows facing the parking lot. The McCreech family sat around a scarred bar table: Leon, Alice, and Shane, all of them gaping at Russell as he explained his visit to the Hornween house last night.

"Oh, honey," Alice said. "This isn't—I don't know where you got the idea—"

"Russell. My boy." Leon rubbed his fist against his own forehead, reddening, then folded his hands. "You can't speak for us like that—ever."

"I didn't speak for nobody. All I said is that maybe—just maybe—we could help the Hornweens with their problems, if they help us with ours."

"And what if it was one of them that killed Jesse, or your girl? You think of that?" Alice snapped.

"I did, Ma. Damn. Listen—it's a way to get a better idea of what they know. But I don't think they're the killers, okay? And another thing, if Jesse was the one who stole the drugs, why did he bring Bree's car over to have it shredded—with the shipment still in it?"

"Jesse don't always think things through," Alice said.

"Duane nearly lost his mind dealing with that one. Boy was a bit off."

"He ain't *that* dumb, baby," Leon replied.

"Right?" Russell clapped once. "He must have had a reason. I can't believe it's because he just up and killed Bree and happened to have twelve-hundred bucks sitting around to shred her car. Plus, someone got bloodied up at Mike's. Mike's on the run. From who? Point I'm making is this: There's a—what do you call it—a third thing between Bree and Jesse."

Russell looked around the table—hoping things would keep moving, that Leon and Dan would meet, that he was getting closer to the truth and not just building a bridge to an imaginary solution. He'd been blind to so many things, to the secret life of almost everyone he cared about, but maybe he was beginning to see.

"I think this is a good idea, Dad," Shane said.

"Really?" Russell replied, not meaning to sound so shocked.

"We find out who killed our people, Ricky gets his shipment back, the KoS get their money, and whoever stirred up this shit storm gets taken out of the game." Shane shrugged. "Everybody wins."

"I don't think it's that simple, sweetie," Alice said. "You're assuming everybody's going to be straight about his part."

"I'm assuming Dad will be sharp enough to tell who's being straight and who's not," Shane said. "At least we'll get some of their cards on the table."

"There might be something to this," Leon grumbled. "I'm going to talk to Moose, see what Duane has to say."

Moose was the family attorney and their main line of

business-related communication with Duane McCreech in penitentiary, since his conversations were confidential according to attorney-client privilege.

"If you think so, hon. But in the meantime, listen good." She jabbed a long nail at Russell. "You stay the hell away from the Hornween folk. You too, Shane. Let your dad handle it with Duane until you hear otherwise."

A heavy banging fell on the door.

"Buzz off, we're closed," Leon bellowed. "Can't you read?"

A man on the other side hollered back, "Sheriff's Office. Open up, Leon."

"That's Ed Stoltz," Leon said. "Great. Shane?" Leon waved backhandedly at the door. "Let him in."

Shane walked to the door and unbolted it. Detective Stoltz strode in with four uniformed deputies, leaving the door open behind them.

"We're not actually open yet, gentlemen," Leon laughed out, "but I suppose I can make an exception—"

"Can it, McCreech," snapped the detective.

Three deputies surrounded the table, while the fourth squared off with Shane. A brown-uniformed man in a crew-cut loomed behind Russell. Russ glanced back at the open door, hoping to see Deputy Meg, but there was only a white police Bronco with its lights flashing.

"What's this about?" Shane asked.

One of the deputies tried to roughly spin him around, but Shane stepped and ducked, slipping under his arm. The cop lost his footing and stumbled into a barstool, knocking it over. The commotion caused another deputy to draw his pistol and aim at Shane, yelling, "Do not move! Place both of your hands flat on the bartop! Now!"

"Woah," Leon shouted, raising his hands. "Easy, everybody. Looks like we're going on a trip."

"Nobody say shit to these oinkers," Alice said. "We'll be home in time for lunch."

Cold steel clamped around Russell's wrists. When they pulled his father up from his stool, he shot his son a wink and a grin before they threw Leon to the floor, one cop with a knee in his back while the other sat on his legs and Stoltz snapped on the cuffs. Leon didn't make a sound.

"'Fate is a Beast,'" one of the deputies said, smirking as he looked down at the patches on the back of Leon's cut. "What's that supposed to mean?"

"You're all going to find out," Alice said. "I promise."

CHAPTER 9

A moment after Meghan pressed the bell, the French door opened to reveal a young dark-haired woman wearing pink lipstick that matched her yoga pants. She displayed the look of friendly concern one would expect from her situation: a homeowner in an upscale subdivision of Birch Hills encountering a sheriff in dark sunglasses at her doorstep on a Sunday morning.

"Good morning, ma'am. I'm Chief Deputy Meghan Shaw, with the Stanley County Sheriff's Office." She reached out and shook the woman's manicured hand.

"Brandi Stapleton. Nice to meet you. What can I do for you?"

"I'd like a moment with Connor Ferguson. This is his house, correct?"

Megan had followed up with Sara Van Dorne, Angel Five from Dan's club, and learned that a bachelor party for someone named Connor Ferguson had reserved a table on the Monday before last at Lil' Angels. There was also, she said, a girl dancing that night with a bleached mohawk that fit Bree's description. From Myra, she learned that Connor was a good friend of Brad Stoltz and Sean McGuiness—

until his parents moved away in the wake of the Crystal Lewis incident.

"It's our house, yes. We're engaged—getting married in just a few weeks."

"Congratulations," Meg said. "May I come in?"

"Of course. I'll get Connor for you."

She stepped aside to allow the deputy into the spacious and sunlit foyer. When Meg entered, she saw a ginger-haired and clean-shaven man wearing a polo shirt and khaki shorts walking down the hallway, barefoot on the hardwood floor and holding a glass of lemonade.

"Brandi, is everything all right?" he asked.

"Connor Ferguson?" Meg said, as if he was an old school buddy she'd come across in the park.

"I'm sorry, do I know you?"

"I understand you were in the Pike Lake area the Monday before last. I'd like to ask you a few questions if you can spare a moment."

"Oh, sure." He gave a sudden nervous laugh. Brandi looked puzzled. He stammered out, "Could we—come on—let's talk on the back deck, Officer. Brandi, are you still heading off to yoga, baby?"

"What's going on?" Brandi asked, eyes narrowed.

"It's fine, Ms. Stapleton. We had an incident over there, and we're just talking to people who might have been in the area and seen something. Standard procedure."

"I'll tell you all about it when you get back." Connor grinned. "Go on, now."

"You better, mister."

Connor led Meghan through a spacious, marble-and-brushed-steel kitchen, across a cathedral-ceiling family room, and out a sliding glass door onto a poolside deck. He gestured to an umbrella table, and they both sat down. Somewhere, a dog barked over the drone of a lawnmower.

"Didn't want to talk about your bachelor party in front of your fiancée?" Meg smirked.

"Does anyone? It wasn't exactly a G-rated night. But there wasn't anything illegal about it, as far as I know."

"You're from Pike Lake, Mr. Ferguson?"

"Till my junior year. My parents moved us to Birch Hills—felt like Pike Lake was getting, well, you know. Trashy? There's a better way of saying it, I'm sure."

"Don't worry, I know what you mean. How'd you end up in this house, here?"

An automated pool sweeper whirred as it lazily arced across the water's surface.

"I got my associate's degree. Took over one of my dad's dealerships. Met Brandi at the athletic club and decided to get this house. Move in together. Getting married next month—I bet she told you. Not much of a story."

"So, you had your bachelor party out in Pike Lake?"

"I did. Me and some of the boys. Our old stomping ground. Drinking and dumbassery. Can you tell me what this is about?"

"You were at the Lil' Angels Gentlemen's Club that night." Meg called up a picture on her phone of Bree Wells from one of the girl's online social profiles, hair in a liberty-spiked mohawk, raccoon eyeliner, doing her best Sid Vicious sneer. "Recognize this girl? Hair was probably blonde. Large, black bird tattooed on her back. Might have been working that night."

He picked up the phone and peered at it before handing it back. "I don't think so. Honestly, I was wasted by the time we got there. Everyone was buying me shots all night.

It's all kind of a blur. Who is she?"

"Just someone we're trying to find out some things about. Could you tell me who was in your bachelor party group?" She took out her notebook.

"Oh, let's see…" He rattled off several names, counting them out on his fingers. "That covers it."

He sipped his lemonade.

"Thank you, Mr. Ferguson. That's very helpful." She glanced down at the notepad. "Anyone you might have forgotten?"

"Hrmmm. No. Nope. That's about it."

"How about Sean McGuiness and Brad Stoltz?"

"What about them?"

"Well, you see, they ran up a lot of charges that night at the club. Would be quite a coincidence if they just happened to be there, seeing as you guys were buddies back in the day. Student Council. Golf team. All that. It's all in the yearbooks."

"Ooooh, right! Brad and Sean. Duh. Of course. They were there, yes." He circled his pointer finger around his temple. "Like a said, all a blur." He laughed.

"Sounds like it. Why did you have a bachelor party on a Monday at the club?"

"It's the first place we went drinking together on my twenty-first, which also happened to fall on a Monday that year. The amateur night at Angels. So, it was like an old-time's-sake, memory-lane kind of thing. Most of the guys are home from school for the summer, so, what the heck, we made a go of it."

"How fun. Did anyone from the club leave with anyone from your party?"

"Oh, no. I don't think so. Strippers, you know—you won't get laid, but you will get screwed."

"That's funny," Meg said. It was an old joke. "So where

did you go after the club?"

"The lake house. Sean's family's place—that's where we'd been since Saturday night."

"Nice place?"

"Oh yeah. It's great. Dock, big TV, all of that."

"And everyone came back there."

"Yeah. I rode back with Sean. His BMW only seats two. The rest made their own way."

"Thanks for the details. Do you have a card, Connor? In case I need to get a hold of you again?"

"Of course." He moved to stand, but sat again and asked, "Is this about something with the stripper you showed me? I mean, we went out for a guys' night out, but we don't hang out with that kind of people, you know? Strippers, I mean. Working at a place like that, they're probably involved with all kinds of sketchy guys, right?"

Meg gave an interested smile and tilted her head to the side. "Did you have anyone in mind?"

"Who knows? Those redneck bikers on the bad side of the lake and the creepers who live out in the woods. Drug dealers. Juggalos. People like that."

"Oh yeah, I know all about people like that. Right now, I need names." She pointed at the list in her notebook, then waved it away. "I'm just going around ruling people out who don't know something about that girl, so we have a clear path to someone who does."

"Great. Super. Let me get you that card. I'll be right back."

He walked across the deck toward the gabled white house, the green lawn rolling all around it, the sunlight flashing across the sky-blue pool. When Connor turned his back, her smile faded. She removed her sunglasses to reveal her bruised and battered eye.

* * *

Russell sat in the interrogation room, rubbing the red cuff marks on his wrists. He glared across the table at Detective Stoltz, who had a laptop open in front of him, along with a thick folder of papers. A sandy-haired deputy, Williams, stood in the corner behind him.

"Russell, I want you to know that you are not personally a suspect in what happened to Bree," Stoltz said. "But if you don't cooperate, that could mean some serious charges."

"I want a lawyer."

"We found your cap at Mike Morgan's place. It looks like some bloody things went on there."

"Well, then I definitely want a lawyer." He wondered what it was keeping them from charging him if they thought he had something to do with the incident at Mike's. He now wished he hadn't brushed off Deputy Meg. She warned him that if he didn't come in, Stoltz would come after him. Then again, maybe they were working together in a good cop/bad cop scheme.

"Before you shut this conversation down," the detective said, "take a look at this."

He turned the laptop to face Russell, wincing as if it weighed a ton. The screen displayed grainy, black-and-white security footage of a Citgo gas pump.

"This is from early Tuesday morning, at the gas station. You can see from the time/date stamp in the corner. And look what car pulls up." A Honda Civic pulled in, with a scuff on the bumper and a peace symbol sticker in the back window. Passenger seat empty, driver in shadow. Bree's car. "Now look who gets out."

Jesse McCreech stepped out and hurried to the pump.

"That's your cousin. He only put one gallon in the car. Probably because he didn't plan on driving it far. You and I both know who runs the scrapyard in this town, Russell. The state police are there right now, looking for this vehicle." Stoltz pointed at the screen at the car pulling away. "Or what's left of it."

Russell licked his lips before saying, "Lawyer."

"It looks like Jesse killed your girlfriend, son." Stoltz looked down for a moment. "And someone killed Jesse to keep him quiet about it. I can't imagine how that feels, Russell. And I'm so sorry to tell you this. But I think you know, in your heart, the sort of people the Ironwolfs are. Your uncle in prison, your brother just out. Violent charges. History of violence against women, too."

"Got nothing to say to you."

"You're not like this, Russell. This isn't you. You're a better kind of person." Stoltz shook his head and said, "Unless, of course, Jesse was covering up for someone. Your family has always gone a long way to take care of its own, hasn't it? Why don't you run through where you were last week, starting with Sunday night. Take me through it. Day by day."

"Ain't saying shit about shit to you."

"Something you don't want me to know about, son?"

"I ain't your son. Now you mention it, funny how your son and his buddies can swap around dirty pics of middle school girls, and that shit don't stick, but then you come riding in like some kind of white knight to pin a murder on us. Y'all never gave a damn about Bree when she was alive. But I sure as hell did. You're a goddamn fraud, and I ain't playing." Russell folded his arms. "Lawyer."

And with that, the door burst open. A huge man with a

long white beard and his hair in two braids like an Indian, dressed in a double-breasted, pinstriped suit, thrust his finger at Stoltz and shouted, "A minor? With no charges? Have you lost your mind, Detective?"

"Hey, Moose," Russell said, sneering. "There's my lawyer."

Stoltz said, "We were informally questioning—"

"Oh, bullshit, too." Moose grabbed Russell's arm and held it out as if he was a ragdoll. "Cuff marks? You are so fucked. I'm getting pictures of this."

"I can't be accountable when someone in transport chooses to resist his restraints."

"Resist his restraints? I take shits bigger than this kid." He patted Russell's head and said to him, "Sorry, Russ, but I do," and then to Stoltz, "And you tell me you had a problem with resistance? If you come near my client, or anyone else in the McCreech family, I will have you crucified. Do you hear me? I will drag you in front of a judge, along with this clod-hopping mob of bumpkin rejects you call sheriffs, and I will disembowel each one of you and tap dance around in your entrails. In a metaphorical, legal sense, of course. Come on, kid, let's go."

Russell stood, shot a finger gun at Stoltz and the deputy, and walked out the door.

Meghan found Sean McGuiness in the backyard of his family's expansive brickwork manor in the rolling country-side on the outskirts of Pike Lake, whacking golf balls into the meadows behind it. He was a lanky, tanned young man with a hell of a swing. When she called out to him, he lowered his driver and said, "This is private property," before heading up a flagstone path between the hedges.

She walked after him, saying, "I know you were at Lil' Angels on the Monday before last, Sean. Something happened that night. To a girl who was there."

A wren twittered from the brush among the trill of insects. His sparkling blue eyes swept over Meghan before glancing up at the clouds. He yawned.

"You're trespassing," he said, opening the door to a rambling screened-in porch. "If you want to talk, talk to my dad."

"Is he here right now? I'd like that." The screen door banged shut in her face, and she called out after him, "I'll wait out here for him."

Within five minutes, Jim McGuiness, a silver-haired and more deeply tanned version of his son, strode out onto the porch and glared at her through the screen door.

Before she could introduce herself, he said, "I know who you are, and I know why you're here."

"Then you understand how important your son's cooperation is."

"This is ridiculous." He chuckled and shook his head. "I know how much you want to be taken seriously, Deputy. But whatever you're trying to prove by coming out here—"

"I'd like to prove who is responsible for the dead teenage girl we found in a creek yesterday morning, Mr. McGuiness."

"Maybe her parents should have been more responsible and kept better tabs on her."

You bastard, she thought. He was needling her, hoping to escalate it. Get something to add to the complaint.

"Is that your official statement, Jim?"

He clucked his tongue. "Tell you what. Meghan, is it? I'll give Ed Stoltz a call. He's a dear friend of mine. Dale Cunningham, too. I've been a generous supporter of our sheriff from the start. And we'll see who ends up having to make an official statement. I hope you're on good terms with your union rep, Deputy."

He turned his back and began to walk away, freezing for a moment when Meghan called after him, "This one isn't going to go away, like what he did to the Lewis girl," then retreated back into the comforts of his home.

Russell leaned on the tattoo shop's counter, looking over the flash on the walls: eagles and lightning bolts, women and spiders. The neon sign buzzed in the window, tinting everything with a scarlet glow. He didn't have any ink yet, but he'd decided he'd be getting some once this all came to an end—if he was still around to see it. He didn't know what he wanted, but he wouldn't be getting it at Triple Felony Tattoos. That much he was sure of.

Sam hunched over her iPad and said, "So you're sure your dad and uncle have cooled down the Knights of Satan— you're positive."

"Right. Best thing to do, now that we know Bree is dead, is pretend that we're all moping around, being sad if any cops come by."

"Who's pretending?" She looked up from the screen, her eyes deep and dark. "Aren't you sad, Russell?"

"Never said I ain't. But I ain't gonna sit around and cry about it when whoever did it is up and walking around. Cops are keeping an eye on us—and they ain't gonna get the real killer, or killers, I guess, long as they ain't looking at nobody else. They know things got weird at Mike's. They know Jesse took the car. State police are picking through the scrapyard, but that's all clean—we made sure it was all straight as soon as Clint took us to that garage."

"So the KoS supplied Ricky, Ricky handed it off to Bree, and Bree lost it. The car ended up with Jesse, who sent it to Larry to be shredded."

"Yeah. And Larry parted it out instead, and that's how Clint found the molly packed into the door he bought. At least, that's his story."

"And someone picked up Jesse from the scrapyard. And someone shot down Jesse. And someone killed Bree. All the same motherfucker?" She ran her tongue stud between her lips.

"Maybe. Or maybe a few different motherfuckers." His finger traced along a Celtic knot pattern on one of the wall's flash displays. "It's all twisted around itself right now. But we're straightening it out."

"We gotta find Mike. I'm working on Jolene a bit, I think she knows—he's her connect, maybe her boyfriend."

"Jolene is doing Crazy Mike? Really?"

"He's not bad looking." She added, "For an old dude, I mean. Jolene's like what, forty-something?"

He grimaced, not wanting to picture it. "Mike Morgan and Ricky Hornween need to be accounted for—we need to know where those sonsofbitches were when all this went down."

Sam tapped and swiped on her tablet screen and said, "I'm still freaked about those KoS guys coming through. If your dad gave them back the drugs, you think they'd just back off?"

"Maybe. They don't know we have it, just that we have info about it. If it wasn't for my Uncle Duane, they'd probably be skinning us alive to get us to tell them. But they're willing to talk, and so is Dan." He rubbed his temples. "We're gonna have a meeting soon. Long as we're not all locked up."

"The cops don't have dirt on any of us." She tossed back her long black hair. "Else you would all still be in custody. Plus they're trying to figure out the blood at Mike's. Maybe cops got Ricky already."

"Dan would know about that. Or they'd be trying to scare us with what Ricky might say to save his skin. You're right. Stoltz is shooting in the dark, hoping he hits something."

Sam looked past Russell, through the shop's front window. "Head's up, five-o."

"Oh, hell no, I'm done with them." He considered running out the back, or hiding under the counter, but in that moment of hesitation Deputy Meg's cruiser pulled up right at the front door, and he caught her eyes as she stepped out. "I ain't talking. You neither."

Meghan walked in and stood with her hands on her hips. She looked from Russell over to Samantha, blew out a breath and shook her head. "Russell, I had nothing to do with you and your family getting brought in. You know that."

"You're a sheriff, ain't you? I don't see how you can walk on in here with that badge and say you got nothing to do with it."

"I warned you that this is how it might go. You think I wanted Stoltz and the deputies dragging you all in like that? I did everything I could to keep it from happening—but you blew me off. I don't know who you're protecting, or why, but it's not too late to set things right."

"He's protecting himself, ma'am." Sam was calm, but there was an uncharacteristic pointedness to her words. "You aren't trying to solve this thing. You're trying to build a case. It's not the same. That's your job, and we both know it."

"I know you're a smart girl and used to being right, but I promise that this time you're not. So do us both a favor, Samantha. You don't know me, you don't know what this means to me, and you don't know what you're talking about. So don't tell me what my job is or how I go about doing it."

Sam's face flushed and her jaw stuck out. She looked down at her iPad and poked at it.

"My lawyer says not to talk to you, and that you guys all need to stay away from me."

"Fine, Russ." Meghan clapped her hands once. "Before you write me off, you should know I've managed to, as Sam said, build a bit of a case. Now, I know this isn't going to be easy for either of you, but the last time Bree was seen alive, it was at Lil' Angels. Did you know that?"

Russell thought of Dan, his glinting, coked-out eyes as he slouched behind his giant desk. If it was true, he must have known. And he looked right through Russell and didn't say a thing.

"I told her not to," Sam said, quietly. "I did."

"Looks like she didn't listen to you, Samantha. I don't know what else she got herself tangled up in, but I'm going to unravel it sooner or later. But I've said it before: I need you guys. You knew her, and you know more than you're telling me. I need to find out what happened between her leaving that club Monday night and her time of death. If nobody talks, I'm stuck. And that means the investigators are going to work with what they already have. That means Jesse, who had the car, and Mike Morgan—and those who knew them. That includes you two. And I think there's more to it than that. I need to know about some people."

"Like who?" Russ asked.

"Don't, Russ," Samantha said.

"Like Sean McGuiness," she said, "for one."

"Why?" Russ asked.

"We don't know shit about him, other than he's an ass-hole," Samantha cut in. "You think Sean McGuiness ever hung out with us?"

"I know he hung out with one of your friends years ago, and it got pretty ugly. Crystal Lewis."

"Old news." Samantha locked eyes with Russ. "We're not talking to you."

"Did he ever have any connection with Bree?"

"I said we're not talking," Sam said, a sharpness creeping in.

"Wait, why would you ask that?" Russ asked.

"Let's just say I'm interested. I have reason to believe he saw her that night, and he's—uncooperative. You quote me on any of that, I'll deny it. Can you help me with this?"

Russ took a breath, hooked his thumbs in his pockets, and stared down at the floor. When he raised his head to look into Meghan's face, she didn't look angry, expectant, or anything other than exhausted and a bit sad. One of her eyes sat in a smear of plum-colored bruise, and both were shot with red veins. Her skin was sallow, and her hair hung lank against her face.

"You don't get it, Deputy. You need us. But we don't need you," he said. "Don't try to talk to me again."

She turned on her heel and shoved out the front door, not looking back. He wanted to call out something but wasn't sure what, or why. As the car pulled away, he felt like there was something more he should have said, or something else, but there was no undoing it.

"McGuiness," Sam said, breaking the silence. "She'll

never be able to get to him. Guys like that will always get a pass."

He looked over to the flash art, the patterns of colorful scars, until his gaze settled on a skull with a dagger through its eye socket.

"Not from us, they don't."

It used to be something like a dream, the River Run Mall, when Meghan was a kid. Even though it was a thirty-minute drive from Pike Lake, Mom or Dad were usually all right with dropping her off with Myra on a weekend afternoon, as long as the girls had kept up with homework and chores, promised not to leave with anyone, and were sure to be at the JC Penny entrance by eight to be picked back up again. The sisters would spend hours walking among the groups of kids parading in little tribes among the towering displays of athletic shoes and cardboard stand-ups of pop singers, past the backlit posters of movie stars and gleaming walls of sunglasses, looking for a chance to buy a piece of a fantasy, and maybe—just maybe—find a way to live it. At least for a little while.

Just over ten years ago, the last stores in the River Run Mall closed. Like a hulking brown freighter ran aground in a gray sea, it loomed over what seemed to be endless miles of cracked gray asphalt. Dead light poles towered like the masts of sunken ships. Ryan's blue state patrol car and Meghan's beige cruiser, parked in the empty lot, seemed like a pair of lifeboats paralyzed on a dead current. A few yards from their vehicles, they stood gazing at the bulk of the darkened mall as if it might show some signs of life. It did not.

"You were right. The medical examiner says it's definitely

Brianne Wells," Ryan said. "Dental records closed any question of that."

Meghan did not expect a weight to press on her chest when she heard it, but it hit her nonetheless. The feeling of dashed hope was foolish, and she tried to sweep it away. In a world of stolen data, shifting identities, and digital alternation, if there was one thing that could be identified, it was a corpse. And even if somehow it hadn't been Bree, but some other tattooed, bleached blonde washed up by the creek, what then? The case would have merely switched from one dead girl to another. Another grieving family, another damaged community, another broken circle of friends.

"Expected." She shrugged. "Any word on time or cause of death?"

"Week ago, give or take. No water in her lungs, though, so that's interesting. Suggests that she was dumped."

"From the bridge? That's what I was thinking. The rain on Saturday night raised the creek level, washed her down a ways." She chewed a knuckle for moment, thinking. "I know it's unlikely, but could she have struck one of the abutments or the concrete base before falling into the water? Or even cracked her neck against the shallows?"

"Her larynx is crushed. Hyoid bone snapped clean through."

Broken bottles caught the afternoon sun, and windblown trash drifted across the asphalt.

"So she was strangled." Meg took a breath. "Signs of rape?"

"She'd been sexually active, and her underwear was inside out." He turned up his hands. "But condition of the body being what it is..." He trailed off.

"Inconclusive." She cleared her throat. "Semen found?"

"Yes. But degraded. Probably can't be identified, and again, won't tell us whether it was from the murderer, or from a previous encounter, or—"

"I know, I know. Just might get us an idea of who had been in contact with her." Meg looked up at a lonely gull circling the lot. "Phone records?"

"Still waiting. Another two weeks, at least." Ryan saw her annoyance and added, "Sorry. But honestly, who knows if she had another phone, or was using an app to clone a different number, or what? Even cell records aren't as cut and dried as they used to be."

"Toxicology, then? Trace evidence under her nails?" It took a good two minutes to throttle someone to death, even a girl Bree's size. If she wasn't drugged into unconsciousness, it seemed like she would be one to put up a fight.

"You know how lucky we are to even have these preliminary findings so soon."

"I know." Meg shifted her weight from one hip to another. "Why are they trying to push me out, Ryan?"

"The sheriff's office? Oh, come on. You know why. They're intimidated. How would it look if some deputy closed the case all on her own?" He walked over to his car and leaned back on it. "They want your investigation's discoveries—"

"Do they?"

"Sure, but they would prefer to take you out of the lead— even if you built most of the case. Especially because of that, actually." He glanced around the empty lot, then out to the distant interstate. "Jeez. This place is depressing."

"I used to love coming here." She clicked her tongue. "Which is kind of depressing in its own way. It was all such nonsense, but it mattered to us. I don't remember why."

She looked over at Ryan. He'd always been straight with her. Of course, she never told him about the incident that happened on-base when she was in the service. Lot of good toeing that line did for her. But Ryan, he wasn't a part of any of that.

But he wasn't an island—he had built a career. It wasn't as if he was trying to climb the ranks of the Pike Lake Sheriff's Office, though. He was a state trooper, already ranked as an inspector.

She took a breath before asking, "The NEO task force. The informant network. Am I stomping mud across a floor that you guys are trying to mop up?"

"Well, Jesse McCreech got himself ventilated, so that doesn't look good. But he wasn't a CI being handled by the state—he was your county's asset. If anyone is going to eat that shit sandwich, it's Cunningham. That's as high as it would go. But, let's face it, it not like there's going to be any state inquiry into the loss of a guy like Jesse. I doubt he's missed much in Pike Lake, either."

"Do you have a dog in this fight, Inspector?" she asked.

He looked taken aback, saying, "Yeah. Some sicko strangled a young girl and threw her in a creek. I'd like to catch him." He cocked his head as he asked, "What are you getting at, Ice?"

"You first. Tell me the way my office is leaning toward the case."

"Really?" He eyed her, then folded his arms. "Alright. Stoltz thinks that your girl might have tried to get into that strip club, Lil' Angels, with a relative's ID, but was bounced out. She met Jesse McCreech in the lot there, since he's banned from the place, maybe he was bounced out too. Guess he was known to hang around the lot now and again.

She wanted to score some drugs, so he took her out to Mike Morgan's place. Something went bad there, and they killed her."

"That's the scenario?" Meg pursed her lips. "Then what?"

"Why don't you ask Detective Stoltz yourself?"

She lowered her chin and stared at him.

"I get it. Fine." He spread his fingers out in front of him. "So the timeline goes like this, as Stoltz sees it. Jesse shreds her car at McCreech Salvage. Mike pitches her body off the bridge. Mike picks up Jesse at the scrapyard with Jesse's truck. Girl gone, car gone. That's supposed to be the end of it. But Jesse's a tweaker, too paranoid to let it go, and as the week goes on, he starts trying to steal enough shit to get himself a ticket out of town or just hit the road."

"Hence the stolen mower," Meghan said.

"Right. And Jesse doing this stuff makes Mike Morgan nervous. That, and maybe he hears whispers about Jesse being an informant. So, Mike heads down there with a gun, and Jesse is waiting with a gun too. It all hits the fan at Jesse's place. Mike's dog is wounded, and maybe Mike too, but Jesse gets the worst of it. Mike and his dog flee. Jesse dies, holding out that necklace, saying 'It wasn't me' to you and his cousin when you traipse into the mess these geniuses put themselves in."

"So, when Jesse said that, he was trying tell us that it was Mike Morgan that killed Bree?"

"That's the tale as Stoltz tells it. And I've heard worse stories."

"It's a story, alright. And it hinges all on Mike Morgan. Has Stoltz mentioned anything about charge receipts from Dan Hornween's club?"

He shook his head. "The detective says the club is a dead

end, that the girl probably didn't make it in the door. They don't talk to police there, anyway. No sense fighting that battle when we could get Mike Morgan and maybe lean on the McCreeches, find what's left of that car. See if the boy has an inkling of what happened to his girlfriend and might be willing to cooperate."

"Huh." Meghan tucked her thumbs in her belt. "You lost any chance of Russell talking when the sheriffs came in and knocked his family's heads together in front of him."

"Not the way I would have handled it, I'll give you that."

"And Mike Morgan's chances of being taken in alive aren't good, if you ask me."

He blinked. "You think he's going to fire on officers if approached?"

"That's not what I said."

"Ah." He rubbed his chin. "Well, I'll tell you this. If you think there's some dirt on this thing, none of it's on my hands. This county isn't my playground. And if you're not telling me what's going on, I might end up knocked down in the mud and never know who pushed me."

Now or never, she thought.

"Let me tell you how I see it," she said. "But if you screw me over on this, I'm going to take it personally. And I'll settle it that way, too."

"You have my word." He raised his hand. "I'd like to think that after all these years, that's enough for you. Without the threats."

"You've got to give me some backup on this if you say you're in. I'm going to need your help."

"I'm in if you need me. Always."

She took the chance.

CHAPTER 10

The pack of eight motorcycles sounded like a drum corps playing inside a fleet of garbage trucks as they flooded into the lake house's driveway and gathered in a row side-by-side: a regiment of Ironwolfs in full colors, the chrome and steel of their bikes gleaming in the sun. Russell eased the Harley, blatting and growling beneath him, into his place at the end. He did not have an M-class license to ride it, but that was not on his mind as the pack barreled down the road to roll up on a wide, two-level A-frame placed among the lakeside oaks and aspens.

A single BMW coupe sat in the leaning, triangular shadow that spilled from the house and across the driveway. Leon looked around, then pointed down a small peninsula beyond the house. It jutted out into the lake and ended at a wide dock. Russell saw what his dad had spotted: a lone figure crouching beside a boat's stern-drive motor. The figure stood, roused by the noise, and used one of his hands as a visor against the sun as he looked toward the intruders. Leon whirled his hand over his head as if swinging a lasso, twisted his throttle, and took off across the yard toward the dock. The rest of the Ironwolfs followed, fanning out behind him. Russell felt the bike bounce and tip a bit as the tires tore across the lawn, but he steadied it and took his place in the half-circle that formed around the foot of the dock, sealing it off.

Sean McGuiness looked much the way Russell remembered. A handsome, long face. Tall and lean. He wore a college ball cap and a pale-blue button-down over green cargo shorts. He didn't look so much afraid as he did furious. He stomped down the dock, shouting something that could not be discerned over the clattering roar of the motorcycles. Shane was laughing, but everyone else stared dead ahead. Leon gestured for the engines to cut off, and they did.

"Look what you did to the yard! This is private property," Sean screamed, his face red and his voice strained. "Do you know who I am? Do you have any idea whose house this is? Do you?"

Leon stepped off his bike. Two other club members, Shane and Injun, followed. Shane shook with barely contained giggles, but Injun's deep-lined face radiated bad intentions. Sean did a double-take at the bowie knife strapped to Injun's thigh as the three stood around him. The rest of the riders stared him down. Russell folded his arms, his mouth dry, his heart pounding.

"Of course we know who you are, Sean," Leon said as he strode toward him. "You think we showed up here on accident or something?"

"Alright. I don't know what the hell you think you're doing, but I won't be intimidated." He pulled a cell phone from his pocket. "I'm calling the sheriff."

As Sean looked down to dial, Injun lashed out and slapped the phone from his hand. It spun like a boomerang, clanked once against the dock, then bounced into the lake with a *sploosh*.

"Oops," Leon said. "Looks like you dropped your phone. Don't get worked up about it, though. Things get lost in the bottom of this lake all the time. It's a soft-bottomed one. Black silt. Once something's gone down there, it's gone. You should be careful out here."

Sean looked around at the bikers as if seeing them for the first time and asked, "Why are you doing this to me?"

"You know who *we* are, right?"

Sean nodded.

"We just want to have a quick conversation, and then you can get back to working on your boat. Nice boat, by the way." Leon smiled. "So, you tell me what I need to know, and you won't have to worry about us anymore. Think you can pull that off?"

"Yeah," he mumbled.

"I'm sorry, my hearing's not so good these days." Leon cupped a hand to his ear. "What was that?"

"I said yes, okay? What do you want? Money?"

"Shane, show him."

Shane pulled out a folded up piece of paper from his pocket. He, using his thumb and forefinger, slowly and ex-aggeratedly unfolded it, smoothed it on his chest, and then held it out. McGuiness's hand shook slightly when he took it. It was a playbill for the Shattered Dolls amateur contest at Lil' Angels.

"You were at that?" Leon said.

"This was a couple weeks ago. I mean—"

"I'm not hearing a yes or a no."

"Yes. I was there."

"With who?"

"A lot of people. Seriously. It was a bachelor party. Did

something happen?"

"Yeah, one of the girls working that night was found dead, washed up in a creek down from a railroad bridge."

"Whoa. Hold on." He raised his hands, the playbill fluttering in the breeze. "I don't have anything—"

"You remember seeing a girl working that night with a blonde mohawk? Big raven tattooed across her back?"

Sean squirmed. "There were a lot of girls working that night, so—"

"Hrrrm." Leon sighed. "I'd like to take a look at that house back there. Why don't we sit down inside, put on some music, and see what we can work out? It must be nice, being out here away from prying eyes and ears. Is it?"

"Is it what?"

"Is it nice?" Leon swept his arm in a grand gesture across the wooded lake. "This is a place where a guy can just scream and scream, and you ain't gotta worry about nobody hearing."

"Look. I don't know how to help you, but—"

"Injun, help Sean-boy here up to the house. I'd like a tour."

When Injun reached for Sean, the young man stepped back and stammered out, "Listen, listen, take it easy. That girl was there. I didn't have much to do with her. My friends Connor and Brad were into her, dropped a ton of cash on her, till Brad got kicked out."

"For what?" Leon said.

"He was trying to buy drugs off the strippers. Like, really loudly. Just joking, right? He was caught in a loop, just blackout drunk. I thought he was playing up, just to be funny. That's before he fell down and puked all over himself in the lot."

"You saw all this happen?" Leon asked. "You were with him?"

"No, I was with Connor. I wouldn't have let Brad drive if I'd known he was that bad off."

"So, I'm confused, Sean. I ain't the smartest guy. I admit it. Break it down for me. He got kicked out. But you guys all stayed."

"Yeah, we did." Sean's voice shook. "I swear. He texted me, said he'd meet us at the lake house. I'd show you, but my phone—"

"Sad story. Poor phone. How do you know about him throwing up and falling in the lot if you weren't there?"

"I don't *know*, know. You know? That's what he said. Later. I swear. Look, he said he went home to change his clothes because he puked all over himself. Fell down. He looked freaked out. I don't think he knew how wasted he was. Full-on blackout. You've been there, right?"

"No," Leon said.

"Oh."

"Any girls from the club come over? Or you call any in from a service?"

"No, sir. We were all pretty much out of it by then. I'd never seen any of those girls before the club—or after either."

"How long did it take?"

"For what?"

"For everyone to get from the club to here. It's what, a twenty, twenty-five-minute drive?"

"I don't know." When Injun slapped the hat off of Sean, he then elaborated, "Everyone came right back."

"What about Brad? I thought you said he changed his clothes?" Leon stroked his beard.

"Well, not him," he stammered out. "He took longer. I

don't know. I was drunk, just…longer? Okay? I seriously couldn't tell you. I wasn't looking at the time by then."

Leon glanced over to Russell, who gave him a slight nod.

"I think we're about done here." He patted Sean on the shoulder. "Good talking with you. If we need to ask about anything else, don't worry, buddy." Leon rapped his finger on Sean's breastbone. "I promise, we'll always know where to find you."

Leon, Injun, and Shane made their way back to their bikes. As the pack roared away, across the lawn and onto the gravel, Russell glanced over his shoulder to see Sean McGuiness, trembling, sitting down on the dock, staring down at the Shattered Dolls playbill as if were a death warrant.

Connor Ferguson stood up behind his desk and extended his hand in greeting as Meghan walked into his office. When she released his handshake, he fiddled with some pens and documents on his desktop.

"Thanks for coming up to the office to talk," he said. "I mean, it's not the sort of thing that's appropriate for the sales floor."

She scanned the office and was struck by its blandness. In one corner, a case with some golf and tennis trophies. In another, a well-tended fern. On one wall, framed photos of classic automobiles and numerous plaques commending his work performance. Opposite it, a glass wall overlooking the showroom, where a few people walked among the latest models, accompanied by attentive salespeople. Connor did not offer her a seat.

"It's no problem, Mr. Ferguson. I'm sorry to come by your place of business, but there are a few details I need to pin down we didn't get to last time." She took out her notebook and pulled a pen from her breast pocket. "I tried calling you."

"I'm sorry, before you get started, I mean, I just wanted to tell you." His words were halting as he pulled open his desk drawer and rummaged in it. "Ah." He held a business card out to her. "I've been advised to tell you that if you have any questions about that night, you know, to call the number on that card."

She plucked it from his unsteady hand.

Looking down at the card, she read aloud, "James R. McGuiness, Attorney at Law." She clicked her tongue once. Son of a bitch. "So, after we talked, you went and got yourself a lawyer?"

"Hey, now." He placed both his hands on his desk. "That's not what I said—"

"So, James McGuiness contacted you."

"Listen, all I can say is that—"

"I know that his son was there that night, Connor. You're aware of how this looks."

"Now, how it looks, you see, that doesn't matter. What matters is that—"

She leaned in. "A girl was murdered, Connor. That is what matters," she hissed through gritted teeth.

"I never said it didn't." He glanced around, flustered. "But I can't talk to you."

"Her mother is weeping at home, right now, because she will never see, smell, or hold her daughter. Not ever again. Brianne Wells, at seventeen, is dead. She will never grow up. Someone squeezed her throat for so long, and so hard, that her larynx was crushed and her windpipe was flattened. The man who did it then tossed her body into Grass Creek when he was done with her, like a sack of garbage. Do you understand that this is the only thing that matters right now?"

He uttered a cracked single syllable before trying again, saying, "I don't know who did that. I really don't."

"Well, that makes two of us, Connor, but I'd like to find out. You seem like a decent enough man. Not the kind to go around hurting little girls. Or killing them."

"No, of course not."

"The person who did this isn't going to stop. He probably got his start a long time ago."

"There were others?" His eyes widened.

"Maybe. But I bet he got his start bullying. Dominating. Discovering how much he liked it. And how easy it was to get away with." She sought Connor's eyes, and he looked away. "Crystal Lewis was twelve. She never had a chance. I don't know if she ever got over it. But it looks like all of you boys did."

"Whoa." He raised his hands. "I didn't have anything to do with that."

"I'm not sure if that's true. But let's suppose it is. It doesn't change that you know who did it, though. You've always known." She put the card down on the desk. "I'm not calling Jim McGuiness, Connor. And I'm not going to go digging up your past, either. But I'm asking you to please, if you have any decency, help me. This person strangled a girl to death. It wasn't an accident. It wasn't a mistake. And it's going to happen again if we don't do something about it."

She thought he was looking down to avoid her gaze, but then she saw he was staring into the framed photo propped up on his desktop. She could see from its angle that it was a picture of his fiancée, Brandi, smiling on a porch swing.

"I don't know what happened to the girl." He sighed, then swallowed. "I saw her at the club that night though. I didn't even want to go there. I didn't understand why they were insisting on it. Not at first."

"You said it was where you went for your twenty-first birthday," she replied. "Old time's sake."

"Yeah. That's what they told me. But Brad and Sean had other reasons. They found out that Crystal Lewis was working for that Shattered Dolls website. She was part of the touring group. He wanted us to be there—"

"To laugh at her," Meghan finished. "To make her relive it, all over again."

"Maybe. Maybe to remind me that I'm a piece of shit. That I'm a coward. To make it so I couldn't end up back at home without something to feel bad about. Who knows why they do what they do."

She eyed him. She couldn't tell if he was deflecting or not.

"We stayed for the amateur show. That's where I saw the mohawk girl. Brad and Sean were dropping a ton of cash on her. But we never got to see Crystal, if she was even there at all—I didn't even find out that had been the plan until we got back to the lake house. We got bounced, all of us. Maybe it was because we were a mess. Or maybe Crystal had us thrown out."

"Then what? Where did you go after?"

"Like I said, the lake house. Went straight there. Well, not all of us. Brad said he was going to get some ecstasy or something from one of the girls. That he'd bring it back to the place. He said—I don't know. He was really drunk, I think."

"What did he say?"

"He said that he'd bring her back, too."

"Connor, do not lie to me. Do you understand? I can help you—I can keep you from getting in trouble, from this getting back to Brandi. Did he bring Bree Wells out there?"

He waved it off. "No girls were there all weekend. Brad showed up later that night. Much later. He'd thrown up all over himself and collapsed in a parking lot."

"Did this happen at the house by the lake? Did you see it?"

"No," he said. "But I believe him. Or I did, when he told me. He said he'd gone to his dad's house to change his clothes. And bandage his hand."

"Which hand?" Her heart raced. "What happened to it?

"His right. I don't know what happened—he said it was from falling down in his dad's driveway the night before. I didn't notice until the next day, when we were having coffee, that it was bandaged."

"Thank you, Connor." She scribbled furiously in her notepad. "You're doing the right thing. You won't regret this."

"I don't know about that."

The vacant factory floor seemed to Russell a hangar for spacecraft that had left earth in a different age. Long ago, the plant's machines had been sold off to another company, or shipped away to another country, or maybe just sold as scrap. Grime-covered yellow railings enclosed only empty space, and metal stairways led up to nothingness. Birds roosted in the dripping beams high overhead, and graffiti rioted across the walls. From shattered skylights, colossal pale columns poured in, teeming with insects and dust.

Three groups of men gathered in the ghost factory's center, each contingent forming an equilateral triangle's point. Their voices echoed in the abandoned vastness.

From Pike Lake, there were the Ironwolfs MC. Russell stood behind and to the left of Leon, Shane, and Wink.

Representing Detroit's Knights of Satan MC, the walrus-mustached Sergeant-at-Arms known as Paul "Pickaxe" Cross, accompanied by a dark-bearded mammoth of a man and a younger, blond greaser-type with black tears tattooed beneath each eye, all three wearing their club colors.

From parts more local was the Hornween crew: Dan, decked out in mirrored sunglasses, a black cowboy hat, and a purple trench coat over a leopard-print tank top and pin-striped dress pants; Dick, the hulk who tended Dan's bar, in his standard skin-tight black T-shirt and steel-toed boots; and Finch, the burn-scarred nosferatu from the abandoned carnival, who looked even more unnerving in a gray suit with no shirt under its jacket—and still wore no shoes. Dan and his henchmen stood protectively around the positively terrified and dead-tired Ricky Hornween.

Russell burned with fury at the sight of Ricky, but he almost ached at seeing how brought-low the man looked. His hair, normally pasted into perfect conical spikes that gave his skull the look of some post-apocalyptic helmet, was unruly and matted. A few black, wilting spikes struggled to keep their shape among the tangled mess. His normally razor-sharp eyeliner was almost inscrutable through dark rings of exhaustion. The layer of ivory foundation that usu-ally smoothed out the man's clean-shaven face had long since rubbed away, still visible as white spackle in his crow's feet and the lines across his forehead. Gray stubble shadowed Ricky's loose jawline and tattooed throat. He looked as if he'd been panhandling in the track jacket and baggy cam-ouflage shorts that hung rumpled on his hunched form.

"We only want what's ours," Pickaxe said, his arms folded.

"Right. I hear that," Bloody Leon said. "But as Duane made clear with your president, this ain't your territory. Both of our clubs agree. So, when you come riding out here and setting up shop, you need to show proper respect to the dominant club. It's how it's done."

"You think we give a shit about Pike Lake?" Pickaxe barked out a laugh. "Our rockers say Detroit, brother. You can have this hayseed bullshit. We're not supposed to be setting up a damn thing. The merchandise was only passing through. It's that sack of smashed assholes," he said, pointing at Ricky, "that sent this thing down the shitter. And now someone's gotta pay for it."

"Now, we all agree that this could have been handled better," Dan said. "But there have been external players that need to be accounted for."

"You got that right," Pickaxe said. "Viking's in jail because of this fuckery."

"Yeah, well, my nephew Jesse is dead. That's Duane's kid, by the way." Leon added, "And my son's girlfriend got dropped too."

"Gonna have to chalk that up to Not My Problem," Pickaxe said. "Money or merch. That's all I'm here to talk about. The rest ain't my concern, friend."

"Afraid it kind of is," Dan said. "Now, before you go on some hell-on-wheels rampage about it, why don't we let Ricky explain what happened for everyone who might not have been in class lately." Dan looked over his shoulder. "Ricky?"

"So, yeah, it's like this. Viking Dave, you know, he tells me he got a line on that molly and some H from your Canadian people, right? Says maybe I should mention it to Dan, if he wants a little bit, for the events on the property." He sounded as if he had a terrible cold. "But thing is, I know this guy in Chicago who's looking for some weight, because his connect with some Chinese just got taken down by the feds. You might've heard about it. Right before the summer festivals, too. I know Dan doesn't need my help, but I figured I could handle a little something myself."

"Mistake," Shane muttered.

"So, just for this run, I'd take it on down to Chicago myself. It's my thing. At least it was supposed to be. But then I got a call, you see? I got a call to be on this show, a reality show. In L.A."

"What show?" The blond Knight of Satan asked.

"*Tattoo Kings*," Ricky said.

"Shit, really?" Blondie grinned. "That's awesome, bro."

"That reality TV stuff is garbage," the bearded giant said. "I don't know why anyone would watch that when there are so many better shows on."

"Whatever, man. Last season was pretty good," the blond replied.

"Kill the banter," Pickaxe snapped.

Ricky cleared his throat. "Well, anyway, I didn't want to pass it up. But promises were made, and I'd heard from my shop girl, Sam, that her friend was driving down there to see BlocksFest. Good cover, right? So, I made a little transpo deal with the girl. Bree. I put it in her car. In the doors, floorboards. I did it up solid. Give her the connect's info, let him know what's going to go down. She'll roll down with her friends, check them into a hotel like rock stars. The Hard Rock, right on the Loop, then roll by the sale point and unload it. Then back at the fest. Everybody wins."

He wasn't mentioning Sam's cam-ring accounts. Russell wondered if he was trying to protect her or just trying to keep the info from Dan.

"Hold on." Wink scratched his jaw. "You sent a seventeen-year-old girl from Pike Lake to deliver a carload of drugs to a dealer in Chicago?"

"Hey, I know these guys," Ricky said. "They're straight."

"Your shopgirl never sent the cash," Pickaxe said. "You said she'd transfer it through the accounts."

"You were using the shop accounts for this?" Dan snapped.

"No, no, Dan." Ricky kneaded his hands. "Sam, she's like a computer whiz. She has her own thing going on. I wouldn't involve the shop."

"Unless, of course," Pickaxe said, "you count the collateral."

Dan took a deep breath through his nose and out through his mouth before asking, "Say what, now?"

"Your brother put up the shop as collateral on the merchandise," Pickaxe said.

"Tell me this man is mistaken." Dan turned and stepped toward his brother, ever so slightly, as he stared him down. "You did not do that."

"It was just a one-time thing, Dan, just to get me started—"

"This is what I get for having your back? For setting you up with a place and a job? What the fuck, Ricky?" Dan sputtered. "You're lucky Dad isn't around anymore. You know what he would do to you? You have any idea?"

Ricky shrugged and looked down at the floor. "I wanted to do my own deal."

"It's my shop, and you're on parole, you dumb motherfucker." Dan whitened with rage as he slowly turned back to the Knights of Satan bikers. "The studio was not my brother's to promise."

"That don't change the fact that promises were made," Pickaxe said.

"Someone killed the girl," Shane said. "The one that was supposed to make the delivery. After she was at your club, Dan."

"Looks like it," Dan said. "And, I might add, her car goes poof."

"And my goods, too," Ricky said.

"Fuck your 'goods,' you half-assed wanna-be," Russell snarled.

"Take it easy, boy," Leon said. "Someone took a lot of interest in her at the club that night, Dan."

"Well, she was a very interesting girl," Dan replied.

"Brad Stoltz," Ricky said. "It was him, right?"

A chill rippled down Russell's spine. "That cop's son, right."

Leon put his hands on his hips. "Ricky. What made you say that?"

"She texted me. Said that he was there being all creepy, trying to score, and—"

"Wait." Dan held up a finger. "You knew there was an underage girl in my club, and you didn't tell me?"

"I was in L.A., dude. And I didn't even see the texts until the next morning, besides."

"Y'all can have a family dispute on your own time," Leon said. "What did she say?"

"Was just one message. Said there was a cop's son there trying to score some candy."

"Did she meet him after?" Russell asked.

"Dude, I don't know." Ricky sighed. "That's the last I heard from her. I thought she took off with the drugs. That she and my shopgirl burned me. Or she got snatched up by the pigs. That's what I thought right up to when I heard Bree was dead." He glanced over at Russell and then back away. "I'm sorry. You gotta believe I never meant for it to go like that."

"Fuck you, Ricky." Russ spat.

"Signs point to yes on her meeting with Brad Stoltz, then," Leon said.

"How you know it wasn't a burn?" Pickaxe asked. "We've been wanting to have a talk with that shopgirl, till Duane and our prez put things on hold, pending this here sit-down."

"Because I know exactly where the drugs are, and there is only one way you're gonna get that bit of information out of me," Leon said. "You need to help set right what your bad business has cost my family. We never had shit to do with it. Not till you brought it here. We lost people because of it. And I want to make sure those debts are paid, so I need some answers direct from the horse's mouth before I'm telling you guys shit."

"I'm listening," Pickaxe said, "but don't go testing my patience."

"I want Brad Stoltz, wrapped up with a fucking bow on him," Leon said. "He's out in Mount Pleasant, going to college. Summer session. Do that, and the goods that started this mess are back in the picture—how y'guys want to settle that, well, that's on you, you know?"

"You're asking us to kidnap a law-enforcement officer's son and deliver him to a criminal gang?" Dan whistled. "And I imagine he's going to have a bad time with you folks."

"Looks like he tossed my son's girlfriend off a bridge. Might have set up my nephew, too." Leon shrugged. "Take it or leave it."

Pickaxe turned away to mutter with his companions, revealing the sword-wielding devil patch on his back. When he faced back again, he said, "It's not like we're going after a federal judge or some shit. We're in if the Hornweens are."

"Goddamn it." Dan rubbed his goatee. "I'll take Leon at his word. McCreech's are assholes, but they're not liars. Fine, we're in."

"Nice." Leon lit a cigarette, took a drag, and exhaled. "See what folks can accomplish if they work together?"

"Yeah, it's all real inspiring." Dan sighed. "Let's get this shit in motion. We got work to do. I'm not just dropping the cop's kid off, though. I'm seeing this through. In for a nickel and all that."

Leon reached over and clasped Russell's shoulder, and though it struck him like a thunderbolt that burned the flesh from his bones, he did not shrink from his father's grasp.

The staccato snapping of Meghan's last combo into the heavy bag—jab, jab, hook, straight—echoed across the empty room in the county recreation center. When she spotted the uniformed man watching her from the doorway, she lowered her gloves and called out to him.

"Sheriff?"

"Thought I'd find you here." Dale Cunningham gave her a wave and stepped into the room. As he walked between two rolled-up tumbling mats, he said, "Looking good. You're fast, and clean, too."

"Thanks. My dad taught me," she said. "We had a bag in the garage and a lot of his old gear."

"Part of him wanted a boy, eh?"

"I think he wanted a girl who could throw a punch, that's all." She sat down beside her gym bag on a bench. After pulling free a glove's knot with her teeth, she unlaced it with the other's thumb. "What brings you out here, sir?"

"I want you to know that you did a great job in the early phases of this investigation," the sheriff said. "We all think so."

"Thank you, sir. I look forward to assisting in any way I can."

"Well." Cunningham's knees cracked as he sat down on the bench's opposite end. "I appreciate your enthusiasm, but let's face it. You've been through a lot lately."

"I'm sorry, sir?" She put her gloves in the duffel.

"First on the scene at the McCreech homicide. The injury you sustained apprehending the suspect at Ricky Hornween's place the other night. Identifying the Wells girl and being the liaison with her mother." He tsked once and looked at her pityingly. "I'm sure it's been a heckuva strain."

"It's part of the job, sir." Meg began unwrapping her right hand.

"Not usually part of it out here in Pike Lake. It can hit you hard when you're not ready for it."

"I've seen plenty of bodies." As she spoke, she rolled both hand-wraps into tight cylinders. "And more than that."

"Well, I imagine that's the sort of thing that can stay with you, too." He cleared his throat. "Regardless, I think you should take some time."

"Time, sir?" She took a breath. "Are you suspending me?"

"No, no." He chuckled. "Medical leave."

"I'm sorry? For this?" She pointed at her eye. "I'm not concussed, and it's not affecting my vision."

"Sure, sure. But Meg. You're clearly exhausted. How many hours have you logged in the past week?"

"Deputies aren't eligible for overtime, sir."

"But all staff are required to log hours."

"Right." She rolled a shoulder. "Is anyone processing the logs?"

"Doing what now?"

"The logs." She laced her fingers and cracked their knuckles. "Could you tell me where these logs are supposed to be submitted and who is their custodian? Because I've never seen or heard of salaried deputies logging hours in all my years on the job. Now, I have case notes, and I've—"

"You need rest, Meg." He raised an eyebrow. "We both know what I'm talking about."

"I'm not sure we do, sir."

"It's a few things. First of all, I hear you got a bit rough with some of the staff at the club out on Deerfield Road."

"You're putting me on leave on the recommendation of Dan Hornween?" She zipped the duffel with a sharp yank.

"No, Meg. But they have the security footage, and it doesn't look good."

"I think plenty of worse things than a scuffle with some bouncers have gone on at that club, sir. You know about the victim's presence there the night she disappeared."

"We do. Now, there's also the matter of you going around interviewing people who have never been considered persons of interest—"

"Sir? You interview to identify persons of interest. Not the other way around."

"Let me finish, Deputy. You're stirring people up and muddying the waters. Did you call a reality TV show in L.A. asking about Ricky Hornween?"

"I was only attempting to verify his whereabouts."

"Well, it's also contacting the media. More immediately, though, we can't have you riding around to every town in the county, showing up on people's doors or at their workplaces, accusing them of this and that. This is a delicate thing."

"I'm not accusing. I'm investigating."

"I don't know how else to tell you this. It's not your investigation. You're on leave." He raised a hand before she could protest. "I hear about you visiting anyone else on this case, or dredging up old high school gossip, or any of that, and we'll have to take this to another level. For now, get some rest. We will be in touch. Understand?"

"Oh, I understand exactly what this is." She stood and threw the bag's strap over her shoulder. "You're better than this, sir."

He called after her as she shoved through the metal gym door and out into the hall, but her ears rang, and all of her shook. She didn't break pace when she nearly collided with a group of children carrying plastic cones and soccer balls on the sidewalk as she half-ran to her truck, her sweat chilling in the breeze. She slammed the truck door behind her, hyperventilating, squeezing the wheel until her knuckles turned white.

Finally, when she had calmed, she called her sister.

"Myra, remember when you said to call you if I ever felt like I might do something I'll regret? Well, that's what I'm doing right now..."

Within the hour, Meghan was home, showered, changed, and sitting on the couch in her living room as her sister poured two cups of jasmine iced tea in the kitchenette. Mr. Purrs sat in the corner, noisily grooming his hindquarters.

"You should have seen how scared Connor looked, sis.

And I don't think it was of me, or of the law. I think he's scared of crossing these guys. They obviously have some reach, at least around here. Stoltz and McGuiness were able to knock me out of play pretty quick."

"So, what now?" Myra set both glasses on the coffee table and sat down beside her. "Take it to a journalist?"

"Wouldn't matter much now. We have plenty of dirt but no real evidence. I want convictions, not scandals." Meg flexed her bare toes against the carpet. "I think Ryan still has my back. Don't know about the rest of the state boys, though. Still, it has the makings of a corruption case. Problem is, there's not a ton of cash involved, and that's what makes for good cases."

"How about murder and rape? Doesn't that count?"

"Maybe if it happened to—I don't know—a different kind of people."

"Jesus." Myra looked over at her sister. "You actually think so?"

"Sure. You ever watch those true-life detective shows? *Crime Science Files* and all that?"

"I think that show went off the air fifteen years ago, Meg. They're all podcasts now."

"Whatever, you know the type. You notice how it's always some saint who gets killed at the start—some smiling, fit young wife or high school honor student who plays the cello and teaches pottery classes to handicapped kids?"

"I always thought they picked those cases because they had more dramatic effect."

"Maybe. But they're also the cases that get intensive investigations. You want good police work on your behalf, well, you better look like a good girl. Or even a good guy. Bree Wells, Jesse McCreech—they're not the right kind of victims. No outcry, no outrage. So, that means—"

Meg stopped mid-sentence, then raised a finger to silence her sister before pointing to the front door. Meg stood up and crept to the kitchenette, where she pulled her pistol from the holster on the countertop. The creak of a footfall shifted on the front porch. Myra's eyes widened. Meg gestured for her sister to retreat into the bathroom. A shadow darkened the peephole, then moved away. Meg crouched, making her way to the door, her weapon at low-ready. She took a breath, stood to the side, and threw open the door.

There, standing on the porch, was Samantha Black. Dark mascara tears ran down her face. Meg slid the pistol into the back of her waistband to hide it from the girl. The teenager quaked from head to toe and clutched her hands in front of her.

"Samantha. Come on inside, sweetie." Meg reached out, took her by the arm, and led her inside. "My sister's here. You know Myra—Ms. Shaw, from school?"

Sam sniffled and nodded. As she walked in, she sobbed out, "I'm so sorry, I didn't know where to go. It's all my fault—and I'm so scared, and it's all my fault. I don't know what to do."

"Don't be scared, Sam." Myra stepped from the bathroom doorway. "You're safe here. And it's not your fault."

"It *is*, though," Sam croaked out. "It was all my idea, get it? *All my idea…*"

CHAPTER 11

Dan Hornween stood over a crooked desk in the dead factory's office, and Russell was struck by how focused, how absorbed in his work he seemed, like a zombie businessman oblivious to the fact that he was dead and all of civilization had collapsed years ago. Stroking his goatee, he scanned a tablet screen propped up in its smooth leather case, displaying credit data, criminal records, and DMV info in overlapping windows. Broken chairs were strewn about the room, and burned-out light fixtures dangled from the ceiling. Moldy papers and damp leaves covered the floor, and the night wind whistled through a bathtub-sized hole in the ceiling.

Dan switched on a battery-powered lantern, moved it slightly to his left, and then placed an open wallet beside it. Bugs swarmed the sallow light. Like a fortune-teller laying out a tarot spread, he arranged the wallet's contents in neat rows.

The lantern illuminated the shapes of Pickaxe and Bloody Leon, who stood nearby. Russell watched his father slouch in the corner and smoke, his cigarette ember's flare setting his face aglow. Pickaxe peered over Dan's shoulder at the screen and the wallet's contents.

"Hovering," Dan sang out, annoyed.

"Deal with it," Pickaxe growled.

"This is our guy, all right." Dan scrolled through some of the data on the touchscreen with a long, thin finger, white rectangles reflecting in his sunglasses. "I see the charges at my club, and some other bars and party stores that night. Lots of bars and liquor stores in the days after, too. Also an ER visit a few days ago. This kid's a walking disaster."

"Who snatched him up?" Russell's voice sounded muffled inside his own head.

"I had Blondie from my crew work with one of yours," Pickaxe said. "Short, tough-looking dude. All beat to shit, though."

"Larry," Leon said. "Looking to get back in our good graces."

A door on the opposite end of the room groaned open. Finch shuffled in, moving around pillars and trash heaps. He seemed like a wraith; a crooked, thin shape among gloom, lugging what seemed to be a child-sized coffin. The red dot of his low-intensity flashlight drifted toward the makeshift workstation.

At last, Finch entered the pool of electric lantern-light in the corner, dressed in olive coveralls and carrying a massive red tool chest as if it weighed nothing at all. Eyes like damp, blue stones glinted from his half-melted face. The cross inked on his forehead seemed to glisten. Metal clanked on concrete when he set down the box. Russell noticed that Finch wore surgical gloves.

"He's ready." Finch's words were wet with spittle. "I'll handle the mechanics as usual, Mr. Hornween. But I don't know what to ask."

"I want to be there," Russell said, his stomach flipping

once. "I want to ask the questions."

Dan's head swiveled, and he trained his dark lenses on the boy. "I'm not sure that you do, kid."

"If my son says that's what he wants," Leon said, "then that's what he wants. He's earned it."

"Fine," Dan said. "Thought I'd save the boy from some nightmares."

"Get yourself your own kid," Leon said.

"Well, I want to hear what this bastard has to say, too," Pickaxe said. "It'll be a crowded show. Let's get this thing started."

Dan gave a small nod to Finch, who slobbered, "Masks and gloves," as he opened the chest. The lid faced Russell. He could not see what it held inside, but Pickaxe gave a low whistle and said, "That'll do it."

The scarred man pulled a box of latex gloves from the container and passed it around. They all snapped on a pair. They felt dry and constricting on Russell's hands, like a dead man's skin over his own, held in place by rubber bands around the wrists.

Finch handed each person an elastic, fabric mask. Dan tucked his sunglasses into his breast pocket.

"They're all the same," Finch waved his claw around the circle. "Put 'em on now. Don't take 'em off. He's been bagged since we grabbed him. He sees a face, that means he dies, got it? Hornweens leave no witnesses. And lose your vests."

"Fuck that," Pickaxe said. "I don't hide my colors."

"Wearing a mask doesn't have much of a point if you're wearing a vest with your name, organization, and location on it, friend," Dan said. "So do it, or don't, but you're not walking in there wearing it."

"Just turn it inside out, okay?" Leon said as he pulled off

and reversed his own. "There's no one here to rep for."

As Pickaxe removed his cut, he glared around at the others and said, "You better never tell anyone about this."

They bowed their heads and masked themselves. The skin-tight fabric clung to Russell's face like an alien parasite. He adjusted the eyeholes and looked around. Each man wore the yellowed face of a cartoonish scarecrow with a wide, stitched smile.

Dan did a little jig and sang, *"If we only had some brains…"*

"Cute. Where is he?" Leon asked.

Dan plucked up the electric lantern as Finch closed and latched the chest.

"Follow me." Dan's voice echoed as he stalked away. *"Follow, follow, follow the yellow brick road…"*

Russell stayed close to his dad as they trailed the swaying lantern through a back corridor and down a set of fire stairs until they came to what once had been a locker room. Patches of mold and water stains ran from floor to ceiling on the cement block walls, giving the impression of giant, greenish faces in the lantern's passing light. Their feet slapped through the puddles covering the broken tiles. The tang of urine seeped through the damp reek of decay as the masked men approached the shower room. Russell heard muffled gasps coming from the black shadows, quickening as the men walked among the rusting stalls.

It was apparent Brad Stoltz was bound and hooded, but not immediately evident how badly he had been hurt. Staring through the mask's eyeholes, Russell felt washed out at the sight of the man, as if part of his mind had shut down. He felt immaterial. The sound of water dripping, and the dank stink, made it feel as if he'd drifted into a cavernous tomb.

Finch yanked off the captive's black hood. Brad's eyes bulged as he shrank from Dan's light, their whites startlingly bright among the dark blood crusted over his face. Drool ran out from beneath the gag, and his breath shuddered wetly through his shattered nose. He sat on a large plastic sheet in the middle of the shower room, hunched forward with his knees against his chest. Finch had zip-tied the young man's wrists behind his back. Another tie held his ankles. Brad Stoltz was a broad, powerfully built guy but, broken as he was, he exuded no strength.

One of his bare feet had been broken, the left one. It swelled up from the ankle to the toes like a purple balloon. Brad's right hand was broken as well, the fingers hanging at odd, dead angles. A filthy bandage hung from it. Russell saw the cold logic of the initial crippling. Even if the captive escaped his bonds, he would not be able to fight or run— not in any way that mattered. Finch dropped the tool chest next to Brad, and it boomed like thunder through the dark- ness. The captive wept piteously, squalling through his gag, and Russell suddenly wanted nothing more than for all of this to stop.

Finch, placing a finger to his scarecrow mask's lips, stooped over Brad and removed the gag. Brad gurgled out a sob. Russell became aware of the three identical blank, smiling masks looming around the gasping captive, looking at Russell as if expectant. It took him a moment to remem- ber that he was a scarecrow too.

He felt a heavy, reassuring hand on his back, and looked over his shoulder to see his scarecrow-father towering over him. It nodded and said with Leon's voice, "Ask what you want to know."

Russell stepped forward, feeling like a spook house

animatronic drifting toward the crippled man.

"You were at the club a couple weeks ago. Lil' Angels. You tell me everything that happened that night. If I think you're lying, we will hurt you."

"Don't hurt me anymore." Brad's voice trembled. "Please."

"If you lie, we will hurt you until I believe you again."

"Okay," he said, nodding, then, "Okay, okay, okay, okay…"

"I'm listening," Russell said, cupping a hand to the side of his head.

"We were already drunk when we got there. It was the end of the night. We heard a girl from our high school was going to be there, on stage, it was supposed to be a surprise. For Connor. Connor Ferguson."

"Her name?"

"Crystal." He coughed and spat out some blood. "Crystal Lewis. She started doing porno stuff after she dropped out. We wanted—"

"We know what you and Sean did to her, Brad."

"It was ninth grade, for God's sake. I was fifteen." He sniffled. "Is that what this is about? Are you insane?"

Finch kicked Brad's broken foot, and his scream tore at something in Russell's head.

"You don't ask questions," Finch said. "You answer them."

"I'm sorry," he cried. "I'm sorry, I'm sorry…"

For a second, Russell forgot why this was happening. He felt dizzy, things whirled around him. He saw Dan leaning forward, speaking to the bound, bloody man, but Russell couldn't make out what he was saying.

Then Brad was talking again, saying, "She said she'd meet me on the logging trail. Sell me some capsules. She was all flirty about it. I just went there to buy pills—that's all I did, I just bought some pills—"

"*Liar,*" Russ screamed. "You lying sack of shit!"

"Get started," Dan said to Finch.

A small flat-bladed screwdriver appeared in Finch's hand. He knelt behind Brad and, in a swift motion, used it to peel off the captive's index fingernail. Brad wailed.

"It was an accident." Brad's sobs broke like waves from the depths of his chest. "You have to believe me."

"There, there," Dan reached out and patted Brad's head with a gloved hand, his mouth working behind the mask's frozen smile. "Settle down, Bradley. You want to go home? To see your dad?"

"I want to go home," he cried. "I want to see my dad."

"Well, then." Dan pointed to Russell. "Tell the little one what happened."

"I don't know." Brad rocked back and forth. "I don't know. I don't know…"

"Yes. You do," Leon said.

"Don't let them hurt me." Brad, snot running from his nose, looked over to Dan, then to Pickaxe. "You can stop this."

"Oh, damn, kid," Dan said, pointing at his own mask. "Can't you see we're all the same?"

Russ shuddered. Months ago, Bree had looked so small with that guitar in her lap, a bony girl in a frayed T-shirt and pajama pants with her fingers nimble on the fretboard. G, C, D. Swaying with her eyes closed on an unmade bed. Such a beautiful voice. Russell couldn't remember what she sang, only how it felt.

Finch flipped the metal chest's latches. The lid screeched as he opened it. He stooped over, tools clattering as he rummaged, ignoring the captive's pleas. Finch stood, holding a cordless circular saw, its teeth flashing in the light as he turned to face the bound young man. The blade whirred to shrieking life.

Russell lunged, grabbing Brad by the shirt, screaming in his face, "*Last chance, you son of a bitch. What happened to her?*"

The saw wound down, and Brad was howling, "I'll tell you everything, everything, everything…"

Leon strolled over, his boot heels clacking on the tiles until he crossed onto the plastic tarp. He took Russell by the arm, stood him up, and led him away a few steps. The boy's legs felt weak, and his heart hammered in a single, aching drone. He found himself part of the ring standing around Brad, who quaked and bled and hyperventilated beneath them. Leon cupped a hand to the side of his head and said, "We're listening."

"We were parked on the old logging trail. Standing outside, between the cars. It was very dark, but the moon. The moon." He sniffled. "She said it made everything blue and silver, and I said she was beautiful. She gave me the capsules when I showed the cash. I knew I was paying too much. Way too much, but I was there for her, not the drugs. When we handed them off, I took her arm. I don't remember. I tried to kiss her, but she pulled back, said she had a boyfriend." His eyes swam in place, like a dog's when dreaming. "I couldn't let her go. I told her to come with me to see the lake house. Come out on the boat. Said we had money for her. Said we had everything. I don't remember. Couldn't let her go. I was kissing her and we fell, we were on the ground, I was on top and then she was screaming. I thought they were good screams. Then I realized they weren't.

Everything was blue and silver, spinning. Like a giant drain. I couldn't stand up. And she wouldn't stop screaming." There was a hitch in his voice, he swallowed. "I put my hand over her mouth. And she bit me, she wouldn't let go, and I just wanted it to finish. When I could stand, she wouldn't wake up. The blood on my hand looked black. It was all over her chin and mouth. Dark. Shining. I pulled up my pants and then I was sick all over myself and fell down beside her. I told her I was sorry. I thought she was pretending. But she wouldn't wake up." He looked from blank mask to blank mask, his eyes unfocused and glistening. Tears streamed down his cheeks. "That's all I remember."

"What did you do then?" asked a soft voice. Russ realized that it was his own, emanating from beneath his mask.

"I called my dad. He brought me clean clothes, helped me change. He cleaned and bandaged my hand, made me drink a bottle of water. I threw most of it back up. He was very calm. Very sad." Brad shuddered. "He told me to go to the lake house, told me what to say. Told me to leave in the morning and never talk about what happened ever again. I asked, even to him? And he said yes, even to him. Only to God. So I went straight to the lake house, then left town the next morning. I don't know what happened to the car or the girl after that. He didn't do anything. He was just trying to take care of me. He's my dad." Brad began to sob again. "My mom's gone already. Please don't hurt my dad…"

Meghan was driving, deep in the woods, when she got the call from Ryan. The phone, set to speaker, bounced and shimmied on the dashboard as she rolled over the dirt road's potholes and navigated the meandering curves. Long morning light flashed and rolled through the treetops.

"You were right." His voice sounded scratchy and clipped. "We canvassed some mid-Michigan ERs and got a hit. Brad Stoltz came into one, just a few days ago. Guess his injury."

"His hand, right?"

"A bite, a deep nasty one. Infected. At first, I thought maybe the dog from Mike's. But timeline isn't right. It was infected as hell. It's written up as 'possibly human.'"

"That's a hell of a good lead, Ryan." She grinned, despite herself.

"There's more. Guess what we found in the victim's autopsy."

"I'm on my way to talk to some people involved in the case. I don't have time to guess."

"Her nails were cleaned out pretty good, but there's human tissue in her mouth and throat. It's not a large sample, but I think enough to get a DNA match."

Meg's heart skipped as she said, "Snatch him up. Ryan, you hear me, *today*. Get a sample. Hold Brad Stoltz until you get a warrant if he refuses—"

"We tried. He's gone."

She struck the steering wheel. "What do you mean, gone?"

"I mean he didn't come home from a bar last night. O'Kelly's. He was supposed to be on the way to hook up with a girl after, but he never showed up. His car is still outside. His frat brothers haven't seen him, either."

"Did word get to him? Do we have a leak?" She cursed. "Tell me he's not on the run."

"Troopers are hunting for him. It's not a big city, but we don't have a lot of people on this. I'm going to be knocking on doors there myself. Who are you meeting with?"

"It's a long shot, don't even worry about it. Keep me

informed, and I'll do the same."

At the black-boned skeleton of a cabin that had burned long ago, she pulled to the roadside. Her revolver was hip-holstered under a loose-fitting, light flannel, and a knife was sheathed in her combat boot. Being out of uniform made her feel less protected but more dangerous. She had the grim thought that this was how it felt to be a criminal. When she stepped out of the truck and approached the weed-choked ruin, a redheaded older woman rounded the brick chimney's remains. Meghan raised her hand in greeting and called out, "Jolene?"

The woman gave a nod. She'd been hit for possession or DUIs once or twice but had settled down a bit recently since she'd had a kid. Waitressed at the Chinese place, had a little girl. Meghan scanned the trees and listened to the hushed roar of the woods before asking, "You alone?"

"For now. But Mike's out there. And some of his people, maybe."

"Mike Morgan? Samantha Black said you could put me in touch with him." Meghan squared off, about fifteen feet from Jolene. "I'd like to know what he saw the night Jesse McCreech was killed."

"You think he did it."

"No, ma'am. I don't know who killed Jesse," Meghan said. "But Sam tells me that you say that Mike does. It's pretty clear he was there."

"You here as a cop? You're not in uniform."

The question tripped Meg up. "Someone killed a girl. And then someone killed Jesse. If I can set that right as a cop, I will. If not, I guess I'll have to handle it some other way."

"Oh, I think it's being handled." Jolene gave a cold smile. "You're from around here, right? You know how it works."

"Yes, I do. But the law's the law. I like to make work for people if I can."

"They say you're one of the good ones. Went a bit hard on Rodney Bunker last year, though. Beat him like a rented mule."

"No worse than he beat his wife and those kids. I shouldn't have done it, but he had it coming. I'm fair. My reputation backs it up."

"That's what I hear. But what's a reputation? Nothing but how deep you bury your shit."

"When can I talk with Mike?"

"Now, if you want." She hitched a thumb up the wooded hill. "Walk on up there."

"How will I find him?"

"Oh." Jolene laughed. "Don't you worry. He'll find you."

"You're not setting me up, are you? I'm playing this straight with you."

"If they wanted to drop you, you're standing out in the open right now." Jolene sat down on a boulder. "Go on."

Meghan stepped through the underbrush and made her way into the woods. The thick loam silenced her footfalls as she bent saplings and stepped over fallen branches. Sunlight dappled the ground in scattered patches, streaming through the muttering canopy overhead. A freight train's horn wailed in the distance, and a crow cawed overhead. She took even breaths, stepping carefully. From the corner of her vision, something glistened. She pivoted and found herself looking into the net of an orb weaver's spider web, droplets of condensation like diamonds backlit by the sun.

A gun's cold muzzle pressed against the back of her neck, and a craggy voice said, "Easy now. Don't move."

She froze, steeled herself, and lifted her hands. "Mike?

I'm here to talk. Remember me? Meghan Shaw. My sister is Myra. Our mom and dad used to buy firewood from you sometimes."

"Hold on. Gotta cover my bases, hon." He patted her down, pulling the revolver from the holster and the knife from her boot. She heard him swing the cylinder open and empty out the shells. "Now turn around. Slowly. Then sit down, Indian style."

She did. Mike stood over her in full camouflage, pointing a massive handgun that she assumed was configured to fire a rifle shell. His silver shaggy hair hung loose under a cap, and his face was a net of wrinkles and creases above a long white beard. He was well over six feet and thin as a rail.

"Single-shot?" She nodded at his pistol.

"It's a .243, and I don't miss." He handed back her Colt, the cylinder open, then kicked the knife over to her. "Don't do anything dumb with those while I'm here."

"I just want to know what happened to Jesse. And the girl."

"They're trying to pin it on me. Knew that's how it was going to shake out the minute it hit the fan." He looked at her skeptically. "You still with the department?"

"Officially, yes. But they put me on leave."

"For what?"

"Asking the wrong kind of questions. Crossing the wrong people."

"Yup. That's how it always goes. Shit never ends, does it?" He lowered the pistol but kept it at ready. "You want to talk. Let's talk. First off, Jesse was working for the narcs."

"What makes you say that?"

"It's true, right?"

"He was informing, yes." Meg folded her hands in her

laps. "He got busted for heroin and made a deal. I don't know how much he gave them, so don't ask. I'm only a deputy."

"How much you think, though?"

"Honestly, not much. He didn't have much to tell. Gave up a lab in Woodham, but as far as I know, not much else."

"Who else is ratting?" Mike's brow knitted.

"I told you. I'm not part of those operations. I'm sitting here disarmed and alone, out of uniform, being held at gunpoint in the woods."

"And so?"

"And so the sheriff obviously isn't keeping me close."

"You on the take?"

"Never."

"Ed Stoltz is dirty. Was dirty in Detroit, is dirty here. You know that, right?"

"Who owns him?"

"It's not like that out here." Mike Morgan swept an arm at the woods. "Stoltz works for Stoltz. And if he gets you for something, he might let you go—but you'll owe him. But you never really can get it paid off if you start playing with him. Ironwolfs always told him to fuck off. Jesse, well, he made a deal he couldn't get out of."

"Wait," Meghan said. "Did he kill the girl *for* Stoltz? To shut her up?"

"Don't think so. Dig this. Jesse came by my cabin the day before he got shot down, asking if he could buy a gun from me, a clean one. I said sure, but he didn't have the money on him. He told me to come by late night, like 3:30 a.m. I said sure, if he'd have the cash. And I brought him that shotgun. Private sale, by the way. All legit. Me and Vince, my dog, walked on down there. I brought him that double-barrel."

"That's a pretty early time to rise."

"I don't sleep at night much. Haven't for decades. You know?"

"I know it. Don't sleep so well at night myself."

"War?"

She nodded. "So, you brought down the shotgun. Were you carrying besides that?"

"No. I carry when I'm working and when things get hot. Rest of the time, I always have my dog, and I'm plenty good with a knife, even at this age. Learned from the best and had plenty of practice."

"Special Forces?"

"Life." He yawned. "Anyway. I get there, and Jesse's freaked out. He doesn't have the money, but he has a push mower. Like I need a mower. So I says he should put the thing back where he took it from. He's falling down drunk. Scared. I always felt bad for Jesse. He was never cut out for the sort of shit Duane, Leon, Shane, and all those boys were into. Part of me is worried that he's gonna use that shotgun to hold a place up or blow his brains out. So, after I drag that damn mower back onto the truck, I walk him into the house. I sit him down. And I says, what is going down, man? And he hands me the flyer, the one of the missing girl and her car. Leon's kid's girlfriend: Bree. And he says, 'They made me crush this car. I know it was her car.' And at first I think he means the McCreeches made him, but then he goes, 'Stoltz got me with some skag, and they'll send me up if I don't do what they say.' Which jibes with your story."

Mike Morgan hunkered down, keeping his pistol resting on his knee.

"You believed him?" she asked.

"Nobody admits being a narc unless they think they're

gonna end up dead anyhow. So Jesse tells me Stoltz gave him money and made him take the car out to McCreech Salvage to shred it. Jesse found a necklace in the seat, checking the thing for change. Then, a few days later, the posters came out. Jesse knew it was Bree's car. He had the necklace in the picture that's on the flyer. He was fucked. It looked like Jesse killed Russell's girlfriend, or covered it up, or whatever. He wanted me to help him. Honestly, I wasn't sure of any way out. In earlier days, I probably would have reached out, snapped Jesse's neck, and then tossed him down the basement stairs. End of story."

"Why didn't you?"

"He let me watch movies on his TV. Always did right by me. He's Duane's boy. And I've seen enough kids die. I thought I might be able to fix it, with a bit of thinking." He spat. "And then I heard Vince bark, over Jesse's dumbass dog, and a shot right after, and I was out the back with my blade."

"Not the shotgun?"

"Left that for Jesse. Figured I'd loop around, close on whoever it was, and take them down with the knife. When I rounded the house, I saw Stoltz kicking in the front door, and he and Jesse blasting it out."

"Hold on. You're *sure* it was Stoltz?"

"Oh, I know that mofo alright. I was closing on him with the knife. I wanted to make sure it was a clean kill. I thought he was heading inside, but he stumbled back to the car before I could get to him and tore away. Not sure if he saw me or not. I looked in on Jesse and, well, he was done for." He clucked his tongue once. "Found Vince on the porch. He took one in the gut. Carried him back to my place, tried to patch him up. He was a good boy. He didn't make it."

He could be trying to turn her against Ed—exploiting her suspicions. A good con knows the best way to get what he wants is to tell you what you want to hear. A few people had come together to lead her here. She could not be sure where else she was being led, or why.

"What was Russell doing out at your cabin?"

"Probably looking for his girl. Didn't recognize him till after I knocked his ass out."

"Why didn't you go to Leon, or anybody else in…" She hunted for the right words. "Your community."

"Because there are narcs out there, and I don't know who's working for who. I went into the woods and decided I'd take care of it on my own time."

"You willing to testify to all this?"

"Now," Mike Morgan said with a smile, "why would I go and do a thing like that?"

"Because I can close this case with your testimony. The state knows the sheriffs are dirty out here, Mike, and they've already settled on a suspect for Bree's murder. It's not Jesse, or Russ, or you. This isn't some Stanley County good-ol'-boy bullshit. It's the state, and it's for real. If you help, the prosecutors can get a conviction on Stoltz for this business with Jesse. We'll put him away. And it ends."

"Law has never been on my side—and excuse me if I think this sure as shit sounds like a case where I'll get a raw deal. Who will listen to me? They call me Crazy Mike. And the others? We're the bad guys."

"That's not true."

"You know it is. We're not the kind of folks who do well in court. And I know what I need to know. Ed Stoltz killed Jesse. And he killed my dog. And he aims to kill me." He stood up and holstered his pistol. "He's not going to get that opportunity."

"That won't end it," she said. "Right or wrong, the law will come back at you hard."

"That may well be." He reached up and touched his hat brim in a quick salute. "I'm going to walk away now. Good talking with you, ma'am."

"I can't let you assassinate a detective over this, Mike. Even a dirty one. Don't put me in the middle of you two."

"Don't put yourself there. Me and Stoltz, we'll both step over your body to settle this if it comes to that. Don't doubt it." As he turned away, he said over his shoulder, "Now gather up your gear, and get the hell out of my woods."

Russell slid his left hand deep into the neck-hole of the wolf mask, holding it steady under a magnifying lamp as his right hand glided the paintbrush over its sharp teeth. Aside from the lamp's glow at his workbench, his bedroom was submerged in darkness. Plastic fangs set in rubber gums, enlarged and bending beneath the lens, transfixed him. Sculpted by his own hand, the maw gained a further semblance of life with each brushstroke. He breathed deeply of the poisoned scents of enamel and turpentine as screeching throats and grinding instruments stormed from speakers lurking deep in the gloom.

A presence lumbered through his doorway. Without turning, he knew his brother by the smell of his oily boots and the murk of his sweat. Russell swiveled in his work stool, the brush poised in one hand, the wolf mask like a decapitated trophy in the other. Shane stood with his arm frozen mid-reach, poised to tap his younger brother on the shoulder. He gave an awkward smile as he withdrew it.

Russ did not return the expression.

"Could you turn this shit down a bit?" Shane hollered over the music.

Russ stared.

"Russ, I ain't joking. Shut it down or I smash the thing."

Russ swiveled back to the worktable. After cleaning his brush and placing it on a square of paper towel, then resting the mask on a stand, he plucked up his phone and remotely lowered the speakers' volume. Without turning back around he asked, "What do you need, Shane?"

"I don't *need* anything. I want to talk to you about what happened. Out at the old factory. I'm sorry I wasn't there. We needed someone to watch over Mom and Samantha, and someone to make sure the club and businesses were covered."

"Mom and Samantha are plenty tough."

"Yeah, well, Samantha's gone."

"I know where she's at."

"Great. Anyway, Dad told me what went down." Shane folded his arms. "You don't have to do this kind of shit. You know that, right?"

"I know." Russell stared at the comic book and horror movie posters covering the wall, the red tableaux of blood and blades, the monsters and mutilation, all of it seeming somehow more frightening in its unreality than ever before.

"Look, I know I give you a lot of shit. About your bicycle and your music and art stuff, and, like, I shouldn't. You should be yourself. You don't have to be like me."

"You think I want to be like you?" Russell loosed a chattering, cruel giggle that sounded like a voice not his own.

"I just mean—I'm not good at finding the right way to say shit, okay? All I'm saying is I've done some things that

I wish I hadn't. After Roy died, I went kinda crazy. We all did. Our family being how it is, it just seemed like good old hell-raising. Till I broke."

"That why you beat up that girl?"

"Trish?" Shane grunted, shrugged. "I only hit her once, because she was trying to pull me off of that other shithead. Harder than I needed to, I will say that."

"You didn't need to hit her at all."

"You're right. And I did my time and more for that." Shane rubbed the back of his neck. "Thing is, I don't know why I was stomping that man, neither. Thought it was because of him coming between me and Trish. But you know, Trish and me weren't even really a thing no more. And when I think about her, I don't feel a goddamn thing. I don't remember her voice. Hell, I might not recognize her if I passed her on the street. You know?"

"What you did, and what's going on now—they're not the same." Russell coughed. "At all. Someone murdered Bree and we know who. And whoever killed Jesse is still out there. Your shit was—"

"Crazy. That's what I'm saying. But it felt right. Crazy sneaks up on you. I thought it was what I had to do. Fuck if I know why. All I remember is getting locked up. All I got is a record. This business, with the club and the McCreeches and the Knights of Satan and all that—it's all I can do. That's what I got left."

"So?"

"You should leave it be."

"Why should I? No one handled what happened to Roy. Whoever hit his bike—"

"Was killed for it," Shane said.

Russell spun around on the stool, a cold lump in his

throat, his heart racing. "What?"

"Uncle Duane drove a four-ton tow truck at sixty miles an hour into a Chevy Lumina without even tapping the breaks. Crushed it flat with a man inside. Duane, who could hold his liquor as well as any man who ever lived and had been driving trucks since before we was even born. You think that was an accident?"

"How did we know it was the guy?"

"That dumb bastard hit Roy and drove off. Later, he took his damaged car to our shop to get it fixed. Had no idea what he'd stepped in. The family looked into it. Found out what we needed to. Dad wanted to handle it himself. But Uncle Duane, being the oldest, didn't want Dad to go away for it. So Duane got in his 'accident.'"

"Good," Russ said.

"You think so? He took the manslaughter charge, got ten years. Duane's own son was killed while Duane sat inside. And our club lost its leader, pretty much. Dad had to work twice as hard to keep it all running, and we never see him no more. And do you feel better knowing that some man who never meant to kill nobody, that we never knew, got smashed into pulp for killing Roy? For an accident?"

After a long moment, Russell said, "I don't know how I feel about it."

"I don't think Roy would have wanted that. And well, it never did much for me. I still went on the warpath. Doing bad things, seeing bad things—it gets inside of you. You never asked for any of this. You saw Jesse die. And Larry get stomped. And you shouldn't have been at that factory. It ain't right. You already seen too much."

Russell remembered Jesse's head, dead-eyed, lolling over like a puppet's. The crack of fists and boot heels. Brad Stoltz's wailing pleas as he trembled in the moldering shower room. He could not picture Bree, but he remembered the smell of her hair, like autumn leaves and strawberry ice cream, and then his mind drifted to the reek of piss, shit, and blood of wounded and dying men.

Russell said, "You get used to it."

"Oh, I know it. Spend a few years inside. You'll meet folks that ain't nothing but animals or dead men walking around, too mad or too stupid to lay down. I know you're dying inside about what happened to Bree. And Jesse. And Roy. But if you don't move on, you're just gonna keep on dying. I don't know much, but I know this: Being dead inside, being an animal—it ain't no kind of life. Not for you. Don't let Dad, or nobody, make you be something you don't want to be. It ain't right, putting the decision about what happens next on you."

Russell turned away. Before Shane could say anything more, Russ turned up the music to drown out his brother's words. He uncapped a bottle of scarlet paint, lifted the wolf's head from its stand, and returned to his work, keeping his head down until his brother's presence drifted away and he was alone again in the dark, with the music and his masks.

Rock radio ads hollered over the gas station's sound system as Meghan stepped around the spinner rack of cheap sunglasses, strode down an aisle of colorful two-liter pop bottles, took a turn at a display of sunblock and bug spray, and then pulled open a stand-up cooler's glass door. She leaned through the blast of cold air to pick up a forty-ouncer of malt liquor. It was cold and slick against her palm, golden under the fluorescent lights.

She glanced up into the security camera set into the corner. Its lens seemed to strip her down, leaving her guilty and exposed. She shivered, feeling the phantom pressure of Crazy Mike's pistol against her head again, as she had so many times in the hours since her encounter with him. She put the bottle back.

When she walked to counter, the clerk smiled. He was the usual night guy, Brian, an acne-spotted twenty-something who wore too much styling paste in his hair. He usually tucked his work polo into black cotton pants with a metal-studded belt and exuded the smell of sports deodorant and marijuana.

"Hey, Deputy Shaw, almost didn't recognize you without your uniform," he said. "Pump two?"

Thunder rumbled like distant ordnance detonating.

"Yup." She glanced up to see her pickup in the gray, glowing screen of the security monitor over his head. "You were working the night Jesse McCreech came in here with that lawnmower. You remember that night?"

"The night he got shot? Yes, ma'am." The register beeped as he poked its keypad. Lightning flashed, the glass door's panes blinked black-white-black. He lowered his voice and added, "I was working the night he came in with Bree's Honda, too. You think he did it?"

"Did what?"

"You know."

"Well, that's what we're trying to find out." She pulled out her wallet.

"I knew something was wrong the second I saw him driving that girl's car. I mean, I know Bree. She's kinda hard to miss. Anyway, she was always nice to me. We talked about TV shows now and then, back when she used to hang around outside the store." He added with a bit of pride, "Me and her were both watching *Supernatural* on Netflix."

"Why didn't you call in a tip?"

"I did," he said. "You know I always tell you what's up when I see you. But I didn't see you that night." He looked around and lowered his voice. "I called it in later."

Meg blinked. "To the tipline?"

"No, this was before those posters went up; that wasn't till after Jesse got shot. Might've been that same day, though. Her boyfriend came in the day before that, saying nobody had seen Bree for a few days. Asked if I had. I didn't say anything to him about Jesse with Bree's car, because, well, you know—I didn't want to get involved. McCreeches. But I had real bad dreams that night. Took it as a sign, maybe. So I called it in to the cops the next afternoon when I got up." He scratched at the pit of his chest. "Your gas is twenty thirty-eight."

"Hold on," she said. "When did you make that call? Who did you talk to?"

"I talked to a detective," he stammered. "Is something wrong? I mean, I figured it was the right thing to do. The detective came on by that afternoon and took the tape. Big older guy, never seen him on patrol. When you came later that night, I assumed it was because of the tape. So I told you I saw him in a truck with that mower. It wasn't because of the tape the detective got?"

It was Stoltz. Crazy Mike was right. "Have you told anyone else about this?"

"About tipping off the cops? You think I'm crazy?" He cleared his throat. "Yeah, no ma'am. Anyway. Your total is twenty thirty-eight."

As she handed him the money, her phone buzzed in her pocket. She almost jumped from the surprise of seeing who it was—Deputy Mark Williams.

"Stoltz got a tip that Mike Morgan is at his cabin," Mark said. "He made a call for backup, but I'm all the way out by White Brook, and he knows it. The other deputy is responding to an accident out on the highway. You said you wanted to know if I heard anything—"

"I'm at the Citgo, not too far from there." She hurried toward the door, her heart pounding, "Thanks, Mark."

Brian the clerk called after her, waving her few singles of change. She shouted over her shoulder for him to keep it. Outside, rain soaked through her clothes within a few steps after she shoved her way through the door.

"Be careful, Shaw," Mark said. "Ed's not going to be happy to have you responding. You're supposed to be on leave."

"Like it or not, I'm still a cop." She jogged across the parking lot to her truck, her boots splashing in the puddles on the asphalt. "See you there."

Her truck tore down the winding road, the trees rushing by, her pistol on the passenger seat beside her. Windshield wipers clacked and shrieked over the engine's steady growl. A cold single-mindedness settled on her, the way her training took over when she first came under fire in Iraq—the icy splash of panic rolling away and replaced by something immediate and ingrained. Her actions felt automated as she wove around the taillights that came flying toward her windshield like red eyes charging through the night, and she drove under the overpass without a single flutter in her chest.

She turned onto the winding two-track leading up through the hills, deep into the woods, to Mike Morgan's cabin. The truck bounded over the chuckholes and rocks, her seatbelt barely holding her in place. In the pouring rain, the road-way—if you could even consider it one—was turning into a brown riverbed.

If what Mike Morgan and the clerk told her was true, then Ed Stoltz had been covering up for his son all along. And Ed couldn't have Mike Morgan talking. There wasn't time to get the troopers out to the cabin. She had to get there first, somehow, and hope she could get the drop on Mike and bring him to the State Police. But who saw Mike at the cabin? Who called in the tip, and why? She had the sinking realization that this had the makings of an ambush—but who was being set up? Her or Ed?

She swerved around a chuckhole the size of a mortar crater, glimpsing the watery pit in the headlights as she passed. Then, the whole truck shuddered and dropped.

The front end swung wildly, and with the rending of metal, her wheels' bare rims ground into the dirt. The seat-belt yanked tight around her shoulder as she was thrown forward, her stomach floating, weightless for a sickening moment, the lights swinging into the sky as the truck rock-eted up on a roadside embankment and came crashing back down. She kept a grip on the wheel, trying to turn into the skid as the rear fishtailed and the axle snapped. The truck's sagging front end scraped across the ground, spraying stones and mud up onto the hood until it slammed into a tree and expired.

Wincing, she released the seatbelt before groping into the dark passenger footwell to retrieve her pistol. The door groaned as she pushed her way out. She clicked on her flash-light and looked down the road the way she had come, peering through the blinding rain, then swept it across her truck's wheels. The rubber of each was shredded—as if she had run over a set of tire spikes. If this was a setup, it was too late to back out now. Best not to linger too long in any one place.

She continued down the road, slogging through ankle-deep mire. Each step brought a bright twinge of pain in her shoulder, and her ribs were ablaze. At last, she saw Mike's cabin. A dull light glowed through the window's shrouds. Ed Stoltz's Buick LaCrosse, running dark, rolled up to the timber-beam gate.

Had he spiked the road behind him to keep others out? Or had someone else done it to keep him in?

Hunched in a rain poncho, he stepped from the Buick. In a flash of lightning, she saw the .45 in his hand. A blast of thunder drowned her voice as she shouted his name.

She flashed her light on him, but he didn't take notice as he ducked under the gate and hurried toward the cabin in a low crouch, his weapon at the ready. Meghan splashed across the yard after him as Ed took the front steps. He tore the web of yellow police tape crisscrossing the door into tattered streamers, then moved to force his way inside.

Before he could throw his shoulder into the door, she shouted his name, holding her ribs in one hand, her pistol in the other. Staggered by mud, she slipped just before the porch steps, scraping her palm against the rickety wooden stair, one knee slopping deep into the muck. She looked up to see that Ed had turned, startled.

His huge pistol was aimed at her face.

"Don't shoot," she cried, struggling to her feet. "I'm here to help."

"Stay back, Shaw."

Stoltz spun around to face the door, kicked it open, and charged inside. Beyond the splintered frame, she saw him pivot right, drop to one knee, and fire. She took porch steps in a single leap not a second later.

The peal of the gunshot still rang in the air when she crossed the threshold, sweeping the safety zones with her gun's sights before turning her aim to where Ed had fired. There, beyond the timber-frame sofa, in the darkened bathroom doorway, stood a tall, gray-bearded figure dressed in camouflage, the hood of his hunting jacket pulled up and dark glasses concealing his eyes. He stood stock-still with his empty hands by his side, a dark stain spreading from the wound in his chest. Stoltz stayed on one knee before him, his pistol still aimed. She reached out with her free hand and placed it gently on top of Stoltz's pistol, forcing him to lower it, while keeping her own by her side.

"Mike." She crept toward him, her hand raised for calm, "It's going to be okay. I'll get you to a hospital. Lay down on the floor."

But he did not move, only wavered jerkily back and forth. Why didn't the .45 knock him down? As she drew nearer, her confusion swelled. The beard was Mike Morgan's, but Morgan was tall, skinny; this man was broader. The wounded man made a muffled grunting sound. As she closed in from his left, she saw bindings around his hands and legs, fixing him in place. He'd been strapped, standing upright, onto a wheeled cargo dolly.

"It's not Mike, Ed. He's someone else. Someone tied up."

"What?"

She rushed over, yanked down the jacket's hood, and knocked away the sunglasses. Weeping terrified eyes looked into hers. The beard, she saw now, was false.

"It's okay," she said softly as the man wheezed. "We'll get you down from there and to a hospital."

"What do you mean?" Ed said, fear rising in his voice. He stood, his gun trembling in his hand. "Who is that?"

The captive's head drooped forward as she gently pulled the beard away, the sticky gum used to attach it leaving behind strands as it peeled free from his skin. The man was young, his face swollen from beatings.

"Oh, God," Ed said. "Oh my God."

A wave of revulsion hit her when she saw the black ball-gag filling the captive's mouth like an apple in a roasted pig. She reached behind his sweat-soaked head and unhooked its buckle, and it tumbled to the floor.

Brad Stoltz, tied up like a scarecrow in another man's clothes, lifted his head and looked past Meghan.

"Oh, oh, oh no, Jesus Christ." Ed ran to his son and pressed both hands against the flowing hole in the boy's chest. "You're going to be okay, son. Stay with me. Bradley, stay with me."

Brad's cracked lips drifted into a childlike smile of relief. A rivulet of blood trickled from his mouth.

"Dad?"

The gleam of life faded from his tear-damp eyes. A low groan flooded out from somewhere deep inside Ed Stoltz. A chill wormed its way through Meghan's bones as he wrapped his arms around the dead son who stood before them. Ed Stoltz buried his face in the boy's shoulder as blood drummed against the floorboards, streaming from between them.

CHAPTER 12

Russell sat on the roof of his family's house, the sun beating down on its black shingles and rising up again, and watched the police vehicles roll in: two sheriff's Broncos, two cruisers, and two state police trucks. He moved back toward the attic window and climbed inside.

After the incident at Mike Morgan's cabin, the cops were snatching up everybody they could get their hands on. He'd heard they knocked down the gates of the Hornween property with an armored personnel carrier borrowed from a neighboring county, which Dan had apparently foreseen, as it encountered a tangle of flatbed trucks laden with carnival rides barricading his driveway halfway up the hill. When it attempted to maneuver around, its front end tumbled into a ten-foot-deep trench hidden in the tall grass, where it would remain until a crane or perhaps another tank could be obtained to remove it.

Soon after, the Hornween crew—showered, shaven, and accompanied by their lawyers—walked into the State Police post to submit to questioning. Meanwhile, sheriffs and troopers raided the Ironwolfs clubhouse and Lil' Angels, closed down the Hobble Inn and Triple Felony Tattoos, suspended the license of the gun shop, and extended their occupation of McCreech Salvage to include Hornween's No-Question Self-Storage. Mike Morgan could not be found. Word had it that Crazy Mike, perhaps not so crazy, was no longer in Michigan or even America. The McCreech family—accompanied by their lawyer, Ted "Moose" Schneider, and his two "investigators," a disgraced MMA fighter and a convicted data thief—were taken into custody without incident.

Russell found himself in the back of Deputy Shaw's cruiser, just as he had been two weeks before on the morning that his cousin Jesse had been shot, but this time in handcuffs. It seemed so long ago. His car was third in the convoy, behind the one holding his mom and dad and the other holding Shane and Larry.

As they turned onto the main highway, he said to Deputy Meg, "Y'guys are gonna kill us all, ain't you?"

Through the cage, he saw her glance up in the rearview. "What makes you say that?"

"You killed Jesse."

"No, I didn't," she said flatly.

"Your people, then."

"Russell, I don't know what to say anymore." She leaned back, her hands firmly on the wheel. "I tried to help you. I had a case, a real case, and now this. You blew it up. Do you know how much harder this makes it? This isn't a threat, but it's going to get really bad. I expect the FBI is going to be looking into this."

"Stoltz ain't gonna have a good time with that, is he?"

"Russell, I know you might not understand how awful what happened is, but I was there. Whatever you think Brad did—"

"Aw, hell. If you don't know, I think you can guess."

"Whatever you think he did, what happened to him, and to Ed, was cold-blooded. Brad was kidnapped. Tortured. And then to make a man do that to his own child…" She trailed off as the convoy passed beneath the overpass, its shadow rolling over them. "It's sick."

"You tell that to Bree, or Jesse. Or their moms and dads. You tell them how sick what happened to him is. You think I don't get how bad what happened to the Stoltzes is? I do." Russell had affixed the beard to Brad's battered face and slid the sunglasses over the captive's tear-streaming eyes before they rolled him away on the dolly like a Halloween decoration. "I just don't care."

"Someday you will. It will stay with you. It's this you'll remember. Not Jesse. And not Bree."

"We don't got nothing to do with it, Deputy. Plenty of bad folks out here. And I'll tell you what I remember. I remember—" He searched for a moment but heard only the roll of the wheels on the road, the chatter on her radio, then said, "I remember seeing my cousin die in that chair, with that necklace in his hand. She was wearing it when she said the last thing she ever said to me. You know what that was?"

The deputy didn't answer.

"It was, 'I love you too.' Right before she drove away in that little purple car. And then I never saw her again."

The deputy brought the car to a halt as the convoy came to an intersection.

"It was the first time saying that, you know. For me, anyway." He pressed his face against the cage and strained his wrists against the cuffs until his arms ached. "Not just to her. To anybody. It just, I don't know, popped out there. Couldn't keep it in any longer." A shudder quaked through him. "Anyway. Yeah. Damn shame about Brad."

"This wasn't all about you and how you feel about it," she snapped. She was quiet for a moment before sighing out, "Stoltz is going to come after you."

"I'll be waiting."

"You make masks, Russell. You told me so. The disguise on Brad didn't come from a joke shop."

His heart galloped, but he steadied his voice, "You gonna come at me, then? And how you gonna do that without going after Stoltz? Whose side you on, anyway?"

"The victim's," she snapped. "And the law's."

"Law don't mean shit. Once you're a victim, it's already too late, ain't it? What can you do for a dead girl?"

"How about get justice for *her*? Instead, what are we left with? Nothing but revenge."

"Same thing."

"Oh. You're a child." She shook her head. "Do you even know the difference? Justice is for *everybody*. Revenge? That's something for *you*. Someday you might get that."

He collapsed back into his seat and remained silent all the way to the county jail.

Soon, she was back on the road. Meghan made a gentle turn onto Kickapoo Drive, passing a squadron of BMX bikes that clipped along in the opposite direction. The beaming kids waved to her cruiser, their bare legs pumping. She gave them a nod and a wave. Ed Stoltz's dark blue Buick sat in his open garage, and Meghan parked behind it.

Hedges that flanked the porch now sprawled shabby and wild. Mud and matted leaves lined the sidewalk where bright marigolds once bloomed. A country-craft welcome sign hung beside the door, and a tattered American flag waved listlessly on its pole. The curtains were drawn.

Though over twenty people had been brought in for questioning, she doubted any of them could be held for long—they were, each and every one, lawyered-up and not talking. They were prepared. She doubted Ed Stoltz would be, but he was a lawman, and he knew the game. Cunningham and the deputies would do their damnedest to protect one of their own, so the sooner she could get him away from the rest of them, the better. Ryan, along with two other units of State Police, was positioned just a couple streets over. She took a breath, rehearsing in her head how to bring him in—especially with his son still cooling in the morgue. It was such a nice day, too.

She rapped her knuckles on the storm door, the inner door hanging open to let in the breeze. Stoltz bellowed from inside, "Go away."

"Ed, it's Deputy Meghan Shaw. I'm afraid it's urgent."

There was no response. The kids on their bikes zipped past again, laughing brightly. In a neighboring yard, a radio called out a play-by-play of the Tigers game. The smoky aroma of an outdoor grill drifted on the breeze. After she called through the screen again, Ed hollered back, "Fine, fine, fine. Door's open."

She stepped into the entryway and looked into the living room, where newspapers and junk mail, case files and forms, mugshots and photo arrays, pizza boxes and beer cans, and God knows what else seemed to have fallen in an avalanche stretching from the couch to the opposite wall. A TV soundlessly played a soap opera to an empty rocking chair.

She called out to Ed again as she crept across the room. A three-photo frame sat atop the ancient television, the first showing his oldest daughter with her grinning husband and sleepy new baby, which Meghan guessed was taken about ten years ago. Another showed Ed and Gladys with stiff smiles, standing at Niagara Falls. The third, at center, was a senior photo of Brad—suit and tie, close-cut hair, a wide-shouldered and bullet-headed Michigan boy with a tough-guy smirk. The favorite son. The one who left his DNA behind in a dead girl's mouth and spent some of his last moments on earth propped up like a Hogan's Alley target in his father's sights.

A shelf displayed trophies for everything from Boy Scout pine-box derby races to golf meets to wrestling to football, a loving altar of achievement beneath a dusty square on the wall where a photo once hung.

"In here," Ed called from an adjacent room.

She found him in his shirtsleeves, sitting in the dining room, gazing down at the framed photo he held in his thick hands, his .45 resting beside a cocktail glass and a mostly drained fifth of Popov on the table.

"What you got there, Ed?"

"His varsity picture." He turned it to her, then laid it facedown on the table. "You know, he nearly quit. You know that, Shaw?" His voice was slurred by drink, his face red. "I never pulled strings to get him off the bench. He put his shoulder to the sled every afternoon, and dammit, when they made him a starter, he was a monster on the field."

And off of it, too. "I know you and Gladys loved him very much."

"He was our boy. I did my best. You know what it's like to lose a mother." He poured another drink, and Meghan kept her eye on his pistol. "I think, well, it took a toll on him. Maybe more than he let on. I know it did on me."

"I can't imagine the pain you're in right now, Ed. I truly can't. We won't stop trying to find who's responsible. What happened to him wasn't right."

He downed the vodka and licked his lips, then fixed Meghan with a watery, red-eyed stare. "You hated him."

"I didn't know him, Ed. But I know what he did, and I think you do too. I know that must be a terrible thing to carry, and I think it led you to make some terrible decisions."

"Oh, cut it out. Yeah, I'm drunk. Yeah, I'm sitting here trying to decide which dirtbag in this town I should turn this gun on first. I'm a mess. But I'm not stupid. I'm not spilling my guts to the first woman who walks in with a kind word for me. You got nothing, Shaw. Get out of my house."

"Listen to me, Ed. The state boys have this already. Brad had a bite on his hand. It got infected. There are ER records. They're matching the bite pattern to Bree Wells, and they found tissue in her mouth that will be matched to him too."

"Isn't it enough that he's dead? And how he died, what they made me—" He loosed a rough sigh. "My son got himself mixed up with a drug-dealing stripper who, word has it, was part of some online prostitution ring. And now you're going to drag his name through the mud? For what?"

"And then there's the matter of Jesse McCreech."

"Oh, what a tragedy, Jesse. That scumbag—"

"Was your CI, Ed. You sent him out to get rid of that car after Brad killed Bree Wells. We thought the blood on the porch had been contaminated with your DNA. Well, the blood that wasn't from the dog. It's your blood. I bet under that shirt, your left side is peppered with buckshot. Makes it real uncomfortable to wear a shoulder holster. That's why you stopped. Who patched you up?"

"Well, aren't you real police?" He laughed bitterly. "I

patched it up myself. Was an army medic. You were in the army, right?"

"The troopers have units positioned nearby, but nobody wants it to go like that. You, cuffed and led away, in front of the whole neighborhood. I figured you could come in with me, on your own accord, with respect. Stand up and step away from the weapon, Ed."

"Well, first of all, I don't know if I can stand up. But I'll tell you how it's going to go. I like you, Shaw. I actually do. So will you listen to me?"

"I'd be a better listener without that .45 on the table. Why don't you tell me about it in the car?"

"I didn't think to check if the girl's car was running on empty, you see. Didn't know that Jesse, the dumb hick, stopped at the gas station on his way to the scrapyard. He didn't say a thing about it when I picked him up afterward. When the call about the security tape came in, I went straight down to the Citgo and snatched it up."

She had him talking, just like he said he wouldn't. If that gave him the feeling that he was in control of the situation, she would see how long she could keep it going. But if his hand went for the gun...

"Who dumped her body?" she asked.

"It was not easy for me. None of this was, Shaw. She was already dead. Why ruin two lives—"

"Are you going to tell me about the body or not?"

"I wrapped it in plastic and put it in my trunk. Thought I'd be able to destroy the corpse, but I just didn't have it in me. You know what that involves. So I cleaned out the fingernails and sponged it down, but I couldn't decide where to bury it. I guess I just didn't want to deal with it anymore. It sat in my trunk for almost a week."

Meghan kept a neutral expression, even as a tingling chill crept down her back. How many times had she walked past Ed Stoltz's Buick, never knowing he had a dead girl in his trunk?

"Until you put it in the creek. Why the creek?"

"Figured the water would cover up anything I missed. But that wasn't my original plan. I was hoping people would think she up and ran off. But then it became clear I couldn't cover up the tape of Jesse with the girl's car. Too many people knew about it. It wouldn't be long before Jesse was brought in—and that would be the end of the runaway story. I couldn't have him talking. And then it became so obvious. I'd take him out and then put the body in his basement. Then, stash some item of hers in the house. I'd say I saw it when I came to investigate after viewing the tape, that he grabbed for a gun, and I took him out. But when I came to Jesse's house—"

"Crazy Mike's dog attacked you. You shot it, and then they both knew you were coming. And Jesse winged you before you could kill him."

"I didn't know how bad I was hit, but it hurt a lot. Never been shot before. I knew Mike Morgan had to be around. The dog was never far from him. Crazy Mike might kill me off right there. I panicked. Went home and patched up my wound as best I could. And then you walked in looking for the mower before I could return to the scene. Funny thing is, Jesse already had her necklace. I wouldn't have had to plant a damn thing other than the body. Just picked the wrong night. I dumped the body in Grass Creek a day later. Figured I could still pin it on Jesse and Mike, long as I could get Mike out of the picture too. Didn't want to look too eager at first, so made a show of pushing against connecting the two. I thought you would end up steering toward it. But you were just too goddamn smart. Weren't you, Shaw?"

"Thank you for telling me this. Let's head down to the state police post and make an official statement."

"I wanted you to have the whole story. You're a good cop." He lifted the glass of vodka to his lips and swallowed. "But I'm not going with you."

"Hold on now, Ed." She reached out, slowly, her fingers splayed wide, gesturing for calm. "I can call in the troopers if you need me to—"

"Here we are at high noon. And this is how it's going to go. I'm going to grab up that .45. And we're going to see who shoots first."

"You don't want that, Ed." Her whole body stilled as she spoke, her voice measured and warm. "You're not going to shoot me. I know you. You've had more things happen to you than most folks could deal with, and you lost your way. What you've been through, it will play well to a jury. Lost a wife. A son. But besides that, you're not a bad man—certainly not the kind who would look a woman and a fellow sheriff in the face and put a bullet in her. So come with me, okay?"

He bowed his head, breathing deeply, steadily.

"Every night while that body was in the trunk, I had dreams about that girl. Bree," he said. "Wandering through my house like a ghost, or her corpse sitting at my desk in my office, or worse. Sick things." He poured some vodka in the glass, then gazed at the bottle in his grip as he spoke. "After the night I dumped her in the creek, I stopped dreaming about her. But I had other nightmares. About scarecrows. Like the one I saw on Jesse's porch that night—you see that thing? I'd dream about armies of scarecrows coming to drag my son away, and in those dreams, there was nothing I could do to save him. Last night, I didn't dream about anything at all."

He looked up, sniffed, and then hurled the bottle at her head. She stepped back and dropped to one knee, her hand flying to her weapon as the bottle shattered against the wall, but the .45 was already in his grip. Before her gun could clear its holster, Ed Stoltz shoved his semiautomatic's barrel into his own mouth and fired.

CHAPTER 13

Meghan sat on the bed in her room at the Travelodge, watching a cable television reporter who could have passed as a runway model stand in front of the Stanley County courthouse. In a perky-serious tone, the reporter bantered with a host in a Los Angeles studio about "the chain of bloody events that have rocked this tight-knit Michigan community."

The details surrounding Brad's death had leaked to the media after Ed's suicide a week ago, and suddenly the mystery surrounding what happened to Bree became something worth reporting. No one had been charged, and journalists desperately constructed a story based on informed conjecture as best they could. The primary theory suggested that Ed and his son had colluded with Bree Wells, Jesse McCreech, and a ring of unknown drug traffickers to establish a line of heroin distribution running through rural Michigan as a waypoint between Detroit and Chicago. The fact that Brad was about to be charged in Bree's murder, and his dad was about to be arrested for Jesse McCreech's killing, gave it enough heft to seem credible. Everyone involved was tight-lipped, only adding to the mystery of the possible hidden players, who ranged from biker gangs to human traffickers to right-wing militias. But the main enigma was Mike Morgan, an elderly recluse who had vanished and some presumed dead.

At the end of the day, though, everyone thought Meghan Shaw knew more than she was letting on. For this reason, she was booked under a fake name in a cheap motel twenty miles outside the county line. The moment she was awakened by a camera crew from Channel 7 Action News pounding on her door, she knew she needed to get out of town. At least she was still officially on paid medical leave.

The cable news transitioned to covering America's latest mass shooting, this time at a waterpark in Wisconsin. She changed the channel, settling on a PBS nature documentary.

Crows, like humans, are social animals, the narrator said over a shot of black birds hopping around a barn's cupola.

On the nightstand, her phone buzzed a message notification. As she rose and made her way over to it, the TV narrator continued, *The bonds of family and friendship encourage togetherness, but they can also lead to conflict. Corvids do fight among themselves, and on occasion, these altercations turn deadly.*

She glanced down at her phone. It was Ryan, saying he would be at her door in a few minutes. Meg picked up her holstered weapon and clipped it to her belt. She wasn't afraid of her old friend, but better safe than sorry. There were still a lot of wildcards out there.

Protecting a mate or preserving sexual access to them, as well as the defense of territorial resources, can lead to intra-species violence, the TV droned.

She drew her pistol, chambered a shell, disengaged the safety, and re-holstered it.

Fights inside family units are relatively rare and tend to be short-lived. However, battles between opposing familial or social groups can be lengthy and are often fatal…

Someone knocked at the door. She glanced through the peephole and let Ryan inside. It was odd to see him out of uniform, dressed in a tight gray T-shirt, Levis, and a pair of Nikes.

"This place isn't as shabby as I expected. Can I sit down?"

She pointed to the room's one chair, and he eased into it.

"Reporters still camped out at my place?" She perched on the corner of the bed.

"They're still all over town, but it's thinning out a bit. That rampage in Wisconsin, you know."

"Right. First one at a waterpark." She picked up the remote and clicked off the television. "What's the latest with the case?"

"Nothing good." He turned up his hands. "No sign of the girl's car anywhere. Mike Morgan is as gone as gone can be. All the folks with direct motive to grab up Brad have solid alibis. And the bodies are in a closed-loop leading to other bodies. It's pretty clear who killed who."

"That doesn't mean we know why. Someone snatched Stoltz's son away and set the boy up to get shot."

"Well, with Stoltz and his son both up on murder charges, your office has dummied up and isn't too keen on looking into it. Honestly, whoever did a number on those two did the Stanley County sheriffs a huge favor—along with anyone connected to the Stoltzes. We're stuck."

"There's another way in."

She hadn't said anything about Russell, or his masks, in her statement. And Samantha Black had, when she weepily appeared on Meg's door, told her tales of sex cam rings and hidden accounts after being convinced Meg would keep it all confidential if, and only if, Sam could get Meg a meeting with Mike Morgan. She had hoped to keep the two teens out of it—but back then, she imagined someone could be charged without their testimony. Now it seemed like Russell and Sam might be the only avenue to finding out what happened. But it meant pulling those kids in and using everything they had told her against them. Ryan raised an eyebrow, waiting for her to continue.

"It's going to involve some of the younger suspects in a way that I hoped to avoid. But it starts with Ricky Hornween. Now, he was supposedly in Los Angeles—"

He raised his hand. "Let me stop you there."

She scoffed. "Could you hold your questions until the end, Inspector?"

"I think I know where this is going. You know about Ricky's status. I swear, I only found out yesterday."

Her stomach lurched, and he scrutinized her face.

"Quit fishing, Ryan. I don't do that to you. Say it or don't."

He raised his hands. "Years ago, Ricky Hornween got nailed on a lot more than that possession charge. It's all sealed, but word has it that it was pretty bad stuff. He made a deal. He did a short stretch inside and came out as a federal asset. Drug and online sex crime informer, placed deep. The thing with the show audition in LA was a cover story while he was held in protective custody. He set up an interstate drug buy between the Knights of Satan gang and some up-and-comers in Chicago."

She swallowed the lump in her throat and said, "You motherfuckers."

"State police didn't know, Meg. I swear, when you asked—"

"They let Ricky dupe Bree Wells into interstate drug trafficking? She's seventeen."

"No one could have seen that she would get killed, Meg. Brad Stoltz threw a wrench in the whole operation—"

"Threw a wrench? Brad raped and murdered her. When they were probably high on the drugs that the feds set her up with to sell. And what if she had gone through with it? They'd lock that poor girl up in prison for it? And Samantha? Was she going to get taken down too?"

Ryan looked down and said, "Samantha Black is probably running a prostitution ring. She covers her tracks. Neither we nor the feds can draw a line to connect her directly. The money from the drug sale would have gone through an account she handles back to Ricky, and that would have incriminated her. I know you're upset, but these aren't some innocent kids we're talking about."

"I think you should go."

"Ricky's still a federal asset. That's confidential. Feds want to keep him inside, see if there's some other way he can bring down a syndicate. If either of us goes to the press—"

"Get. Out."

He opened his mouth to say something but stopped when she walked over to the door and stood by it. He sighed and rose to his feet.

"I don't like some of the things we have to do, Meg. And this is FUBAR, I agree. A carload of drugs lost. Four dead. And shit all over everybody. But if you know anything more that could help bring in anyone, please say something. You cut down a tree by sawing at the bottom. These kids made choices, and they're not your friends. They're nobody's friends."

"If you won't leave, then I guess I will." She took her

jacket from the hook.

"Fine." He stomped past her to the door. He paused for a moment when he grabbed the knob, then turned to her. "I talked to Cunningham, by the way. You're off medical leave and can go back on patrol anytime. You're a good cop. I know it. And you know it."

"That's what they tell me," she said softly. Her throat was tight and dry. "I'm not quitting. You can count on that."

"God, I hope so. You've always been someone I could count on." He reached out and put his hand on her shoulder, and she looked up into his clear blue eyes. "I need you. Maybe more than you know. But this case is still open. Can I count on you to help salvage this operation?"

She placed her hand over his and pressed its warmth against her shoulder. She stood on her toes, kissed him on the cheek, and then leaned into his ear to whisper, "*No.*"

Russell tossed another mask onto the fire, where it flared in a white sheet of flame before sagging into a blackened heap. The blaze roared toward the stars and spilled its colors out across the black surface of Pike Lake. Beyond the pyre, firelight gleamed on the chrome and steel of his motorcycle. It was a humid summer night. Sweat stung his eyes and plastered his bangs to his forehead. A black trash bag slumped at his feet, filled with things from his bedroom—from his life—that he wanted to disappear. The flames hissed and crackled, and the night sounds whirled around him.

Bree had told him the upside of being in high school was the same as the downside: Everything seemed to last so long. When he last saw her sitting in her little purple car and looking up at him as he leaned over her open window, her voice, her eyes, her body, her dreams had forever been part of his life—in middle school, when he eyed her drawing griffins in her journal or winding a lock of amber hair around her fingertip, or when she had curled naked beside him atop a blanket in the woods, or when she sent him a string of emojis at some strange hour, or played some silly pop song on her guitar, or when she had tried to explain the convoluted plot of the latest book she imagined writing someday—always involving a half-demon girl, scarred and deadly, seeking to settle a score or save the world or survive the perils of fame— Bree Wells had meshed with the totality of his past and his future, and together they would escape the dreariness and depression of Pike Lake to rejoice and to conquer. And he had said, "I love you," and for a moment of shrieking terror she was silent until a smile dimpled her cheeks and she said, "I love you too." Then she turned the key and drove away.

That had been a thousand years ago. It seemed as if she had always been dead, as if he had always been grieving. And he could not imagine ever loving anyone else again.

He pulled another mask from the trash bag: Michael Myers. The killer was actually called "The Shape," and it was evil, pure evil—Michael was only the body in which the darkness lived. It was Russell's favorite movie monster— after Dracula, but only little kids admitted Dracula was their favorite. He tossed it on the bonfire.

He wondered what had happened to the pink teddy bear he'd given Bree for Valentine's Day. She'd looked at it quiz- zically for a moment after unwrapping, gazing down at it in her hands as if he'd given her a paint roller or a socket set, and then her eyes sparkled, and she said, "A guy has never given me something like this before." She put her smooth, warm palm on his cheek and said, "You're a sweet boy."

The fire warped and weaved in red and gold. He heard someone step from the trail, twigs snapping as the person moved through the brush. He glanced over and saw Samantha approaching, tree-shadows swaying all around her. He gazed into the flames as she took a place beside him.

"You got a full Ironwolf vest," she said.

"Dad made me an official member. Seeing how I helped get things handled and everything."

"Why is that on there?" She pointed to a shield-shaped patch on the front. It read KoS above, and 666 beneath, a crossed sword and pitchfork. "That's a Knights of Satan crest, isn't it?"

"Duane and Dad worked something out with them, so they're an allied club now. We'll be working together. Cops shut our businesses down, and they might be that way for a while. Money has to start coming back in somehow. I guess Dad wants the Ironwolfs to be more 'active.' Whatever that means."

"You good with that?"

He shrugged. "Guess I'll find out."

"What's in the bag?"

"My masks." He pointed to one of the blackened, melting faces in the bonfire. "Burning them."

She gasped, "Why?"

"Evidence."

"Of what?"

"Of me."

A meteor streaked overhead, and an owl hooted from its hidden perch. He looked over to Sam. Dark hair framed a face painted golden by firelight, like something on the sarcophagus of an Egyptian queen, and her lips were full and red.

"I'm sorry." She wiped a black-mascara tear from the

corner of her eye. "For all of this."

"We all did what we did, and Bree did too. I don't blame you."

"Thank you," she said, and then added, "I'm glad Brad is dead. And his dad, too."

"So am I."

"I quit working at Ricky's shop. I know you're not crazy about it, but I'm still running my thing. Dan's backing me now."

"I think maybe he's always been backing you more than you let on." He shrugged. "You do what you want. Ain't up to me."

"I need your help."

He turned to her. "For what?"

"For protection. And it could be good for you, too. If your club and the KoS are working together, you could use me. I could help handle your accounts, taxes. And if they're going to be moving any weight, I can help you guys get it into Dan's events or maybe even his nightclub. Dan respects you."

He gazed up at the whirling sparks. There was a time when he thought he was going to work in the movies. Special effects. It seemed to him a stupid idea now, like how kindergarteners all say they want to be astronauts or firemen, as if anyone who wants to can grow up to explore outer space or save lives.

"You won't have to deal with Ricky. I don't blame you for hating him," she said. "It will be a long time before Dan lets him have a hand in anything after everything that happened. You and me—we work well together. You have to admit it."

"I'll think on it."

He pulled another mask from the bag and held it up. The Big Bad Wolf. Sam reached out and grabbed it by the fur between the ears.

"No," she said. "Not this one."

"Why?"

"It's the best one."

He looked at the misshapen canine face gripped in her hand and in his. It was startlingly lifelike, as if it had been peeled from the bone and flesh of a fairytale boogeyman, its teeth glinting like crystalline shards.

"Will you put it on?" Her dark, gleaming eyes locked with his. "I want to see it. Please."

When he lifted it to his chin, he had the fleeting urge to hurl it into the flames, but instead found himself dragging it over his head, feeling his own hot breath gather in its snout and dampen his face. Through the eyeholes, he saw her smile.

"It's amazing," she said. "It's you."

She reached out and wrapped her arms around him, then pressed her cheek against his hammering heart. His breath rasped inside the mask. He stroked her hair, the heat of the bonfire at his back, the wind coming in from the lake beyond, and stared out to the woods. Dark figures gained definition as they emerged from the gloom beneath the trees. Leon walked with a folding chair under one arm and the other slung across his wife's shoulders. Russell could not hear Alice's words, but his mom grinned as she spoke, loosely holding a bottle of whiskey as she strolled beside his dad. Shane followed, booming out a laugh with Larry, who hurried along beside him, lugging a case of beer with a picnic blanket slung over his shoulder.

"Hey, Wolfman," Leon called out. "Hope you don't

mind if we join your party."

Russell stepped away from Sam, but he kept a hand around her wrist. He shook his shaggy head and, beneath the mask, he felt himself smile as he spoke:

"Fate is a Beast."

ACKNOWLEDGMENTS

This novel, like most, owes its existence in part to all of those who helped it come to life in various ways. Numerous fellow writers were kind enough to read this work and offer feedback, including Jamison Spencer, Jana Dawson, April Newman, James Lower, Molly Each, Rob Duffer, and David Peak. Special thanks to Jesse Jordan, who was there from my earliest pages to my final proofreading, and who proved time and time again to be an invaluable audience, editor, and friend. Thanks to Eric Campbell, Lance Wright, Kate Hofmeister, and everyone at Down & Out Books for all the hard work that went into helping this book become a reality.

Several books and resources informed this work, including *Under and Alone* by William Queen, *Soldier Girls: The Battles of Three Women at Home and at War* by Helen Thorpe, and *Forensics: What Bugs, Burns, Prints, DNA, and More Tell Us About Crime* by Val McDermid. Thanks to Sgt. Joe McKinney for taking the time to answer some procedural questions and for making sure it's called a "sheriff's office."

Thanks to my family and teachers, and to all the teachers in my family.

Thanks most of all to Karen Hyatt. I made this for you.

GEOFF HYATT worked as a ghostwriter for a YA horror series before the release of his first novel, *Birch Hills at World's End*. Following that, he served as an editor for an independent press while teaching college courses in film and fiction writing. Currently, he scripts online educational courseware and writes content for a toy company. His hobbies include running tabletop roleplaying games, playing guitar, and collecting toys, vintage psychedelic posters, and horror comics. He lives in Chicago.

GeoffHyatt.com

On the following pages are a few
more great titles from the
Down & Out Books publishing family.

For a complete list of books and to
sign up for our newsletter,
go to DownAndOutBooks.com.

All of Them to Burn
Beau Johnson

Down & Out Books
February 2020
978-1-64396-091-3

Darkness is an attribute most of us rally against. It can consume. It can achieve. But if we so choose, it can also be held at bay.

Enter Bishop Rider and the evil he's chosen to obliterate since his family is taken from him. Operating outside the law, circumventing a system beyond repair, Bishop stalks this darkness the only way he knows how. Not only because these men deserve what he's become, but because of a message he attempted to create has come back to haunt him, now, after all these years. It's this story, along with other, unconnected tales that populate *All of Them to Burn.*

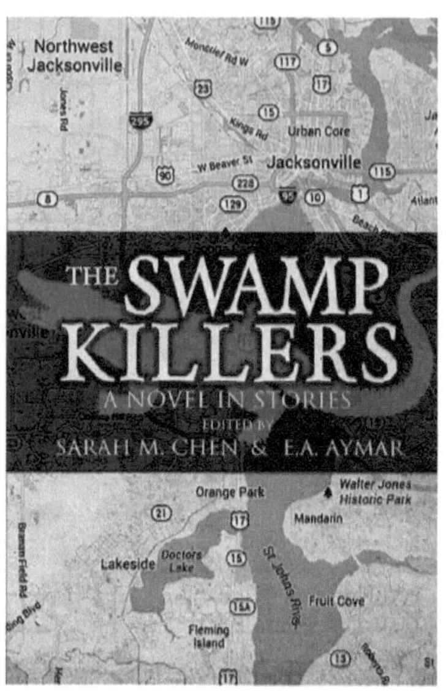

The Swamp Killers
A Novel in Stories
Sarah M. Chen and E.A. Aymar, editors

Down & Out Books
March 2020
978-1-64396-082-1

Timmy Milici, a low-level hitter with the infamous Atlanta-based Duplass crime family, ran off with Melody Duplass to Jacksonville, Florida. Olivia Duplass, her mother and head of the Duplass family, was incensed, and put a price on Timmy—a hundred thousand for his corpse, but with explicit instructions that her daughter not be harmed.

We know that's true. Or, at least, we think we do.

Sixteen writers tell their versions of what happened those fateful days in this gripping novel-in-stories, brought to you from the team behind *The Night of the Flood*.

Man of the World
Paul D. Brazill

All Due Respect, an imprint of
Down & Out Books
April 2020
978-1-64396-099-9

Ageing hit-man Tommy Bennett left London and returned to his hometown of Seatown, hoping for respite from the ghosts of the violent past that haunted him. However, things don't go to plan and trouble and violence soon follow Tommy to Seatown.

Tommy is soon embroiled in Seatown's underworld and his hopes of a peaceful retirement are dashed. Tommy deliberates whether or not to leave Seatown and return to London. Or even leave Great Britain altogether. So, he heads back to London where violence and mayhem await him.

Kraj the Enforcer: Stories
Rusty Barnes

Shotgun Honey, an imprint of
Down & Out Books
October 2019
978-1-64396-059-3

Meet Kraj, low-level errand boy and hitman for Tricky Ricky Gutierrez. In upstate New York Kraj strongarms his way through the ranks of Ricky's shabby organization until he is ultimately committing murder for the man in charge.

Follow him in his adventures with his girlfriend Cami and night club manager Mikael on a trail of equal parts savage lechery and even more savage murder.

www.ingramcontent.com/pod-product-compliance
Lightning Source LLC
Chambersburg PA
CBHW021229060726
47590CB00005B/1683